Young's Literal Translation of the Bible

———

The Four Gospels

By Robert Young

Adansonia
Press

Published in 2018

Logo art adapted from work by Bernard Gagnon

ISBN-13: 978-1-387-99905-7

First published in 1862

Contents

Matthew

Matthew 1:1. A roll of the birth of Jesus Christ, son of David, son of Abraham.

Matthew 1:2 Abraham begat Isaac, and Isaac begat Jacob, and Jacob begat Judah and his brethren,

Matthew 1:3 and Judah begat Pharez and Zarah of Tamar, and Pharez begat Hezron, and Hezron begat Ram,

Matthew 1:4 and Ram begat Amminadab, and Amminadab begat Nahshon, and Nahshon begat Salmon,

Matthew 1:5 and Salmon begat Boaz of Rahab, and Boaz begat Obed of Ruth, and Obed begat Jesse,

Matthew 1:6 and Jesse begat David the king. And David the king begat Solomon, of her [who had been] Uriah's,

Matthew 1:7 and Solomon begat Rehoboam, and Rehoboam begat Abijah, and Abijah begat Asa,

Matthew 1:8 and Asa begat Jehoshaphat, and Jehoshaphat begat Joram, and Joram begat Uzziah,

Matthew 1:9 and Uzziah begat Jotham, and Jotham begat Ahaz, and Ahaz begat Hezekiah,

Matthew 1:10 and Hezekiah begat Manasseh, and Manasseh begat Amon, and Amon begat Josiah,

Matthew 1:11 and Josiah begat Jeconiah and his brethren, at the Babylonian removal.

Matthew 1:12 And after the Babylonian removal, Jeconiah begat Shealtiel, and Shealtiel begat Zerubbabel,

Matthew 1:13 and Zerubbabel begat Abiud, and Abiud begat Eliakim, and Eliakim begat Azor,

Matthew 1:14 and Azor begat Sadok, and Sadok begat Achim, and Achim begat Eliud,

Matthew 1:15 and Eliud begat Eleazar, and Eleazar begat Matthan, and Matthan begat Jacob,

Matthew 1:16 and Jacob begat Joseph, the husband of Mary, of whom was begotten Jesus, who is named Christ.

Matthew 1:17 All the generations, therefore, from Abraham unto David [are] fourteen generations, and from David unto the Babylonian removal fourteen generations, and from the Babylonian removal unto the Christ, fourteen generations.

Matthew 1:18. And of Jesus Christ, the birth was thus: For his mother

Mary having been betrothed to Joseph, before their coming together she was found to have conceived from the Holy Spirit,

Matthew 1:19 and Joseph her husband being righteous, and not willing to make her an example, did wish privately to send her away.

Matthew 1:20 And on his thinking of these things, lo, a messenger of the Lord in a dream appeared to him, saying, `Joseph, son of David, thou mayest not fear to receive Mary thy wife, for that which in her was begotten [is] of the Holy Spirit,

Matthew 1:21 and she shall bring forth a son, and thou shalt call his name Jesus, for he shall save his people from their sins.'

Matthew 1:22 And all this hath come to pass, that it may be fulfilled that was spoken by the Lord through the prophet, saying,

Matthew 1:23 `Lo, the virgin shall conceive, and she shall bring forth a son, and they shall call his name Emmanuel,' which is, being interpreted `With us [he is] God.'

Matthew 1:24 And Joseph, having risen from the sleep, did as the messenger of the Lord directed him, and received his wife,

Matthew 1:25 and did not know her till she brought forth her son--the first-born, and he called his name Jesus.

Matthew 2:1. And Jesus having been born in Beth-Lehem of Judea, in the days of Herod the king, lo, mages from the east came to Jerusalem,

Matthew 2:2 saying, `Where is he who was born king of the Jews? for we saw his star in the east, and we came to bow to him.'

Matthew 2:3 And Herod the king having heard, was stirred, and all Jerusalem with him,

Matthew 2:4 and having gathered all the chief priests and scribes of the people, he was inquiring from them where the Christ is born.

Matthew 2:5 And they said to him, `In Beth-Lehem of Judea, for thus it hath been written through the prophet,

Matthew 2:6 And thou, Beth-Lehem, the land of Judah, thou art by no means the least among the leaders of Judah, for out of thee shall come one leading, who shall feed My people Israel.'

Matthew 2:7 Then Herod, privately having called the mages, did inquire exactly from them the time of the appearing star,

Matthew 2:8 and having sent them to Beth-Lehem, he said, `Having gone--inquire ye exactly for the child, and whenever ye may have found, bring me back word, that I also having come may bow to him.'

Matthew 2:9. And they, having heard the king, departed, and lo, the star, that they did see in the east, did go before them, till, having come, it stood over where the child was.

Matthew 2:10 And having seen the star, they rejoiced with exceeding great joy,

Matthew 2:11 and having come to the house, they found the child with Mary his mother, and having fallen down they bowed to him, and having opened their treasures, they presented to him gifts, gold, and frankincense, and myrrh,

Matthew 2:12 and having been divinely warned in a dream not to turn back unto Herod, through another way they withdrew to their own region.

Matthew 2:13. And on their having withdrawn, lo, a messenger of the Lord doth appear in a dream to Joseph, saying, `Having risen, take the child and his mother, and flee to Egypt, and be thou there till I may speak to thee, for Herod is about to seek thechild to destroy him.'

Matthew 2:14 And he, having risen, took the child and his mother by night, and withdrew to Egypt,

Matthew 2:15 and he was there till the death of Herod, that it might be fulfilled that was spoken by the Lord through the prophet, saying, Òut of Egypt I did call My Son.'

Matthew 2:16. Then Herod, having seen that he was deceived by the mages, was very wroth, and having sent forth, he slew all the male children in Beth-Lehem, and in all its borders, from two years and under, according to the time that he inquired exactly from the mages.

Matthew 2:17 Then was fulfilled that which was spoken by Jeremiah the prophet, saying,

Matthew 2:18 À voice in Ramah was heard--lamentation and weeping and much mourning--Rachel weeping [for] her children, and she would not be comforted because they are not.'

Matthew 2:19. And Herod having died, lo, a messenger of the Lord in a dream doth appear to Joseph in Egypt,

Matthew 2:20 saying, `Having risen, take the child and his mother, and be going to the land of Israel, for they have died--those seeking the life of the child.'

Matthew 2:21 And he, having risen, took the child and his mother, and came to the land of Israel,

Matthew 2:22 and having heard that Archelaus doth reign over Judea instead of Herod his father, he was afraid to go thither, and having been divinely warned in a dream, he withdrew to the parts of Galilee,

Matthew 2:23 and coming, he dwelt in a city named Nazareth, that it might be fulfilled that was spoken through the prophets, that À Nazarene he shall be called.'

Matthew 3:1. And in those days cometh John the Baptist, proclaiming in the wilderness of Judea,

Matthew 3:2 and saying, `Reform, for come nigh hath the reign of the heavens,'

Matthew 3:3 for this is he who was spoken of by Isaiah the prophet, saying, À voice of one crying in the wilderness, Prepare ye the way of the Lord, straight make ye His paths.'

Matthew 3:4 And this John had his clothing of camel's hair, and a girdle of skin round his loins, and his nourishment was locusts and honey of the field.

Matthew 3:5 Then were going forth unto him Jerusalem, and all Judea, and all the region round about the Jordan,

Matthew 3:6 and they were baptized in the Jordan by him, confessing their sins.

Matthew 3:7. And having seen many of the Pharisees and Sadducees coming about his baptism, he said to them, `Brood of vipers! who did shew you to flee from the coming wrath?

Matthew 3:8 bear, therefore, fruits worthy of the reformation,

Matthew 3:9 and do not think to say in yourselves, A father we have-- Abraham, for I say to you, that God is able out of these stones to raise children to Abraham,

Matthew 3:10 and now also, the axe unto the root of the trees is laid, every tree therefore not bearing good fruit is hewn down, and to fire is cast.

Matthew 3:11 Ì indeed do baptize you with water to reformation, but he who after me is coming is mightier than I, of whom I am not worthy to bear the sandals, he shall baptize you with the Holy Spirit and with fire,

Matthew 3:12 whose fan [is] in his hand, and he will thoroughly cleanse his floor, and will gather his wheat to the storehouse, but the chaff he will burn with fire unquenchable.'

Matthew 3:13. Then cometh Jesus from Galilee upon the Jordan, unto John to be baptized by him,

Matthew 3:14 but John was forbidding him, saying, Ì have need by thee to be baptized--and thou dost come unto me!'

Matthew 3:15 But Jesus answering said to him, `Suffer now, for thus it is becoming to us to fulfil all righteousness,' then he doth suffer him.

Matthew 3:16 And having been baptized, Jesus went up immediately from the water, and lo, opened to him were the heavens, and he saw the Spirit of God descending as a dove, and coming upon him,

Matthew 3:17 and lo, a voice out of the heavens, saying, `This is My Son--the Beloved, in whom I did delight.'

Matthew 4:1. Then Jesus was led up to the wilderness by the Spirit, to be tempted by the Devil,

Matthew 4:2 and having fasted forty days and forty nights, afterwards he did hunger.

Matthew 4:3 And the Tempter having come to him said, Ìf Son thou art of God--speak that these stones may become loaves.'

Matthew 4:4 But he answering said, Ìt hath been written, Not upon bread alone doth man live, but upon every word coming forth from the mouth of God.'

Matthew 4:5 Then doth the Devil take him to the [holy] city, and doth set him on the pinnacle of the temple,

Matthew 4:6 and saith to him, Ìf Son thou art of God--cast thyself down, for it hath been written, that, His messengers He shall charge concerning thee, and on hands they shall bear thee up, that thou mayest not dash on a stone thy foot.'

Matthew 4:7 Jesus said to him again, Ìt hath been written, Thou shalt not tempt the Lord thy God.'

Matthew 4:8 Again doth the Devil take him to a very high mount, and doth shew to him all the kingdoms of the world and the glory of them,

Matthew 4:9 and saith to him, Àll these to thee I will give, if falling down thou mayest bow to me.'

Matthew 4:10 Then saith Jesus to him, `Go--Adversary, for it hath been written, The Lord thy God thou shalt bow to, and Him only thou shalt serve.'

Matthew 4:11 Then doth the Devil leave him, and lo, messengers came and were ministering to him.

Matthew 4:12. And Jesus having heard that John was delivered up, did withdraw to Galilee,

Matthew 4:13 and having left Nazareth, having come, he dwelt at Capernaum that is by the sea, in the borders of Zebulun and Naphtalim,

Matthew 4:14 that it might be fulfilled that was spoken through Isaiah the prophet, saying,

Matthew 4:15 `Land of Zebulun and land of Naphtali, way of the sea, beyond the Jordan, Galilee of the nations! --

Matthew 4:16 the people that is sitting in darkness saw a great light, and to those sitting in a region and shadow of death--light arose to them.'

Matthew 4:17 From that time began Jesus to proclaim and to say, `Reform ye, for come nigh hath the reign of the heavens.'

Matthew 4:18. And Jesus, walking by the sea of Galilee, saw two brothers, Simon named Peter and Andrew his brother, casting a drag into the sea--for they were fishers--

Matthew 4:19 and he saith to them, `Come ye after me, and I will make you fishers of men,'

Matthew 4:20 and they, immediately, having left the nets, did follow him.

Matthew 4:21 And having advanced thence, he saw other two brothers, James of Zebedee, and John his brother, in the boat with Zebedee their father, refitting their nets, and he called them,

Matthew 4:22 and they, immediately, having left the boat and their father, did follow him.

Matthew 4:23. And Jesus was going about all Galilee teaching in their synagogues, and proclaiming the good news of the reign, and healing every disease, and every malady among the people,

Matthew 4:24 and his fame went forth to all Syria, and they brought to him all having ailments, pressed with manifold sicknesses and pains, and demoniacs, and lunatics, and paralytics, and he healed them.

Matthew 4:25 And there followed him many multitudes from Galilee, and Decapolis, and Jerusalem, and Judea, and beyond the Jordan.

Matthew 5:1. And having seen the multitudes, he went up to the mount, and he having sat down, his disciples came to him,

Matthew 5:2 and having opened his mouth, he was teaching them, saying:

Matthew 5:3. `Happy the poor in spirit--because theirs is the reign of the heavens.

Matthew 5:4 `Happy the mourning--because they shall be comforted.

Matthew 5:5 `Happy the meek--because they shall inherit the land.

Matthew 5:6 `Happy those hungering and thirsting for righteousness--because they shall be filled.

Matthew 5:7 `Happy the kind--because they shall find kindness.

Matthew 5:8 `Happy the clean in heart--because they shall see God.

Matthew 5:9 `Happy the peacemakers--because they shall be called Sons of God.

Matthew 5:10 `Happy those persecuted for righteousness' sake--because theirs is the reign of the heavens.

Matthew 5:11 `Happy are ye whenever they may reproach you, and may persecute, and may say any evil thing against you falsely for my sake--

Matthew 5:12 rejoice ye and be glad, because your reward [is] great in the heavens, for thus did they persecute the prophets who were before you.

Matthew 5:13. `Ye are the salt of the land, but if the salt may lose savour, in what shall it be salted? for nothing is it good henceforth, except to be cast without, and to be trodden down by men.

Matthew 5:14 `Ye are the light of the world, a city set upon a mount is not able to be hid;

Matthew 5:15 nor do they light a lamp, and put it under the measure, but on the lamp-stand, and it shineth to all those in the house;

Matthew 5:16 so let your light shine before men, that they may see your good works, and may glorify your Father who [is] in the heavens.

Matthew 5:17. `Do not suppose that I came to throw down the law or the prophets--I did not come to throw down, but to fulfil;

Matthew 5:18 for, verily I say to you, till that the heaven and the earth may pass away, one iota or one tittle may not pass away from the law, till that all may come to pass.

Matthew 5:19 `Whoever therefore may loose one of these commands-- the least--and may teach men so, least he shall be called in the reign of the heavens, but whoever may do and may teach [them], he shall be called great in the reign of the heavens.

Matthew 5:20 `For I say to you, that if your righteousness may not abound above that of the scribes and Pharisees, ye may not enter to the reign of the heavens.

Matthew 5:21. `Ye heard that it was said to the ancients: Thou shalt not kill, and whoever may kill shall be in danger of the judgment;

Matthew 5:22 but I--I say to you, that every one who is angry at his brother without cause, shall be in danger of the judgment, and whoever may say to his brother, Empty fellow! shall be in danger of the sanhedrim, and whoever may say, Rebel! shall be indanger of the gehenna of the fire.

Matthew 5:23 Ìf, therefore, thou mayest bring thy gift to the altar, and there mayest remember that thy brother hath anything against thee,

Matthew 5:24 leave there thy gift before the altar, and go--first be reconciled to thy brother, and then having come bring thy gift.

Matthew 5:25 `Be agreeing with thy opponent quickly, while thou art in the way with him, that the opponent may not deliver thee to the judge, and the judge may deliver thee to the officer, and to prison thou mayest be cast,

Matthew 5:26 verily I say to thee, thou mayest not come forth thence till that thou mayest pay the last farthing.

Matthew 5:27. `Ye heard that it was said to the ancients: Thou shalt not commit adultery;

Matthew 5:28 but I--I say to you, that every one who is looking on a woman to desire her, did already commit adultery with her in his heart.

Matthew 5:29 `But, if thy right eye doth cause thee to stumble, pluck it out and cast from thee, for it is good to thee that one of thy members may perish, and not thy whole body be cast to gehenna.

Matthew 5:30 Ànd, if thy right hand doth cause thee to stumble, cut it off, and cast from thee, for it is good to thee that one of thy members may perish, and not thy whole body be cast to gehenna.

Matthew 5:31 Ànd it was said, That whoever may put away his wife, let him give to her a writing of divorce;

Matthew 5:32 but I--I say to you, that whoever may put away his wife,

save for the matter of whoredom, doth make her to commit adultery; and whoever may marry her who hath been put away doth commit adultery.

Matthew 5:33. Àgain, ye heard that it was said to the ancients: Thou shalt not swear falsely, but thou shalt pay to the Lord thine oaths;

Matthew 5:34 but I--I say to you, not to swear at all; neither by the heaven, because it is the throne of God,

Matthew 5:35 nor by the earth, because it is His footstool, nor by Jerusalem, because it is a city of a great king,

Matthew 5:36 nor by thy head mayest thou swear, because thou art not able one hair to make white or black;

Matthew 5:37 but let your word be, Yes, Yes, No, No, and that which is more than these is of the evil.

Matthew 5:38. `Ye heard that it was said: Eye for eye, and tooth for tooth;

Matthew 5:39 but I--I say to you, not to resist the evil, but whoever shall slap thee on thy right cheek, turn to him also the other;

Matthew 5:40 and whoever is willing to take thee to law, and thy coat to take--suffer to him also the cloak.

Matthew 5:41 Ànd whoever shall impress thee one mile, go with him two,

Matthew 5:42 to him who is asking of thee be giving, and him who is willing to borrow from thee thou mayest not turn away.

Matthew 5:43. `Ye heard that it was said: Thou shalt love thy neighbour, and shalt hate thine enemy;

Matthew 5:44 but I--I say to you, Love your enemies, bless those cursing you, do good to those hating you, and pray for those accusing you falsely, and persecuting you,

Matthew 5:45 that ye may be sons of your Father in the heavens, because His sun He doth cause to rise on evil and good, and He doth send rain on righteous and unrighteous.

Matthew 5:46 `For, if ye may love those loving you, what reward have ye? do not also the tax-gatherers the same?

Matthew 5:47 and if ye may salute your brethren only, what do ye abundant? do not also the tax-gatherers so?

Matthew 5:48 ye shall therefore be perfect, as your Father who [is] in the heavens is perfect.

Matthew 6:1. `Take heed your kindness not to do before men, to be seen by them, and if not--reward ye have not from your Father who [is] in the heavens;

Matthew 6:2 whenever, therefore, thou mayest do kindness, thou mayest not sound a trumpet before thee as the hypocrites do, in the synagogues, and in the streets, that they may have glory from men; verily I say to you--they have their reward!

Matthew 6:3 `But thou, doing kindness, let not thy left hand know what thy right hand doth,

Matthew 6:4 that thy kindness may be in secret, and thy Father who is seeing in secret Himself shall reward thee manifestly.

Matthew 6:5. Ànd when thou mayest pray, thou shalt not be as the hypocrites, because they love in the synagogues, and in the corners of the broad places--standing--to pray, that they may be seen of men; verily I say to you, that they have their reward.

Matthew 6:6 `But thou, when thou mayest pray, go into thy chamber, and having shut thy door, pray to thy Father who [is] in secret, and thy Father who is seeing in secret, shall reward thee manifestly.

Matthew 6:7 Ànd--praying--ye may not use vain repetitions like the nations, for they think that in their much speaking they shall be heard,

Matthew 6:8 be ye not therefore like to them, for your Father doth know those things that ye have need of before your asking him;

Matthew 6:9. thus therefore pray ye: Òur Father who [art] in the heavens! hallowed be Thy name.

Matthew 6:10 `Thy reign come: Thy will come to pass, as in heaven also on the earth.

Matthew 6:11 Òur appointed bread give us to-day.

Matthew 6:12 Ànd forgive us our debts, as also we forgive our debt-ors.

Matthew 6:13 Ànd mayest Thou not lead us to temptation, but deliver us from the evil, because Thine is the reign, and the power, and the glory-- to the ages. Amen.

Matthew 6:14 `For, if ye may for-give men their trespasses He also will forgive you--your Father who [is] in the heavens;

Matthew 6:15 but if ye may not for-give men their trespasses, neither will your Father forgive your tres-passes.

Matthew 6:16. Ànd when ye may fast, be ye not as the hypocrites, of sour countenances, for they disfig-ure their faces, that they may appear to men fasting; verily I say to you, that they have their reward.

Matthew 6:17 `But thou, fasting, anoint thy head, and wash thy face,

Matthew 6:18 that thou mayest not appear to men fasting, but to thy Father who [is] in secret, and thy Father, who is seeing in secret, shall reward thee manifestly.

Matthew 6:19. `Treasure not up to yourselves treasures on the earth, where moth and rust disfigure, and where thieves break through and steal,

Matthew 6:20 but treasure up to yourselves treasures in heaven, where neither moth nor rust doth disfigure, and where thieves do not break through nor steal,

Matthew 6:21 for where your treasure is, there will be also your heart.

Matthew 6:22 `The lamp of the body is the eye, if, therefore, thine eye may be perfect, all thy body shall be enlightened,

Matthew 6:23 but if thine eye may be evil, all thy body shall be dark; if, therefore, the light that [is] in thee is darkness--the darkness, how great!

Matthew 6:24 `None is able to serve two lords, for either he will hate the one and love the other, or he will hold to the one, and despise the oth-er; ye are not able to serve God and Mammon.

Matthew 6:25. `Because of this I say to you, be not anxious for your life, what ye may eat, and what ye may drink, nor for your body, what ye may put on. Is not the life more than the nourishment, and the body than the clothing?

Matthew 6:26 look to the fowls of the heaven, for they do not sow, nor reap, nor gather into storehouses, and your heavenly Father doth nourish them; are not ye much better than they?

Matthew 6:27 Ànd who of you, being anxious, is able to add to his age one cubit?

Matthew 6:28 and about clothing why are ye anxious? consider well the lilies of the field; how do they grow? they do not labour, nor do they spin;

Matthew 6:29 and I say to you, that not even Solomon in all his glory was arrayed as one of these.

Matthew 6:30 Ànd if the herb of the field, that to-day is, and to-morrow is cast to the furnace, God doth so clothe--not much more you, O ye of little faith?

Matthew 6:31 therefore ye may not be anxious, saying, What may we eat? or, What may we drink? or, What may we put round?

Matthew 6:32 for all these do the nations seek for, for your heavenly Father doth know that ye have need of all these;

Matthew 6:33 but seek ye first the reign of God and His righteousness, and all these shall be added to you.

Matthew 6:34 Be not therefore anxious for the morrow, for the morrow shall be anxious for its own things;

sufficient for the day [is] the evil of it.

Matthew 7:1. `Judge not, that ye may not be judged,

Matthew 7:2 for in what judgment ye judge, ye shall be judged, and in what measure ye measure, it shall be measured to you.

Matthew 7:3 Ànd why dost thou behold the mote that [is] in thy brother's eye, and the beam that [is] in thine own eye dost not consider?

Matthew 7:4 or, how wilt thou say to thy brother, Suffer I may cast out the mote from thine eye, and lo, the beam [is] in thine own eye?

Matthew 7:5 Hypocrite, cast out first the beam out of thine own eye, and then thou shalt see clearly to cast out the mote out of thy brother's eye.

Matthew 7:6 `Ye may not give that which is [holy] to the dogs, nor cast your pearls before the swine, that they may not trample them among their feet, and having turned--may rend you.

Matthew 7:7. Àsk, and it shall be given to you; seek, and ye shall find; knock, and it shall be opened to you;

Matthew 7:8 for every one who is asking doth receive, and he who is seeking doth find, and to him who is knocking it shall be opened.

Matthew 7:9 Òr what man is of you, of whom, if his son may ask a loaf--a stone will he present to him?

Matthew 7:10 and if a fish he may ask--a serpent will he present to him?

Matthew 7:11 if, therefore, ye being evil, have known good gifts to give to your children, how much more shall your Father who [is] in the heavens give good things to those asking him?

Matthew 7:12. Àll things, therefore, whatever ye may will that men may be doing to you, so also do to them, for this is the law and the prophets.

Matthew 7:13 `Go ye in through the strait gate, because wide [is] the gate, and broad the way that is leading to the destruction, and many are those going in through it;

Matthew 7:14 how strait [is] the gate, and compressed the way that is leading to the life, and few are those finding it!

Matthew 7:15. `But, take heed of the false prophets, who come unto you in sheep's clothing, and inwardly are ravening wolves.

Matthew 7:16 From their fruits ye shall know them; do [men] gather from thorns grapes? or from thistles figs?

Matthew 7:17 so every good tree doth yield good fruits, but the bad tree doth yield evil fruits.

Matthew 7:18 A good tree is not able to yield evil fruits, nor a bad tree to yield good fruits.

Matthew 7:19 Every tree not yielding good fruit is cut down and is cast to fire:

Matthew 7:20 therefore from their fruits ye shall know them.

Matthew 7:21. `Not every one who is saying to me Lord, lord, shall come into the reign of the heavens; but he who is doing the will of my Father who is in the heavens.

Matthew 7:22 Many will say to me in that day, Lord, lord, have we not in thy name prophesied? and in thy name cast out demons? and in thy name done many mighty things?

Matthew 7:23 and then I will acknowledge to them, that--I never knew you, depart from me ye who are working lawlessness.

Matthew 7:24 `Therefore, every one who doth hear of me these words, and doth do them, I will liken him to a wise man who built his house upon the rock;

Matthew 7:25 and the rain did descend, and the streams came, and the winds blew, and they beat on that house, and it fell not, for it had been founded on the rock.

Matthew 7:26 Ànd every one who is hearing of me these words, and is not doing them, shall be likened to a foolish man who built his house upon the sand;

Matthew 7:27 and the rain did descend, and the streams came, and the winds blew, and they beat on that house, and it fell, and its fall was great.'

Matthew 7:28 And it came to pass, when Jesus ended these words, the multitudes were astonished at his teaching,

Matthew 7:29 for he was teaching them as having authority, and not as the scribes.

Matthew 8:1. And when he came down from the mount, great multitudes did follow him,

Matthew 8:2 and lo, a leper having come, was bowing to him, saying, `Sir, if thou art willing, thou art able to cleanse me;'

Matthew 8:3 and having stretched forth the hand, Jesus touched him, saying, Ì will, be thou cleansed,' and immediately his leprosy was cleansed.

Matthew 8:4 And Jesus saith to him, `See, thou mayest tell no one, but go, thyself shew to the priest, and bring the gift that Moses commanded for a testimony to them.'

Matthew 8:5. And Jesus having entered into Capernaum, there came to him a centurion calling upon him,

Matthew 8:6 and saying, `Sir, my young man hath been laid in the house a paralytic, fearfully afflicted,'

Matthew 8:7 and Jesus saith to him, Ì, having come, will heal him.'

Matthew 8:8 And the centurion answering said, `Sir, I am not worthy that thou mayest enter under my roof, but only say a word, and my servant shall be healed;

Matthew 8:9 for I also am a man under authority, having under myself soldiers, and I say to this one, Go, and he goeth, and to another, Be coming, and he cometh, and to my servant, Do this, and he doth [it].'

Matthew 8:10 And Jesus having heard, did wonder, and said to those following, `Verily I say to you, not even in Israel so great faith have I found;

Matthew 8:11 and I say to you, that many from east and west shall come and recline (at meat) with Abraham, and Isaac, and Jacob, in the reign of the heavens,

Matthew 8:12 but the sons of the reign shall be cast forth to the outer darkness--there shall be the weeping and the gnashing of the teeth.'

Matthew 8:13 And Jesus said to the centurion, `Go, and as thou didst believe let it be to thee;' and his young man was healed in that hour.

Matthew 8:14. And Jesus having come into the house of Peter, saw his mother-in-law laid, and fevered,

Matthew 8:15 and he touched her hand, and the fever left her, and she arose, and was ministering to them.

Matthew 8:16 And evening having come, they brought to him many demoniacs, and he did cast out the spirits with a word, and did heal all who were ill,

Matthew 8:17 that it might be fulfilled that was spoken through Isaiah the prophet, saying, `Himself took our infirmities, and the sicknesses he did bear.'

Matthew 8:18. And Jesus having seen great multitudes about him, did command to depart to the other side;

Matthew 8:19 and a certain scribe having come, said to him, `Teacher, I will follow thee wherever thou mayest go;'

Matthew 8:20 and Jesus saith to him, `The foxes have holes, and the birds of the heaven places of rest, but the Son of Man hath not where he may lay the head.'

Matthew 8:21 And another of his disciples said to him, `Sir, permit me first to depart and to bury my father;'

Matthew 8:22 and Jesus said to him, `Follow me, and suffer the dead to bury their own dead.'

Matthew 8:23. And when he entered into the boat his disciples did follow him,

Matthew 8:24 and lo, a great tempest arose in the sea, so that the boat was being covered by the waves, but he was sleeping,

Matthew 8:25 and his disciples having come to him, awoke him, saying, `Sir, save us; we are perishing.'

Matthew 8:26 And he saith to them, `Why are ye fearful, O ye of little faith?' Then having risen, he rebuked the winds and the sea, and there was a great calm;

Matthew 8:27 and the men wondered, saying, `What kind--is this, that even the wind and the sea do obey him?'

Matthew 8:28. And he having come to the other side, to the region of the Gergesenes, there met him two demoniacs, coming forth out of the tombs, very fierce, so that no one was able to pass over by that way,

Matthew 8:29 and lo, they cried out, saying, `What--to us and to thee, Jesus, Son of God? didst thou come hither, before the time, to afflict us?'

Matthew 8:30 And there was far off from them a herd of many swine feeding,

Matthew 8:31 and the demons were calling on him, saying, Ìf thou dost cast us forth, permit us to go away to the herd of the swine;'

Matthew 8:32 and he saith to them, `Go.' And having come forth, they went to the herd of the swine, and lo, the whole herd of the swine rushed down the steep, to the sea, and died in the waters,

Matthew 8:33 and those feeding did flee, and, having gone to the city, they declared all, and the matter of the demoniacs.

Matthew 8:34 And lo, all the city came forth to meet Jesus, and having seen him, they called on [him] that he might depart from their borders.

Matthew 9:1. And having gone to the boat, he passed over, and came to his own city,

Matthew 9:2 and lo, they were bringing to him a paralytic, laid upon a couch, and Jesus having seen their faith, said to the paralytic, `Be of good courage, child, thy sins have been forgiven thee.'

Matthew 9:3 And lo, certain of the scribes said within themselves, `This one doth speak evil.'

Matthew 9:4 And Jesus, having known their thoughts, said, `Why think ye evil in your hearts?

Matthew 9:5 for which is easier? to say, The sins have been forgiven to thee; or to say, Rise, and walk?

Matthew 9:6 `But, that ye may know that the Son of Man hath power upon the earth to forgive sins-- (then saith he to the paralytic) --

having risen, take up thy couch, and go to thy house.'

Matthew 9:7 And he, having risen, went to his house,

Matthew 9:8 and the multitudes having seen, wondered, and glorified God, who did give such power to men.

Matthew 9:9. And Jesus passing by thence, saw a man sitting at the tax-office, named Matthew, and saith to him, `Be following me,' and he, having risen, did follow him.

Matthew 9:10 And it came to pass, he reclining (at meat) in the house, that lo, many tax-gatherers and sinners having come, were lying (at meat) with Jesus and his disciples,

Matthew 9:11 and the Pharisees having seen, said to his disciples, `Wherefore with the tax-gatherers and sinners doth your teacher eat?'

Matthew 9:12 And Jesus having heard, said to them, `They who are whole have no need of a physician, but they who are ill;

Matthew 9:13 but having gone, learn ye what is, Kindness I will, and not sacrifice, for I did not come to call righteous men, but sinners, to reformation.'

Matthew 9:14. Then come to him do the disciples of John, saying, `Wherefore do we and the Pharisees fast much, and thy disciples fast not?'

Matthew 9:15 And Jesus said to them, `Can the sons of the bride-chamber mourn, so long as the bridegroom is with them? but days shall come when the bridegroom may be taken from them, and then they shall fast.

Matthew 9:16 And no one doth put a patch of undressed cloth on an old garment, for its filling up doth take from the garment, and a worse rent is made.

Matthew 9:17 `Nor do they put new wine into old skins, and if not--the skins burst, and the wine doth run out, and the skins are destroyed, but they put new wine into new skins, and both are preserved together.'

Matthew 9:18. While he is speaking these things to them, lo, a ruler having come, was bowing to him, saying that `My daughter just now died, but, having come, lay thy hand upon her, and she shall live.'

Matthew 9:19 And Jesus having risen, did follow him, also his disciples,

Matthew 9:20 and lo, a woman having an issue of blood twelve years, having come to him behind, did touch the fringe of his garments,

Matthew 9:21 for she said within herself, If only I may touch his garment, I shall be saved.'

Matthew 9:22 And Jesus having turned about, and having seen her, said, `Be of good courage, daughter, thy faith hath saved thee,' and the woman was saved from that hour.

Matthew 9:23 And Jesus having come to the house of the ruler, and having seen the minstrels and the multitude making tumult,

Matthew 9:24 he saith to them, `Withdraw, for the damsel did not die, but doth sleep,' and they were deriding him;

Matthew 9:25 but, when the multitude was put forth, having gone in, he took hold of her hand, and the damsel arose,

Matthew 9:26 and the fame of this went forth to all the land.

Matthew 9:27. And Jesus passing on thence, two blind men followed him, calling and saying, `Deal kindly with us, Son of David.'

Matthew 9:28 And he having come to the house, the blind men came to him, and Jesus saith to them, `Believe ye that I am able to do this?' They say to him, `Yes, sir.'

Matthew 9:29 Then touched he their eyes, saying, According to your faith let it be to you,'

Matthew 9:30 and their eyes were opened, and Jesus strictly charged them, saying, `See, let no one know;'

Matthew 9:31 but they, having gone forth, did spread his fame in all that land.

Matthew 9:32 And as they are coming forth, lo, they brought to him a man dumb, a demoniac,

Matthew 9:33 and the demon having been cast out, the dumb spake, and the multitude did wonder, saying that Ìt was never so seen in Israel:'

Matthew 9:34 but the Pharisees said, `By the ruler of the demons he doth cast out the demons.'

Matthew 9:35. And Jesus was going up and down all the cities and the villages, teaching in their synagogues, and proclaiming the good news of the reign, and healing every sickness and every malady among the people.

Matthew 9:36 And having seen the multitudes, he was moved with compassion for them, that they were faint and cast aside, as sheep not having a shepherd,

Matthew 9:37 then saith he to his disciples, `The harvest indeed [is] abundant, but the workmen few;

Matthew 9:38 beseech ye therefore the Lord of the harvest, that he may put forth workmen to His harvest.'

Matthew 10:1. And having called to him his twelve disciples, he gave to them power over unclean spirits, so as to be casting them out, and to be healing every sickness, and every malady.

Matthew 10:2 And of the twelve apostles the names are these: first, Simon, who is called Peter, and Andrew his brother; James of Zebedee, and John his brother;

Matthew 10:3 Philip, and Bartholomew; Thomas, and Matthew the tax-gatherer; James of Alpheus, and Lebbeus who was surnamed Thaddeus;

Matthew 10:4 Simon the Cananite, and Judas Iscariot, who did also deliver him up.

Matthew 10:5. These twelve did Jesus send forth, having given command to them, saying, `To the way of the nations go not away, and into a city of the Samaritans go not in,

Matthew 10:6 and be going rather unto the lost sheep of the house of Israel.

Matthew 10:7 Ànd, going on, proclaim saying that, the reign of the heavens hath come nigh;

Matthew 10:8 infirm ones be healing, lepers be cleansing, dead be raising, demons be casting out-- freely ye did receive, freely give.

Matthew 10:9 `Provide not gold, nor silver, nor brass in your girdles,

Matthew 10:10 nor scrip for the way, nor two coats, nor sandals, nor staff--for the workman is worthy of his nourishment.

Matthew 10:11 Ànd into whatever city or village ye may enter, inquire ye who in it is worthy, and there abide, till ye may go forth.

Matthew 10:12 And coming to the house salute it,

Matthew 10:13 and if indeed the house be worthy, let your peace come upon it; and if it be not worthy, let your peace turn back to you.

Matthew 10:14 Ànd whoever may not receive you nor hear your words, coming forth from that house or city, shake off the dust of your feet,

Matthew 10:15 verily I say to you, It shall be more tolerable for the land of Sodom and Gomorrah in the day of judgment than for that city.

Matthew 10:16. `Lo, I do send you forth as sheep in the midst of wolves, be ye therefore wise as the serpents, and simple as the doves.

Matthew 10:17 And, take ye heed of men, for they will give you up to sanhedrims, and in their synagogues they will scourge you,

Matthew 10:18 and before governors and kings ye shall be brought for my sake, for a testimony to them and to the nations.

Matthew 10:19 Ànd whenever they may deliver you up, be not anxious how or what ye may speak, for it shall be given you in that hour what ye shall speak;

Matthew 10:20 for ye are not the speakers, but the Spirit of your Father that is speaking in you.

Matthew 10:21 Ànd brother shall deliver up brother to death, and father child, and children shall rise up against parents, and shall put them to death,

Matthew 10:22 and ye shall be hated by all because of my name, but he who hath endured to the end, he shall be saved.

Matthew 10:23 Ànd whenever they may persecute you in this city, flee to the other, for verily I say to you, ye may not have completed the cities of Israel till the Son of Man may come.

Matthew 10:24 À disciple is not above the teacher, nor a servant above his lord;

Matthew 10:25 sufficient to the disciple that he may be as his teacher, and the servant as his lord; if the master of the house they did call Beelzeboul, how much more those of his household?

Matthew 10:26 `Ye may not, therefore, fear them, for there is nothing covered, that shall not be revealed, and hid, that shall not be known;

Matthew 10:27 that which I tell you in the darkness, speak in the light, and that which you hear at the ear, proclaim on the house-tops.

Matthew 10:28 Ànd be not afraid of those killing the body, and are not able to kill the soul, but fear rather Him who is able both soul and body to destroy in gehenna.

Matthew 10:29 Àre not two sparrows sold for an assar? and one of them shall not fall on the ground without your Father;

Matthew 10:30 and of you--even the hairs of the head are all numbered;

Matthew 10:31 be not therefore afraid, than many sparrows ye are better.

Matthew 10:32 Èvery one, therefore, who shall confess in me before men, I also will confess in him before my Father who is in the heavens;

Matthew 10:33 and whoever shall deny me before men, I also will deny him before my Father who is in the heavens.

Matthew 10:34 `Ye may not suppose that I came to put peace on the earth; I did not come to put peace, but a sword;

Matthew 10:35 for I came to set a man at variance against his father, and a daughter against her mother, and a daughter-in-law against her mother-in-law,

Matthew 10:36 and the enemies of a man are those of his household.

Matthew 10:37 `He who is loving father or mother above me, is not worthy of me, and he who is loving son or daughter above me, is not worthy of me,

Matthew 10:38 and whoever doth not receive his cross and follow after me, is not worthy of me.

Matthew 10:39 `He who found his life shall lose it, and he who lost his life for my sake shall find it.

Matthew 10:40 `He who is receiving you doth receive me, and he who is receiving me doth receive Him who sent me,

Matthew 10:41 he who is receiving a prophet in the name of a prophet, shall receive a prophet's reward, and he who is receiving a righteous man in the name of a righteous man, shall receive a righteous man's reward,

Matthew 10:42 and whoever may give to drink to one of these little ones a cup of cold water only in the name of a disciple, verily I say to you, he may not lose his reward.'

Matthew 11:1. And it came to pass, when Jesus ended directing his twelve disciples, he departed thence to teach and to preach in their cities.

Matthew 11:2 And John having heard in the prison the works of the Christ, having sent two of his disciples,

Matthew 11:3 said to him, Àrt thou He who is coming, or for another do we look?'

Matthew 11:4 And Jesus answering said to them, `Having gone, declare to John the things that ye hear and see,

Matthew 11:5 blind receive sight, and lame walk, lepers are cleansed, and deaf hear, dead are raised, and poor have good news proclaimed,

Matthew 11:6 and happy is he who may not be stumbled in me.'

Matthew 11:7. And as they are going, Jesus began to say to the multitudes concerning John, `What went ye out to the wilderness to view? --a reed shaken by the wind?

Matthew 11:8 `But what went ye out to see? --a man clothed in soft garments? lo, those wearing the soft things are in the kings' houses.

Matthew 11:9 `But what went ye out to see? --a prophet? yes, I say to you, and more than a prophet,

Matthew 11:10 for this is he of whom it hath been written, Lo, I do send My messenger before thy face, who shall prepare thy way before thee.

Matthew 11:11 Verily I say to you, there hath not risen, among those born of women, a greater than John the Baptist, but he who is least in the reign of the heavens is greater than he.

Matthew 11:12 Ànd, from the days of John the Baptist till now, the reign of the heavens doth suffer violence, and violent men do take it by force,

Matthew 11:13 for all the prophets and the law till John did prophesy,

Matthew 11:14 and if ye are willing to receive [it], he is Elijah who was about to come;

Matthew 11:15 he who is having ears to hear--let him hear.

Matthew 11:16. Ànd to what shall I liken this generation? it is like little children in market-places, sitting and calling to their comrades,

Matthew 11:17 and saying, We piped unto you, and ye did not dance, we lamented to you, and ye did not smite the breast.

Matthew 11:18 `For John came neither eating nor drinking, and they say, He hath a demon;

Matthew 11:19 the Son of Man came eating and drinking, and they say, Lo, a man, a glutton, and a wine-drinker, a friend of tax-gatherers and sinners, and wisdom was justified of her children.'

Matthew 11:20 Then began he to reproach the cities in which were done most of his mighty works, because they did not reform.

Matthew 11:21 `Woe to thee, Chorazin! woe to thee, Bethsaida! because, if in Tyre and Sidon had been done the mighty works that were done in you, long ago in sackcloth and ashes they had reformed;

Matthew 11:22 but I say to you, to Tyre and Sidon it shall be more tolerable in a day of judgment than for you.

Matthew 11:23 Ànd thou, Capernaum, which unto the heaven wast exalted, unto hades shalt be brought down, because if in Sodom had been done the mighty works that were done in thee, it had remained unto this day;

Matthew 11:24 but I say to you, to the land of Sodom it shall be more tolerable in a day of judgment than to thee.'

Matthew 11:25. At that time Jesus answering said, Ì do confess to Thee, Father, Lord of the heavens and of the earth, that thou didst hide these things from wise and understanding ones, and didst reveal them to babes.

Matthew 11:26 Yes, Father, because so it was good pleasure before Thee.

Matthew 11:27 Àll things were delivered to me by my Father, and none doth know the Son, except the Father, nor doth any know the Father, except the Son, and he to whom the Son may wish to reveal [Him].

Matthew 11:28 `Come unto me, all ye labouring and burdened ones, and I will give you rest,

Matthew 11:29 take up my yoke upon you, and learn from me, because I am meek and humble in heart, and ye shall find rest to your souls,

Matthew 11:30 for my yoke [is] easy, and my burden is light.'

Matthew 12:1. At that time did Jesus go on the sabbaths through the corn, and his disciples were hungry, and they began to pluck ears, and to eat,

Matthew 12:2 and the Pharisees having seen, said to him, `Lo, thy disciples do that which it is not lawful to do on a sabbath.'

Matthew 12:3 And he said to them, `Did ye not read what David did, when he was hungry, himself and those with him--

Matthew 12:4 how he went into the house of God, and the loaves of the presentation did eat, which it is not lawful to him to eat, nor to those with him, except to the priests alone?

Matthew 12:5 Òr did ye not read in the Law, that on the sabbaths the priests in the temple do profane the sabbath, and are blameless?

Matthew 12:6 and I say to you, that a greater than the temple is here;

Matthew 12:7 and if ye had known what is: Kindness I will, and not sacrifice--ye had not condemned the blameless,

Matthew 12:8 for the son of man is lord even of the sabbath.'

Matthew 12:9 And having departed thence, he went to their synagogue,

Matthew 12:10 and lo, there was a man having the hand withered, and they questioned him, saying, Ìs it lawful to heal on the sabbaths?' that they might accuse him.

Matthew 12:11 And he said to them, `What man shall be of you, who shall have one sheep, and if this may fall on the sabbaths into a ditch, will not lay hold on it and raise [it]?

Matthew 12:12 How much better, therefore, is a man than a sheep? --so that it is lawful on the sabbaths to do good.'

Matthew 12:13 Then saith he to the man, `Stretch forth thy hand,' and he stretched [it] forth, and it was restored whole as the other.

Matthew 12:14. And the Pharisees having gone forth, held a consultation against him, how they might destroy him,

Matthew 12:15 and Jesus having known, withdrew thence, and there followed him great multitudes, and he healed them all,

Matthew 12:16 and did charge them that they might not make him manifest,

Matthew 12:17 that it might be fulfilled that was spoken through Isaiah the prophet, saying,

Matthew 12:18 `Lo, My servant, whom I did choose, My beloved, in whom My soul did delight, I will put My Spirit upon him, and judgment to the nations he shall declare,

Matthew 12:19 he shall not strive nor cry, nor shall any hear in the broad places his voice,

Matthew 12:20 a bruised reed he shall not break, and smoking flax he shall not quench, till he may put forth judgment to victory,

Matthew 12:21 and in his name shall nations hope.'

Matthew 12:22. Then was brought to him a demoniac, blind and dumb, and he healed him, so that the blind and dumb both spake and saw.

Matthew 12:23 And all the multitudes were amazed, and said, Ìs this the Son of David?'

Matthew 12:24 but the Pharisees having heard, said, `This one doth not cast out demons, except by Beelzeboul, ruler of the demons.'

Matthew 12:25 And Jesus, knowing their thoughts, said to them, Èvery kingdom having been divided against itself is desolated, and no city or house having been divided against itself, doth stand,

Matthew 12:26 and if the Adversary doth cast out the Adversary, against himself he was divided, how then doth his kingdom stand?

Matthew 12:27 Ànd if I, by Beelzeboul, do cast out the demons, your sons--by whom do they cast out? because of this they--they shall be your judges.

Matthew 12:28 `But if I, by the Spirit of God, do cast out the demons, then come already unto you did the reign of God.

Matthew 12:29 Òr how is one able to go into the house of the strong man, and to plunder his goods, if first he may not bind the strong man? and then his house he will plunder.

Matthew 12:30 `He who is not with me is against me, and he who is not gathering with me, doth scatter.

Matthew 12:31 Because of this I say to you, all sin and evil speaking shall be forgiven to men, but the evil speaking of the Spirit shall not be forgiven to men.

Matthew 12:32 And whoever may speak a word against the Son of Man it shall be forgiven to him, but whoever may speak against the Holy Spirit, it shall not be forgiven him, neither in this age, nor in that which is coming.

Matthew 12:33 Èither make the tree good, and its fruit good, or make the tree bad, and its fruit bad, for from the fruit is the tree known.

Matthew 12:34 `Brood of vipers! how are ye able to speak good things--being evil? for out of the abundance of the heart doth the mouth speak.

Matthew 12:35 The good man out of the good treasure of the heart doth put forth the good things, and the evil man out of the evil treasure doth put forth evil things.

Matthew 12:36 Ànd I say to you, that every idle word that men may speak, they shall give for it a reckoning in a day of judgment;

Matthew 12:37 for from thy words thou shalt be declared righteous, and from thy words thou shalt be declared unrighteous.'

Matthew 12:38. Then answered certain of the scribes and Pharisees, saying, `Teacher, we will to see a sign from thee.'

Matthew 12:39 And he answering said to them, À generation, evil and adulterous, doth seek a sign, and a sign shall not be given to it, except the sign of Jonah the prophet;

Matthew 12:40 for, as Jonah was in the belly of the fish three days and three nights, so shall the Son of Man be in the heart of the earth three days and three nights.

Matthew 12:41 `Men of Nineveh shall stand up in the judgment with this generation, and shall condemn it, for they reformed at the proclamation of Jonah, and lo, a greater than Jonah here!

Matthew 12:42 À queen of the south shall rise up in the judgment with this generation, and shall condemn it, for she came from the ends of the earth to hear the wisdom of Solomon, and lo, a greater than Solomon here!

Matthew 12:43 Ànd, when the unclean spirit may go forth from the man, it doth walk through dry places seeking rest, and doth not find;

Matthew 12:44 then it saith, I will turn back to my house whence I came forth; and having come, it findeth [it] unoccupied, swept, and adorned:

Matthew 12:45 then doth it go, and take with itself seven other spirits more evil than itself, and having gone in they dwell there, and the last of that man doth become worse than the first; so shall it be also to this evil generation.'

Matthew 12:46. And while he was yet speaking to the multitudes, lo, his mother and brethren had stood without, seeking to speak to him,

Matthew 12:47 and one said to him, `Lo, thy mother and thy brethren do stand without, seeking to speak to thee.'

Matthew 12:48 And he answering said to him who spake to him, `Who is my mother? and who are my brethren?'

Matthew 12:49 And having stretched forth his hand toward his disciples, he said, `Lo, my mother and my brethren!

Matthew 12:50 for whoever may do the will of my Father who is in the heavens, he is my brother, and sister, and mother.'

Matthew 13:1. And in that day Jesus, having gone forth from the house, was sitting by the sea,

Matthew 13:2 and gathered together unto him were many multitudes, so that he having gone into the boat did sit down, and all the multitude on the beach did stand,

Matthew 13:3 and he spake to them many things in similes, saying: `Lo, the sower went forth to sow,

Matthew 13:4 and in his sowing, some indeed fell by the way, and the fowls did come and devour them,

Matthew 13:5 and others fell upon the rocky places, where they had not much earth, and immediately they sprang forth, through not having depth of earth,

Matthew 13:6 and the sun having risen they were scorched, and through not having root, they withered,

Matthew 13:7 and others fell upon the thorns, and the thorns did come up and choke them,

Matthew 13:8 and others fell upon the good ground, and were giving fruit, some indeed a hundredfold, and some sixty, and some thirty.

Matthew 13:9 He who is having ears to hear--let him hear.'

Matthew 13:10 And the disciples having come near, said to him, `Wherefore in similes dost thou speak to them?'

Matthew 13:11 And he answering said to them that--`To you it hath been given to know the secrets of the reign of the heavens, and to these it hath not been given,

Matthew 13:12 for whoever hath, it shall be given to him, and he shall have overabundance, and whoever hath not, even that which he hath shall be taken from him.

Matthew 13:13 `Because of this, in similes do I speak to them, because seeing they do not see, and hearing they do not hear, nor understand,

Matthew 13:14 and fulfilled on them is the prophecy of Isaiah, that saith, With hearing ye shall hear, and ye shall not understand, and seeing ye shall see, and ye shall not perceive,

Matthew 13:15 for made gross was the heart of this people, and with the ears they heard heavily, and their eyes they did close, lest they might see with the eyes, and with the ears might hear, and with the heart understand, and turn back, and I might heal them.

Matthew 13:16 And happy are your eyes because they see, and your ears because they hear,

Matthew 13:17 for verily I say to you, that many prophets and righteous men did desire to see that which ye look on, and they did not see, and to hear that which ye hear, and they did not hear.

Matthew 13:18 `Ye, therefore, hear ye the simile of the sower:

Matthew 13:19 Every one hearing the word of the reign, and not understanding--the evil one doth come, and doth catch that which hath been sown in his heart; this is that sown by the way.

Matthew 13:20 And that sown on the rocky places, this is he who is hearing the word, and immediately with joy is receiving it,

Matthew 13:21 and he hath not root in himself, but is temporary, and persecution or tribulation having happened because of the word, immediately he is stumbled.

Matthew 13:22 And that sown toward the thorns, this is he who is hearing the word, and the anxiety of this age, and the deceitfulness of the riches, do choke the word, and it becometh unfruitful.

Matthew 13:23 Ànd that sown on the good ground: this is he who is hearing the word, and is understanding, who indeed doth bear fruit, and doth make, some indeed a hundredfold, and some sixty, and some thirty.'

Matthew 13:24. Another simile he set before them, saying: `The reign of the heavens was likened to a man sowing good seed in his field,

Matthew 13:25 and, while men are sleeping, his enemy came and sowed darnel in the midst of the wheat, and went away,

Matthew 13:26 and when the herb sprang up, and yielded fruit, then appeared also the darnel.

Matthew 13:27 Ànd the servants of the householder, having come near, said to him, Sir, good seed didst thou not sow in thy field? whence then hath it the darnel?

Matthew 13:28 And he saith to them, A man, an enemy, did this; and the servants said to him, Wilt thou, then, [that] having gone away we may gather it up?

Matthew 13:29 Ànd he said, No, lest--gathering up the darnel--ye root up with it the wheat,

Matthew 13:30 suffer both to grow together till the harvest, and in the time of the harvest I will say to the reapers, Gather up first the darnel, and bind it in bundles, to burn it, and the wheat gather up into my storehouse.'

Matthew 13:31 Another simile he set before them, saying: `The reign of the heavens is like to a grain of mustard, which a man having taken, did sow in his field,

Matthew 13:32 which less, indeed, is than all the seeds, but when it may be grown, is greatest of the herbs, and becometh a tree, so that the birds of the heaven do come and rest in its branches.'

Matthew 13:33 Another simile spake he to them: `The reign of the heavens is like to leaven, which a woman having taken, hid in three measures of meal, till the whole was leavened.'

Matthew 13:34 All these things spake Jesus in similes to the multitudes, and without a simile he was not speaking to them,

Matthew 13:35 that it might be fulfilled that was spoken through the prophet, saying, Ì will open in similes my mouth, I will utter things having been hidden from the foundation of the world.'

Matthew 13:36 Then having let away the multitudes, Jesus came to the house, and his disciples came near to him, saying, Èxplain to us the simile of the darnel of the field.'

Matthew 13:37 And he answering said to them, `He who is sowing the good seed is the Son of Man,

Matthew 13:38 and the field is the world, and the good seed, these are the sons of the reign, and the darnel are the sons of the evil one,

Matthew 13:39 and the enemy who sowed them is the devil, and the harvest is a full end of the age, and the reapers are messengers.

Matthew 13:40 Às, then, the darnel is gathered up, and is burned with fire, so shall it be in the full end of this age,

Matthew 13:41 the Son of Man shall send forth his messengers, and they shall gather up out of his kingdom all the stumbling-blocks, and those doing the unlawlessness,

Matthew 13:42 and shall cast them to the furnace of the fire; there shall be the weeping and the gnashing of the teeth.

Matthew 13:43 `Then shall the righteous shine forth as the sun in the reign of their Father. He who is having ears to hear--let him hear.

Matthew 13:44. Àgain, the reign of the heavens is like to treasure hid in the field, which a man having found did hide, and from his joy goeth, and all, as much as he hath, he selleth, and buyeth that field.

Matthew 13:45 Àgain, the reign of the heavens is like to a man, a merchant, seeking goodly pearls,

Matthew 13:46 who having found one pearl of great price, having gone away, hath sold all, as much as he had, and bought it.

Matthew 13:47 Àgain, the reign of the heavens is like to a net that was cast into the sea, and did gather together of every kind,

Matthew 13:48 which, when it was filled, having drawn up again upon the beach, and having sat down, they gathered the good into vessels, and the bad they did cast out,

Matthew 13:49 so shall it be in the full end of the age, the messengers shall come forth and separate the evil out of the midst of the righteous,

Matthew 13:50 and shall cast them to the furnace of the fire, there shall be the weeping and the gnashing of the teeth.'

Matthew 13:51 Jesus saith to them, `Did ye understand all these?' They say to him, `Yes, sir.'

Matthew 13:52 And he said to them, `Because of this every scribe having been discipled in regard to the reign of the heavens, is like to a man, a householder, who doth bring forth out of his treasure things new and old.'

Matthew 13:53. And it came to pass, when Jesus finished these similes, he removed thence,

Matthew 13:54 and having come to his own country, he was teaching them in their synagogue, so that they were astonished, and were saying, `Whence to this one this wisdom and the mighty works?

Matthew 13:55 is not this the carpenter's son? is not his mother called Mary, and his brethren James, and Joses, and Simon, and Judas?

Matthew 13:56 and his sisters--are they not all with us? whence, then, to this one all these?'

Matthew 13:57 and they were stumbled at him. And Jesus said to them, `A prophet is not without honour except in his own country, and in his own house:'

Matthew 13:58 and he did not there many mighty works, because of their unbelief.

Matthew 14:1. At that time did Herod the tetrarch hear the fame of Jesus,

Matthew 14:2 and said to his servants, `This is John the Baptist, he did rise from the dead, and because of this the mighty energies are working in him.'

Matthew 14:3 For Herod having laid hold on John, did bind him, and did put him in prison, because of Herodias his brother Philip's wife,

Matthew 14:4 for John was saying to him, `It is not lawful to thee to have her,'

Matthew 14:5 and, willing to kill him, he feared the multitude, because as a prophet they were holding him.

Matthew 14:6 But the birthday of Herod being kept, the daughter of Herodias danced in the midst, and did please Herod,

Matthew 14:7 whereupon with an oath he professed to give her whatever she might ask.

Matthew 14:8 And she having been instigated by her mother--`Give me (says she) here upon a plate the head of John the Baptist;

Matthew 14:9 and the king was grieved, but because of the oaths and of those reclining with him, he commanded [it] to be given;

Matthew 14:10 and having sent, he beheaded John in the prison,

Matthew 14:11 and his head was brought upon a plate, and was given to the damsel, and she brought [it] nigh to her mother.

Matthew 14:12 And his disciples having come, took up the body, and buried it, and having come, they told Jesus,

Matthew 14:13. and Jesus having heard, withdrew thence in a boat to a desolate place by himself, and the multitudes having heard did follow him on land from the cities.

Matthew 14:14 And Jesus having come forth, saw a great multitude, and was moved with compassion upon them, and did heal their infirm;

Matthew 14:15 and evening having come, his disciples came to him, saying, `The place is desolate, and the hour hath now past, let away the multitudes that, having gone to the villages, they may buy to themselves food.'

Matthew 14:16 And Jesus said to them, `They have no need to go away--give ye them to eat.'

Matthew 14:17 And they say to him, `We have not here except five loaves, and two fishes.'

Matthew 14:18 And he said, `Bring ye them to me hither.'

Matthew 14:19 And having commanded the multitudes to recline upon the grass, and having taken the five loaves and the two fishes, having looked up to the heaven, he did bless, and having broken, he gave the loaves to the disciples, and the disciples to the multitudes,

Matthew 14:20 and they did all eat, and were filled, and they took up what was over of the broken pieces twelve hand-baskets full;

Matthew 14:21 and those eating were about five thousand men, apart from women and children.

Matthew 14:22. And immediately Jesus constrained his disciples to go into the boat, and to go before him to the other side, till he might let away the multitudes;

Matthew 14:23 and having let away the multitudes, he went up to the mountain by himself to pray, and evening having come, he was there alone,

Matthew 14:24 and the boat was now in the midst of the sea, distressed by the waves, for the wind was contrary.

Matthew 14:25 And in the fourth watch of the night Jesus went away to them, walking upon the sea,

Matthew 14:26 and the disciples having seen him walking upon the sea, were troubled saying--Ìt is an apparition,' and from the fear they cried out;

Matthew 14:27 and immediately Jesus spake to them, saying, `Be of good courage, I am [he], be not afraid.'

Matthew 14:28 And Peter answering him said, `Sir, if it is thou, bid me come to thee upon the waters;'

Matthew 14:29 and he said, `Come;' and having gone down from the boat, Peter walked upon the waters to come unto Jesus,

Matthew 14:30 but seeing the wind vehement, he was afraid, and having begun to sink, he cried out, saying, `Sir, save me.'

Matthew 14:31 And immediately Jesus, having stretched forth the hand, laid hold of him, and saith to him, `Little faith! for what didst thou waver?'

Matthew 14:32 and they having gone to the boat the wind lulled,

Matthew 14:33 and those in the boat having come, did bow to him, saying, `Truly--God's Son art thou.'

Matthew 14:34. And having passed over, they came to the land of Gennesaret,

Matthew 14:35 and having recognized him, the men of that place sent forth to all that region round about, and they brought to him all who were ill,

Matthew 14:36 and were calling on him that they might only touch the fringe of his garment, and as many as did touch were saved.

Matthew 15:1. Then come unto Jesus do they from Jerusalem--scribes and Pharisees--saying, **Matthew 15:2** `Wherefore do thy disciples transgress the tradition of the elders? for they do not wash their hands when they may eat bread.'

Matthew 15:3 And he answering said to them, `Wherefore also do ye transgress the command of God because of your tradition?

Matthew 15:4 for God did command, saying, Honour thy father and mother; and, He who is speaking evil of father or mother--let him die the death;

Matthew 15:5 but ye say, Whoever may say to father or mother, An offering [is] whatever thou mayest be profited by me; --

Matthew 15:6 and he may not honour his father or his mother, and ye did set aside the command of God because of your tradition.

Matthew 15:7 `Hypocrites, well did Isaiah prophesy of you, saying,

Matthew 15:8 This people doth draw nigh to Me with their mouth, and with the lips it doth honour Me, but their heart is far off from Me;

Matthew 15:9 and in vain do they worship Me, teaching teachings--commands of men.'

Matthew 15:10. And having called near the multitude, he said to them, `Hear and understand:

Matthew 15:11 not that which is coming into the mouth doth defile the man, but that which is coming forth from the mouth, this defileth the man.'

Matthew 15:12 Then his disciples having come near, said to him, `Hast thou known that the Pharisees, having heard the word, were stumbled?'

Matthew 15:13 And he answering said, Èvery plant that my heavenly Father did not plant shall be rooted up;

Matthew 15:14 let them alone, guides they are--blind of blind; and if blind may guide blind, both into a ditch shall fall.'

Matthew 15:15 And Peter answering said to him, Èxplain to us this simile.'

Matthew 15:16 And Jesus said, Àre ye also yet without understanding?

Matthew 15:17 do ye not understand that all that is going into the mouth doth pass into the belly, and into the drain is cast forth?

Matthew 15:18 but the things coming forth from the mouth from the heart do come forth, and these defile the man;

Matthew 15:19 for out of the heart come forth evil thoughts, murders, adulteries, whoredoms, thefts, false witnessings, evil speakings:

Matthew 15:20 these are the things defiling the man; but to eat with unwashen hands doth not defile the man.'

Matthew 15:21. And Jesus having come forth thence, withdrew to the parts of Tyre and Sidon,

Matthew 15:22 and lo, a woman, a Canaanitess, from those borders having come forth, did call to him, saying, `Deal kindly with me, Sir-- Son of David; my daughter is miserably demonized.'

Matthew 15:23 And he did not answer her a word; and his disciples having come to him, were asking him, saying--`Let her away, because she crieth after us;'

Matthew 15:24 and he answering said, Ì was not sent except to the lost sheep of the house of Israel.'

Matthew 15:25 And having come, she was bowing to him, saying, `Sir, help me;'

Matthew 15:26 and he answering said, Ìt is not good to take the children's bread, and to cast to the little dogs.'

Matthew 15:27 And she said, `Yes, sir, for even the little dogs do eat of the crumbs that are falling from their lords' table;'

Matthew 15:28 then answering, Jesus said to her, Ò woman, great [is] thy faith, let it be to thee as thou wilt;' and her daughter was healed from that hour.

Matthew 15:29. And Jesus having passed thence, came nigh unto the sea of Galilee, and having gone up to the mountain, he was sitting there,

Matthew 15:30 and there came to him great multitudes, having with them lame, blind, dumb, maimed, and many others, and they did cast them at the feet of Jesus, and he healed them,

Matthew 15:31 so that the multitudes did wonder, seeing dumb ones speaking, maimed whole, lame walking, and blind seeing; and they glorified the God of Israel.

Matthew 15:32 And Jesus having called near his disciples, said, Ì have compassion upon the multitude, because now three days they continue with me, and they have not what they may eat; and to let them away fasting I will not, lest they faint in the way.'

Matthew 15:33 And his disciples say to him, `Whence to us, in a wilderness, so many loaves, as to fill so great a multitude?'

Matthew 15:34 And Jesus saith to them, `How many loaves have ye?' and they said, `Seven, and a few little fishes.'

Matthew 15:35 And he commanded the multitudes to sit down upon the ground,

Matthew 15:36 and having taken the seven loaves and the fishes, having given thanks, he did break, and gave to his disciples, and the disciples to the multitude.

Matthew 15:37 And they did all eat, and were filled, and they took up what was over of the broken pieces seven baskets full,

Matthew 15:38 and those eating were four thousand men, apart from women and children.

Matthew 15:39 And having let away the multitudes, he went into the boat, and did come to the borders of Magdala.

Matthew 16:1. And the Pharisees and Sadducees having come, tempting, did question him, to shew to them a sign from the heaven,

Matthew 16:2 and he answering said to them, Èvening having come, ye say, Fair weather, for the heaven is red,

Matthew 16:3 and at morning, Foul weather to-day, for the heaven is red--gloomy; hypocrites, the face of the heavens indeed ye do know to discern, but the signs of the times ye are not able!

Matthew 16:4 À generation evil and adulterous doth seek a sign, and a sign shall not be given to it, except the sign of Jonah the prophet;' and having left them he went away.

Matthew 16:5. And his disciples having come to the other side, forgot to take loaves,

Matthew 16:6 and Jesus said to them, `Beware, and take heed of the leaven of the Pharisees and Sadducees;'

Matthew 16:7 and they were reasoning in themselves, saying, `Because we took no loaves.'

Matthew 16:8 And Jesus having known, said to them, `Why reason ye in yourselves, ye of little faith, because ye took no loaves?

Matthew 16:9 do ye not yet understand, nor remember the five loaves of the five thousand, and how many hand-baskets ye took up?

Matthew 16:10 nor the seven loaves of the four thousand, and how many baskets ye took up?

Matthew 16:11 how do ye not understand that I did not speak to you of bread--to take heed of the leaven of the Pharisees and Sadducees?'

Matthew 16:12 Then they understood that he did not say to take heed of the leaven of the bread, but of the teaching, of the Pharisees and Sadducees.

Matthew 16:13. And Jesus, having come to the parts of Caesarea Philippi, was asking his disciples, saying, `Who do men say me to be--the Son of Man?'

Matthew 16:14 and they said, `Some, John the Baptist, and others, Elijah, and others, Jeremiah, or one of the prophets.'

Matthew 16:15 He saith to them, `And ye--who do ye say me to be?'

Matthew 16:16 and Simon Peter answering said, `Thou art the Christ, the Son of the living God.'

Matthew 16:17 And Jesus answering said to him, `Happy art thou, Simon Bar-Jona, because flesh and blood did not reveal [it] to thee, but my Father who is in the heavens.

Matthew 16:18 And I also say to thee, that thou art a rock, and upon this rock I will build my assembly, and gates of Hades shall not prevail against it;

Matthew 16:19 and I will give to thee the keys of the reign of the heavens, and whatever thou mayest bind upon the earth shall be having been bound in the heavens, and whatever thou mayest loose upon the earth shall be having been loosed in the heavens.'

Matthew 16:20 Then did he charge his disciples that they may say to no one that he is Jesus the Christ.

Matthew 16:21. From that time began Jesus to shew to his disciples that it is necessary for him to go away to Jerusalem, and to suffer many things from the elders, and chief priests, and scribes, and to be put to death, and the third day to rise.

Matthew 16:22 And having taken him aside, Peter began to rebuke him, saying, `Be kind to thyself, sir; this shall not be to thee;'

Matthew 16:23 and he having turned, said to Peter, `Get thee behind me, adversary! thou art a stumbling-block to me, for thou dost not mind the things of God, but the things of men.'

Matthew 16:24. Then said Jesus to his disciples, Ìf any one doth will to come after me, let him disown himself, and take up his cross, and follow me,

Matthew 16:25 for whoever may will to save his life, shall lose it, and whoever may lose his life for my sake shall find it,

Matthew 16:26 for what is a man profited if he may gain the whole world, but of his life suffer loss? or what shall a man give as an exchange for his life?

Matthew 16:27 `For, the Son of Man is about to come in the glory of his Father, with his messengers, and then he will reward each, according to his work.

Matthew 16:28 Verily I say to you, there are certain of those standing here who shall not taste of death till they may see the Son of Man coming in his reign.'

Matthew 17:1. And after six days Jesus taketh Peter, and James, and John his brother, and doth bring them up to a high mount by themselves,

Matthew 17:2 and he was transfigured before them, and his face shone as the sun, and his garments did become white as the light,

Matthew 17:3 and lo, appear to them did Moses and Elijah, talking together with him.

Matthew 17:4 And Peter answering said to Jesus, `Sir, it is good to us to be here; if thou wilt, we may make here three booths--for thee one, and for Moses one, and one for Elijah.'

Matthew 17:5 While he is yet speaking, lo, a bright cloud overshadowed them, and lo, a voice out of the cloud, saying, `This is My Son, --the Beloved, in whom I did delight; hear him.'

Matthew 17:6 And the disciples having heard, did fall upon their face, and were exceedingly afraid,

Matthew 17:7 and Jesus having come near, touched them, and said, `Rise, be not afraid,'

Matthew 17:8 and having lifted up their eyes, they saw no one, except Jesus only.

Matthew 17:9 And as they are coming down from the mount, Jesus charged them, saying, `Say to no one the vision, till the Son of Man out of the dead may rise.'

Matthew 17:10 And his disciples questioned him, saying, `Why then do the scribes say that Elijah it behoveth to come first?'

Matthew 17:11 And Jesus answering said to them, Èlijah doth indeed come first, and shall restore all things,

Matthew 17:12 and I say to you-- Elijah did already come, and they did not know him, but did with him whatever they would, so also the Son of Man is about to suffer by them.'

Matthew 17:13 Then understood the disciples that concerning John the Baptist he spake to them.

Matthew 17:14. And when they came unto the multitude, there came to him a man, kneeling down to him,

Matthew 17:15 and saying, `Sir, deal kindly with my son, for he is lunatic, and doth suffer miserably, for often he doth fall into the fire, and often into the water,

Matthew 17:16 and I brought him near to thy disciples, and they were not able to heal him.'

Matthew 17:17 And Jesus answering said, Ò generation, unstedfast and perverse, till when shall I be with you? till when shall I bear you? bring him to me hither;'

Matthew 17:18 and Jesus rebuked him, and the demon went out of him, and the lad was healed from that hour.

Matthew 17:19 Then the disciples having come to Jesus by himself,

said, `Wherefore were we not able to cast him out?'

Matthew 17:20 And Jesus said to them, `Through your want of faith; for verily I say to you, if ye may have faith as a grain of mustard, ye shall say to this mount, Remove hence to yonder place, and it shall remove, and nothing shall be impossible to you,

Matthew 17:21 and this kind doth not go forth except in prayer and fasting.'

Matthew 17:22. And while they are living in Galilee, Jesus said to them, `The Son of Man is about to be delivered up to the hands of men,

Matthew 17:23 and they shall kill him, and the third day he shall rise,' and they were exceeding sorry.

Matthew 17:24. And they having come to Capernaum, those receiving the didrachms came near to Peter, and said, `Your teacher--doth he not pay the didrachms?' He saith, `Yes.'

Matthew 17:25 And when he came into the house, Jesus anticipated him, saying, `What thinkest thou, Simon? the kings of the earth--from whom do they receive custom or poll-tax? from their sons or from the strangers?'

Matthew 17:26 Peter saith to him, `From the strangers.' Jesus said to him, `Then are the sons free;

Matthew 17:27 but, that we may not cause them to stumble, having gone to the sea, cast a hook, and the fish that hath come up first take thou up, and having opened its mouth, thou shalt find a stater, that having taken, give to them for me and thee.'

Matthew 18:1. At that hour came the disciples near to Jesus, saying, `Who, now, is greater in the reign of the heavens?'

Matthew 18:2 And Jesus having called near a child, did set him in the midst of them,

Matthew 18:3 and said, `Verily I say to you, if ye may not be turned and become as the children, ye may not enter into the reign of the heavens;

Matthew 18:4 whoever then may humble himself as this child, he is the greater in the reign of the heavens.

Matthew 18:5 And he who may receive one such child in my name, doth receive me,

Matthew 18:6 and whoever may cause to stumble one of those little ones who are believing in me, it is better for him that a weighty millstone may be hanged upon his neck, and he may be sunk in the depth of the sea.

Matthew 18:7. `Woe to the world from the stumbling-blocks! for there is a necessity for the stumbling-blocks to come, but woe to that man through whom the stumbling-block doth come!

Matthew 18:8 And if thy hand or thy foot doth cause thee to stumble, cut them off and cast from thee; it is good for thee to enter into the life lame or maimed, rather than having two hands or two feet, to be cast to the fire the age-during.

Matthew 18:9 And if thine eye doth cause thee to stumble, pluck it out and cast from thee; it is good for thee one-eyed to enter into the life, rather than having two eyes to be cast to the gehenna of the fire.

Matthew 18:10 `Beware! --ye may not despise one of these little ones, for I say to you, that their messengers in the heavens do always behold the face of my Father who is in the heavens,

Matthew 18:11 for the Son of Man did come to save the lost.

Matthew 18:12 `What think ye? if a man may have an hundred sheep, and there may go astray one of them, doth he not--having left the ninety-nine, having gone on the mountains--seek that which is gone astray?

Matthew 18:13 and if it may come to pass that he doth find it, verily I say to you, that he doth rejoice over it more than over the ninety-nine that have not gone astray;

Matthew 18:14 so it is not will in presence of your Father who is in the heavens, that one of these little ones may perish.

Matthew 18:15. Ànd if thy brother may sin against thee, go and show him his fault between thee and him alone, if he may hear thee, thou didst gain thy brother;

Matthew 18:16 and if he may not hear, take with thee yet one or two, that by the mouth of two witnesses or three every word may stand.

Matthew 18:17 Ànd if he may not hear them, say [it] to the assembly, and if also the assembly he may not hear, let him be to thee as the heathen man and the tax-gatherer.

Matthew 18:18 `Verily I say to you, Whatever things ye may bind upon the earth shall be having been bound in the heavens, and whatever things ye may loose on the earth shall be having been loosed in the heavens.

Matthew 18:19 Àgain, I say to you, that, if two of you may agree on the earth concerning anything, whatever they may ask--it shall be done to them from my Father who is in the heavens,

Matthew 18:20 for where there are two or three gathered together--to my name, there am I in the midst of them.'

Matthew 18:21. Then Peter having come near to him, said, `Sir, how often shall my brother sin against me, and I forgive him--till seven times?'

Matthew 18:22 Jesus saith to him, Ì do not say to thee till seven times, but till seventy times seven.

Matthew 18:23 `Because of this was the reign of the heavens likened to a man, a king, who did will to take reckoning with his servants,

Matthew 18:24 and he having begun to take account, there was brought near to him one debtor of a myriad of talents,

Matthew 18:25 and he having nothing to pay, his lord did command him to be sold, and his wife, and the children, and all, whatever he had, and payment to be made.

Matthew 18:26 The servant then, having fallen down, was bowing to him, saying, Sir, have patience with me, and I will pay thee all;

Matthew 18:27 and the lord of that servant having been moved with compassion did release him, and the debt he forgave him.

Matthew 18:28 Ànd, that servant having come forth, found one of his fellow-servants who was owing him an hundred denaries, and having laid hold, he took him by the throat, saying, Pay me that which thou owest.

Matthew 18:29 His fellow-servant then, having fallen down at his feet, was calling on him, saying, Have patience with me, and I will pay thee all;

Matthew 18:30 and he would not, but having gone away, he cast him into prison, till he might pay that which was owing.

Matthew 18:31 Ànd his fellow-servants having seen the things that were done, were grieved exceedingly, and having come, shewed fully to their lord all the things that were done;

Matthew 18:32 then having called him, his lord saith to him, Evil servant! all that debt I did forgive thee, seeing thou didst call upon me,

Matthew 18:33 did it not behove also thee to have dealt kindly with thy fellow-servant, as I also dealt kindly with thee?

Matthew 18:34 Ànd having been wroth, his lord delivered him to the inquisitors, till he might pay all that was owing to him;

Matthew 18:35 so also my heavenly Father will do to you, if ye may not forgive each one his brother from your hearts their trespasses.'

Matthew 19:1. And it came to pass, when Jesus finished these words, he removed from Galilee, and did come to the borders of Judea, beyond the Jordan,

Matthew 19:2 and great multitudes followed him, and he healed them there.

Matthew 19:3. And the Pharisees came near to him, tempting him, and saying to him, Ìs it lawful for a man to put away his wife for every cause?'

Matthew 19:4 And he answering said to them, `Did ye not read, that He who made [them], from the beginning a male and a female made them,

Matthew 19:5 and said, For this cause shall a man leave father and mother, and cleave to his wife, and they shall be--the two--for one flesh?

Matthew 19:6 so that they are no more two, but one flesh; what therefore God did join together, let no man put asunder.'

Matthew 19:7 They say to him, `Why then did Moses command to give a roll of divorce, and to put her away?'

Matthew 19:8 He saith to them--`Moses for your stiffness of heart did suffer you to put away your wives, but from the beginning it hath not been so.

Matthew 19:9 Ànd I say to you, that, whoever may put away his wife, if not for whoredom, and may marry another, doth commit adultery; and he who did marry her that hath been put away, doth commit adultery.'

Matthew 19:10 His disciples say to him, Ìf the case of the man with the woman is so, it is not good to marry.'

Matthew 19:11 And he said to them, Àll do not receive this word, but those to whom it hath been given;

Matthew 19:12 for there are eunuchs who from the mother's womb were so born; and there are eunuchs who were made eunuchs by men; and there are eunuchs who kept themselves eunuchs because of the reign of the heavens: he who is able to receive [it] --let him receive.'

Matthew 19:13. Then were brought near to him children that he might put hands on them and pray, and the disciples rebuked them.

Matthew 19:14 But Jesus said, `Suffer the children, and forbid them not, to come unto me, for of such is the reign of the heavens;'

Matthew 19:15 and having laid on them [his] hands, he departed thence.

Matthew 19:16. And lo, one having come near, said to him, `Good teacher, what good thing shall I do, that I may have life age-during?'

Matthew 19:17 And he said to him, `Why me dost thou call good? no one [is] good except One--God; but if thou dost will to enter into the life, keep the commands.'

Matthew 19:18 He saith to him, `What kind?' And Jesus said, `Thou shalt not kill, thou shalt not commit adultery, thou shalt not steal, thou shalt not bear false witness,

Matthew 19:19 honour thy father and mother, and, thou shalt love thy neighbour as thyself.'

Matthew 19:20 The young man saith to him, Àll these did I keep from my youth; what yet do I lack?'

Matthew 19:21 Jesus said to him, Ìf thou dost will to be perfect, go away, sell what thou hast, and give to the poor, and thou shalt have treasure in heaven, and come, follow me.'

Matthew 19:22 And the young man, having heard the word, went away sorrowful, for he had many possessions;

Matthew 19:23. and Jesus said to his disciples, `Verily I say to you, that hardly shall a rich man enter into the reign of the heavens;

Matthew 19:24 and again I say to you, it is easier for a camel through the eye of a needle to go, than for a rich man to enter into the reign of God.'

Matthew 19:25 And his disciples having heard, were amazed exceedingly, saying, `Who, then, is able to be saved?'

Matthew 19:26 And Jesus having earnestly beheld, said to them, `With men this is impossible, but with God all things are possible.'

Matthew 19:27 Then Peter answering said to him, `Lo, we did leave all, and follow thee, what then shall we have?'

Matthew 19:28 And Jesus said to them, `Verily I say to you, that ye who did follow me, in the regeneration, when the Son of Man may sit upon a throne of his glory, shall sit--ye also--upon twelve thrones, judging the twelve tribes of Israel;

Matthew 19:29 and every one who left houses, or brothers, or sisters, or father, or mother, or wife, or children, or fields, for my name's sake, an hundredfold shall receive, and life age-during shall inherit;

Matthew 19:30 and many first shall be last, and last first.

Matthew 20:1. `For the reign of the heavens is like to a man, a householder, who went forth with the morning to hire workmen for his vineyard,

Matthew 20:2 and having agreed with the workmen for a denary a day, he sent them into his vineyard.

Matthew 20:3 Ànd having gone forth about the third hour, he saw others standing in the market-place idle,

Matthew 20:4 and to these he said, Go ye--also ye--to the vineyard, and whatever may be righteous I will give you;

Matthew 20:5 and they went away. Àgain, having gone forth about the sixth and the ninth hour, he did in like manner.

Matthew 20:6 And about the eleventh hour, having gone forth, he found others standing idle, and saith to them, Why here have ye stood all the day idle?

Matthew 20:7 they say to him, Because no one did hire us; he saith to them, Go ye--ye also--to the vineyard, and whatever may be righteous ye shall receive.

Matthew 20:8 Ànd evening having come, the lord of the vineyard saith to his steward, Call the workmen, and pay them the reward, having begun from the last--unto the first.

Matthew 20:9 And they of about the eleventh hour having come, did receive each a denary.

Matthew 20:10 Ànd the first having come, did suppose that they shall receive more, and they received, they also, each a denary,

Matthew 20:11 and having received [it], they were murmuring against the householder, saying,

Matthew 20:12 that These, the last, wrought one hour, and thou didst make them equal to us, who were bearing the burden of the day--and the heat.

Matthew 20:13 Ànd he answering said to one of them, Comrade, I do no unrighteousness to thee; for a denary didst not thou agree with me?

Matthew 20:14 take that which is thine, and go; and I will to give to this, the last, also as to thee;

Matthew 20:15 is it not lawful to me to do what I will in mine own? is thine eye evil because I am good?

Matthew 20:16 So the last shall be first, and the first last, for many are called, and few chosen.'

Matthew 20:17. And Jesus going up to Jerusalem, took the twelve disciples by themselves in the way, and said to them,

Matthew 20:18 `Lo, we go up to Jerusalem, and the Son of Man shall be delivered to the chief priests and scribes,

Matthew 20:19 and they shall condemn him to death, and shall deliver him to the nations to mock, and to scourge, and to crucify, and the third day he will rise again.'

Matthew 20:20. Then came near to him the mother of the sons of Zebedee, with her sons, bowing and asking something from him,

Matthew 20:21 and he said to her, `What wilt thou?' She saith to him, `Say, that they may sit--these my two sons--one on thy right hand, and one on the left, in thy reign.'

Matthew 20:22 And Jesus answering said, `Ye have not known what ye ask for yourselves; are ye able to drink of the cup that I am about to drink? and with the baptism that I am baptized with, to be baptized?' They say to him, `We are able.'

Matthew 20:23 And he saith to them, Òf my cup indeed ye shall drink, and with the baptism that I am baptized with ye shall be baptized; but to sit on my right hand and on my left is not mine to give, but--to those for whom it hath been prepared by my father.'

Matthew 20:24 And the ten having heard, were much displeased with the two brothers,

Matthew 20:25 and Jesus having called them near, said, `Ye have known that the rulers of the nations do exercise lordship over them, and those great do exercise authority over them,

Matthew 20:26 but not so shall it be among you, but whoever may will among you to become great, let him be your ministrant;

Matthew 20:27 and whoever may will among you to be first, let him be your servant;

Matthew 20:28 even as the Son of Man did not come to be ministered to, but to minister, and to give his life a ransom for many.'

Matthew 20:29. And they going forth from Jericho, there followed him a great multitude,

Matthew 20:30 and lo, two blind men sitting by the way, having heard that Jesus doth pass by, cried, saying, `Deal kindly with us, sir--Son of David.'

Matthew 20:31 And the multitude charged them that they might be silent, and they cried out the more, saying, `Deal kindly with us sir--Son of David.'

Matthew 20:32 And having stood, Jesus called them, and said, `What will ye [that] I may do to you?'

Matthew 20:33 they say to him, `Sir, that our eyes may be opened;'

Matthew 20:34 and having been moved with compassion, Jesus touched their eyes, and immediately their eyes received sight, and they followed him.

Matthew 21:1. And when they came nigh to Jerusalem, and came to Bethphage, unto the mount of the Olives, then Jesus sent two disciples,

Matthew 21:2 saying to them, `Go on to the village over-against you, and immediately ye shall find an ass bound, and a colt with her--having loosed, bring ye to me;

Matthew 21:3 and if any one may say anything to you, ye shall say, that the lord hath need of them, and immediately he will send them.'

Matthew 21:4 And all this came to pass, that it might be fulfilled that was spoken through the prophet, saying,

Matthew 21:5 `Tell ye the daughter of Zion, Lo, thy king doth come to thee, meek, and mounted on an ass, and a colt, a foal of a beast of burden.'

Matthew 21:6 And the disciples having gone and having done as Jesus commanded them,

Matthew 21:7 brought the ass and the colt, and did put on them their garments, and set [him] upon them;

Matthew 21:8 and the very great multitude spread their own garments in the way, and others were cutting branches from the trees, and were strewing in the way,

Matthew 21:9 and the multitudes who were going before, and who were following, were crying, saying, `Hosanna to the Son of David, blessed is he who is coming in the name of the Lord; Hosanna in the highest.'

Matthew 21:10 And he having entered into Jerusalem, all the city was moved, saying, `Who is this?'

Matthew 21:11 And the multitudes said, `This is Jesus the prophet, who [is] from Nazareth of Galilee.'

Matthew 21:12. And Jesus entered into the temple of God, and did cast forth all those selling and buying in the temple, and the tables of the money-changers he overturned, and the seats of those selling the doves,

Matthew 21:13 and he saith to them, `It hath been written, My house a house of prayer shall be called, but ye did make it a den of robbers.'

Matthew 21:14 And there came to him blind and lame men in the temple, and he healed them,

Matthew 21:15 and the chief priests and the scribes having seen the wonderful things that he did, and the children crying in the temple, and saying, `Hosanna to the Son of David,' were much displeased;

Matthew 21:16 and they said to him, `Hearest thou what these say?' And Jesus saith to them, `Yes, did ye never read, that, Out of the mouth of babes and sucklings Thou didst prepare praise?'

Matthew 21:17 And having left them, he went forth out of the city to Bethany, and did lodge there,

Matthew 21:18. and in the morning turning back to the city, he hungered,

Matthew 21:19 and having seen a certain fig-tree on the way, he came to it, and found nothing in it except leaves only, and he saith to it, `No more from thee may fruit be--to the age;' and forthwith the fig-tree withered.

Matthew 21:20 And the disciples having seen, did wonder, saying, `How did the fig-tree forthwith wither?'

Matthew 21:21 And Jesus answering said to them, `Verily I say to you, If ye may have faith, and may not doubt, not only this of the fig-tree shall ye do, but even if to this mount ye may say, Be lifted up and be cast into the sea, it shall come to pass;

Matthew 21:22 and all--as much as ye may ask in the prayer, believing, ye shall receive.'

Matthew 21:23. And he having come to the temple, there came to him when teaching the chief priests and the elders of the people, saying, `By what authority dost thou do these things? and who gave thee this authority?'

Matthew 21:24 And Jesus answering said to them, `I will ask you--I also--one word, which if ye may tell me, I also will tell you by what authority I do these things;

Matthew 21:25 the baptism of John, whence was it? --from heaven, or from men?' And they were reasoning with themselves, saying, `If we should say, From heaven; he will say to us, Wherefore, then, did ye not believe him?

Matthew 21:26 and if we should say, From men, we fear the multitude, for all hold John as a prophet.'

Matthew 21:27 And answering Jesus they said, `We have not known.' He said to them--he also--`Neither do I tell you by what authority I do these things.

Matthew 21:28. Ànd what think ye? A man had two children, and having come to the first, he said, Child, go, to-day be working in my vineyard.'

Matthew 21:29 And he answering said, Ì will not,' but at last, having repented, he went.

Matthew 21:30 Ànd having come to the second, he said in the same manner, and he answering said, I [go], sir, and went not;

Matthew 21:31 which of the two did the will of the father?' They say to him, `The first.' Jesus saith to them, `Verily I say to you, that the tax-gatherers and the harlots do go before you into the reign of God,

Matthew 21:32 for John came unto you in the way of righteousness, and ye did not believe him, and the tax-gatherers and the harlots did believe him, and ye, having seen, repented not at last--to believe him.

Matthew 21:33. `Hear ye another simile: There was a certain man, a householder, who planted a vineyard, and did put a hedge round it, and digged in it a wine-press, and built a tower, and gave it out to husbandmen, and went abroad.

Matthew 21:34 Ànd when the season of the fruits came nigh, he sent his servants unto the husbandmen, to receive the fruits of it,

Matthew 21:35 and the husbandmen having taken his servants, one they scourged, and one they killed, and one they stoned.

Matthew 21:36 Àgain he sent other servants more than the first, and they did to them in the same manner.

Matthew 21:37 Ànd at last he sent unto them his son, saying, They will reverence my son;

Matthew 21:38 and the husbandmen having seen the son, said among themselves, This is the heir, come, we may kill him, and may possess his inheritance;

Matthew 21:39 and having taken him, they cast [him] out of the vineyard, and killed him;

Matthew 21:40 whenever therefore the lord of the vineyard may come, what will he do to these husbandmen?'

Matthew 21:41 They say to him, Èvil men--he will evilly destroy them, and the vineyard will give out to other husbandmen, who will give back to him the fruits in their seasons.'

Matthew 21:42 Jesus saith to them, `Did ye never read in the Writings, A stone that the builders disallowed, it became head of a corner; from the Lord hath this come to pass, and it is wonderful in our eyes.

Matthew 21:43 `Because of this I say to you, that the reign of God shall be taken from you, and given to a nation bringing forth its fruit;

Matthew 21:44 and he who is falling on this stone shall be broken, and on whomsoever it may fall it will crush him to pieces.'

Matthew 21:45 And the chief priests and the Pharisees having heard his similes, knew that of them he speaketh,

Matthew 21:46 and seeking to lay hold on him, they feared the multitudes, seeing they were holding him as a prophet.

Matthew 22:1. And Jesus answering, again spake to them in similes, saying,

Matthew 22:2 `The reign of the heavens was likened to a man, a king, who made marriage-feasts for his son,

Matthew 22:3 and he sent forth his servants to call those having been called to the marriage-feasts, and they were not willing to come.

Matthew 22:4 Àgain he sent forth other servants, saying, Say to those who have been called: Lo, my dinner I prepared, my oxen and the fatlings have been killed, and all things [are] ready, come ye to the marriage-feasts;

Matthew 22:5 and they, having disregarded [it], went away, the one to his own field, and the other to his merchandise;

Matthew 22:6 and the rest, having laid hold on his servants, did insult and slay [them].

Matthew 22:7 Ànd the king having heard, was wroth, and having sent forth his soldiers, he destroyed those murderers, and their city he set on fire;

Matthew 22:8 then saith he to his servants, The marriage-feast indeed is ready, and those called were not worthy,

Matthew 22:9 be going, then, on to the cross-ways, and as many as ye may find, call ye to the marriage-feasts.

Matthew 22:10 Ànd those servants, having gone forth to the ways, did gather all, as many as they found, both bad and good, and the marriage-feast apartment was filled with those reclining.

Matthew 22:11 Ànd the king having come in to view those reclining, saw there a man not clothed with clothing of the marriage-feast,

Matthew 22:12 and he saith to him, Comrade, how didst thou come in hither, not having clothing of the marriage-feast? and he was speech-less.

Matthew 22:13 `Then said the king to the ministrants, Having bound his feet and hands, take him up and cast forth to the outer darkness, there shall be the weeping and the gnashing of the teeth;

Matthew 22:14 for many are called, and few chosen.'

Matthew 22:15. Then the Pharisees having gone, took counsel how they might ensnare him in words,

Matthew 22:16 and they send to him their disciples with the Herodians, saying, `Teacher, we have known that thou art true, and the way of God in truth thou dost teach, and thou art not caring for any one, for thou dost not look to the face of men;

Matthew 22:17 tell us, therefore, what dost thou think? is it lawful to give tribute to Caesar or not?'

Matthew 22:18 And Jesus having known their wickedness, said, `Why me do ye tempt, hypocrites?

Matthew 22:19 show me the tribute-coin?' and they brought to him a denary;

Matthew 22:20 and he saith to them, `Whose [is] this image and the inscription?'

Matthew 22:21 they say to him, `Caesar's;' then saith he to them,

`Render therefore the things of Caesar to Caesar, and the things of God to God;'

Matthew 22:22 and having heard they wondered, and having left him they went away.

Matthew 22:23. In that day there came near to him Sadducees, who are saying there is not a rising again, and they questioned him, saying,

Matthew 22:24 `Teacher, Moses said, If any one may die not having children, his brother shall marry his wife, and shall raise up seed to his brother.

Matthew 22:25 Ànd there were with us seven brothers, and the first having married did die, and not having seed, he left his wife to his brother;

Matthew 22:26 in like manner also the second, and the third, unto the seventh,

Matthew 22:27 and last of all died also the woman;

Matthew 22:28 therefore in the rising again, of which of the seven shall she be wife--for all had her?'

Matthew 22:29 And Jesus answering said to them, `Ye go astray, not knowing the Writings, nor the power of God;

Matthew 22:30 for in the rising again they do not marry, nor are they given in marriage, but are as messengers of God in heaven.

Matthew 22:31 Ànd concerning the rising again of the dead, did ye not read that which was spoken to you by God, saying,

Matthew 22:32 I am the God of Abraham, and the God of Isaac, and the God of Jacob? God is not a God of dead men, but of living.'

Matthew 22:33 And having heard, the multitudes were astonished at his teaching;

Matthew 22:34. and the Pharisees, having heard that he did silence the Sadducees, were gathered together unto him;

Matthew 22:35 and one of them, a lawyer, did question, tempting him, and saying,

Matthew 22:36 `Teacher, which [is] the great command in the Law?'

Matthew 22:37 And Jesus said to him, `Thou shalt love the Lord thy God with all thy heart, and with all thy soul, and with all thine under-standing--

Matthew 22:38 this is a first and great command;

Matthew 22:39 and the second [is] like to it, Thou shalt love thy neighbour as thyself;

Matthew 22:40 on these--the two commands--all the law and the prophets do hang.'

Matthew 22:41. And the Pharisees having been gathered together, Jesus did question them,

Matthew 22:42 saying, `What do ye think concerning the Christ? of whom is he son?' They say to him, Òf David.'

Matthew 22:43 He saith to them, `How then doth David in the Spirit call him lord, saying,

Matthew 22:44 The Lord said to my lord, Sit at my right hand, till I may make thine enemies thy footstool?

Matthew 22:45 If then David doth call him lord, how is he his son?'

Matthew 22:46 And no one was able to answer him a word, nor durst any from that day question him any more.

Matthew 23:1. Then Jesus spake to the multitudes, and to his disciples,

Matthew 23:2 saying, Òn the seat of Moses sat down the scribes and the Pharisees;

Matthew 23:3 all, then, as much as they may say to you to observe, ob-serve and do, but according to their works do not, for they say, and do not;

Matthew 23:4 for they bind togeth-er burdens heavy and grievous to be borne, and lay upon the shoulders of men, but with their finger they will not move them.

Matthew 23:5 Ànd all their works they do to be seen by men, and they make broad their phylacteries, and enlarge the fringes of their garments,

Matthew 23:6 they love also the chief couches in the supper, and the chief seats in the synagogues,

Matthew 23:7 and the salutations in the market-places, and to be called by men, Rabbi, Rabbi.

Matthew 23:8 Ànd ye--ye may not be called Rabbi, for one is your director--the Christ, and all ye are brethren;

Matthew 23:9 and ye may not call [any] your father on the earth, for one is your Father, who is in the heavens,

Matthew 23:10 nor may ye be called directors, for one is your director--the Christ.

Matthew 23:11 And the greater of you shall be your ministrant,

Matthew 23:12 and whoever shall exalt himself shall be humbled, and whoever shall humble himself shall be exalted.

Matthew 23:13. `Woe to you, Scribes and Pharisees, hypocrites! because ye shut up the reign of the heavens before men, for ye do not go in, nor those going in do ye suffer to enter.

Matthew 23:14 `Woe to you, Scribes and Pharisees, hypocrites! because ye eat up the houses of the widows, and for a pretence make long prayers, because of this ye shall receive more abundant judgment.

Matthew 23:15 `Woe to you, Scribes and Pharisees, hypocrites! because ye go round the sea and the dry land to make one proselyte, and whenever it may happen--ye make him a son of gehenna twofold more than yourselves.

Matthew 23:16 `Woe to you, blind guides, who are saying, Whoever may swear by the sanctuary, it is nothing, but whoever may swear by the gold of the sanctuary--is debtor!

Matthew 23:17 Fools and blind! for which [is] greater, the gold, or the sanctuary that is sanctifying the gold?

Matthew 23:18 Ànd, whoever may swear by the altar, it is nothing; but whoever may swear by the gift that is upon it--is debtor!

Matthew 23:19 Fools and blind! for which [is] greater, the gift, or the altar that is sanctifying the gift?

Matthew 23:20 `He therefore who did swear by the altar, doth swear by it, and by all things on it;

Matthew 23:21 and he who did swear by the sanctuary, doth swear by it, and by Him who is dwelling in it;

Matthew 23:22 and he who did swear by the heaven, doth swear by the throne of God, and by Him who is sitting upon it.

Matthew 23:23 `Woe to you, Scribes and Pharisees, hypocrites! because ye give tithe of the mint, and the dill, and the cumin, and did neglect the weightier things of the Law--the judgment, and the kindness, and the faith; these it behoved [you] to do, and those not to neglect.

Matthew 23:24 `Blind guides! who are straining out the gnat, and the camel are swallowing.

Matthew 23:25 `Woe to you, Scribes and Pharisees, hypocrites! because ye make clean the outside of the cup and the plate, and within they are full of rapine and incontinence.

Matthew 23:26 `Blind Pharisee! cleanse first the inside of the cup and the plate, that the outside of them also may become clean.

Matthew 23:27 `Woe to you, Scribes and Pharisees, hypocrites! because ye are like to whitewashed sepulchres, which outwardly indeed do appear beautiful, and within are full of bones of dead men, and of all uncleanness;

Matthew 23:28 so also ye outwardly indeed do appear to men right-

eous, and within ye are full of hypocrisy and lawlessness.

Matthew 23:29 `Woe to you, Scribes and Pharisees, hypocrites! because ye build the sepulchres of the prophets, and adorn the tombs of the righteous,

Matthew 23:30 and say, If we had been in the days of our fathers, we would not have been partakers with them in the blood of the prophets.

Matthew 23:31 So that ye testify to yourselves, that ye are sons of them who did murder the prophets;

Matthew 23:32 and ye--ye fill up the measure of your fathers.

Matthew 23:33 `Serpents! brood of vipers! how may ye escape from the judgment of the gehenna?

Matthew 23:34. `Because of this, lo, I send to you prophets, and wise men, and scribes, and of them ye will kill and crucify, and of them ye will scourge in your synagogues, and will pursue from city to city;

Matthew 23:35 that on you may come all the righteous blood being poured out on the earth from the blood of Abel the righteous, unto the blood of Zacharias son of Barachias, whom ye slew between the sanctuary and the altar:

Matthew 23:36 verily I say to you, all these things shall come upon this generation.

Matthew 23:37 `Jerusalem, Jerusalem, that art killing the prophets, and stoning those sent unto thee, how often did I will to gather thy children together, as a hen doth gather her own chickens under the wings, and ye did not will.

Matthew 23:38 Lo, left desolate to you is your house;

Matthew 23:39 for I say to you, ye may not see me henceforth, till ye may say, Blessed [is] he who is coming in the name of the Lord.'

Matthew 24:1. And having gone forth, Jesus departed from the temple, and his disciples came near to show him the buildings of the temple,

Matthew 24:2 and Jesus said to them, `Do ye not see all these? verily I say to you, There may not be left here a stone upon a stone, that shall not be thrown down.'

Matthew 24:3 And when he is sitting on the mount of the Olives, the disciples came near to him by himself, saying, `Tell us, when shall these be? and what [is] the sign of thy presence, and of the full end of the age?'

Matthew 24:4. And Jesus answering said to them, `Take heed that no one may lead you astray,

Matthew 24:5 for many shall come in my name, saying, I am the Christ, and they shall lead many astray,

Matthew 24:6 and ye shall begin to hear of wars, and reports of wars; see, be not troubled, for it behoveth all [these] to come to pass, but the end is not yet.

Matthew 24:7 `For nation shall rise against nation, and kingdom against kingdom, and there shall be famines, and pestilences, and earthquakes, in divers places;

Matthew 24:8 and all these [are] the beginning of sorrows;

Matthew 24:9 then they shall deliver you up to tribulation, and shall kill you, and ye shall be hated by all the nations because of my name;

Matthew 24:10 and then shall many be stumbled, and they shall deliver up one another, and shall hate one another.

Matthew 24:11 Ànd many false prophets shall arise, and shall lead many astray;

Matthew 24:12 and because of the abounding of the lawlessness, the love of the many shall become cold;

Matthew 24:13 but he who did endure to the end, he shall be saved;

Matthew 24:14 and this good news of the reign shall be proclaimed in all the world, for a testimony to all the nations; and then shall the end arrive.

Matthew 24:15 `Whenever, therefore, ye may see the abomination of the desolation, that was spoken of through Daniel the prophet, standing in the holy place (whoever is reading let him observe)

Matthew 24:16 then those in Judea--let them flee to the mounts;

Matthew 24:17 he on the house-top--let him not come down to take up any thing out of his house;

Matthew 24:18 and he in the field--let him not turn back to take his garments.

Matthew 24:19 Ànd woe to those with child, and to those giving suck in those days;

Matthew 24:20 and pray ye that your flight may not be in winter, nor on a sabbath;

Matthew 24:21 for there shall be then great tribulation, such as was not from the beginning of the world till now, no, nor may be.

Matthew 24:22 And if those days were not shortened, no flesh would have been saved; but because of the chosen, shall those days be shortened.

Matthew 24:23 `Then if any one may say to you, Lo, here [is] the Christ! or here! ye may not believe;

Matthew 24:24 for there shall arise false Christs, and false prophets, and they shall give great signs and wonders, so as to lead astray, if possible, also the chosen.

Matthew 24:25 Lo, I did tell you beforehand.

Matthew 24:26 Ìf therefore they may say to you, Lo, in the wilderness he is, ye may not go forth; lo, in the inner chambers, ye may not believe;

Matthew 24:27 for as the lightning doth come forth from the east, and doth appear unto the west, so shall be also the presence of the Son of Man;

Matthew 24:28 for wherever the carcase may be, there shall the eagles be gathered together.

Matthew 24:29 Ànd immediately after the tribulation of those days, the sun shall be darkened, and the moon shall not give her light, and the stars shall fall from the heaven, and the powers of the heavens shall be shaken;

Matthew 24:30 and then shall appear the sign of the Son of Man in the heaven; and then shall all the tribes of the earth smite the breast, and they shall see the Son of Man coming upon the clouds of the heaven, with power and much glory;

Matthew 24:31 and he shall send his messengers with a great sound of a trumpet, and they shall gather together his chosen from the four winds, from the ends of the heavens unto the ends thereof.

Matthew 24:32. Ànd from the fig-tree learn ye the simile: When already its branch may have become tender, and the leaves it may put forth, ye know that summer [is] nigh,

Matthew 24:33 so also ye, when ye may see all these, ye know that it is nigh--at the doors.

Matthew 24:34 Verily I say to you, this generation may not pass away till all these may come to pass.

Matthew 24:35 The heaven and the earth shall pass away, but my words shall not pass away.

Matthew 24:36 Ànd concerning that day and the hour no one hath known--not even the messengers of the heavens--except my Father only;

Matthew 24:37 and as the days of Noah--so shall be also the presence of the Son of Man;

Matthew 24:38 for as they were, in the days before the flood, eating, and drinking, marrying, and giving in marriage, till the day Noah entered into the ark,

Matthew 24:39 and they did not know till the flood came and took all away; so shall be also the presence of the Son of Man.

Matthew 24:40 Then two men shall be in the field, the one is received, and the one is left;

Matthew 24:41 two women shall be grinding in the mill, one is received, and one is left.

Matthew 24:42 `Watch ye therefore, because ye have not known in what hour your Lord doth come;

Matthew 24:43 and this know, that if the master of the house had known in what watch the thief doth come, he had watched, and not suffered his house to be broken through;

Matthew 24:44 because of this also ye, become ye ready, because in what hour ye do not think, the Son of Man doth come.

Matthew 24:45 `Who, then, is the servant, faithful and wise, whom his lord did set over his household, to give them the nourishment in season?

Matthew 24:46 Happy that servant, whom his lord, having come, shall find doing so;

Matthew 24:47 verily I say to you, that over all his substance he will set him.

Matthew 24:48 Ànd, if that evil servant may say in his heart, My Lord doth delay to come,

Matthew 24:49 and may begin to beat the fellow-servants, and to eat and to drink with the drunken,

Matthew 24:50 the lord of that servant will arrive in a day when he doth not expect, and in an hour of which he doth not know,

Matthew 24:51 and will cut him off, and his portion with the hypocrites will appoint; there shall be the weeping and the gnashing of the teeth.

Matthew 25:1. `Then shall the reign of the heavens be likened to ten virgins, who, having taken their lamps, went forth to meet the bridegroom;

Matthew 25:2 and five of them were prudent, and five foolish;

Matthew 25:3 they who were foolish having taken their lamps, did not take with themselves oil;

Matthew 25:4 and the prudent took oil in their vessels, with their lamps.

Matthew 25:5 Ànd the bridegroom tarrying, they all nodded and were sleeping,

Matthew 25:6 and in the middle of the night a cry was made, Lo, the bridegroom doth come; go ye forth to meet him.

Matthew 25:7 `Then rose all those virgins, and trimmed their lamps,

Matthew 25:8 and the foolish said to the prudent, Give us of your oil, because our lamps are going out;

Matthew 25:9 and the prudent answered, saying--Lest there may not be sufficient for us and you, go ye rather unto those selling, and buy for yourselves.

Matthew 25:10 Ànd while they are going away to buy, the bridegroom came, and those ready went in with him to the marriage-feasts, and the door was shut;

Matthew 25:11 and afterwards come also do the rest of the virgins, saying, Sir, sir, open to us;

Matthew 25:12 and he answering said, Verily I say to you, I have not known you.

Matthew 25:13 `Watch therefore, for ye have not known the day nor the hour in which the Son of Man doth come.

Matthew 25:14. `For--as a man going abroad did call his own servants, and did deliver to them his substance,

Matthew 25:15 and to one he gave five talents, and to another two, and to another one, to each according to his several ability, went abroad immediately.

Matthew 25:16 Ànd he who did receive the five talents, having gone, wrought with them, and made other five talents;

Matthew 25:17 in like manner also he who [received] the two, he gained, also he, other two;

Matthew 25:18 and he who did receive the one, having gone away, digged in the earth, and hid his lord's money.

Matthew 25:19 Ànd after a long time cometh the lord of those servants, and taketh reckoning with them;

Matthew 25:20 and he who did receive the five talents having come, brought other five talents, saying, `Sir, five talents thou didst deliver to me; lo, other five talents did I gain besides them.

Matthew 25:21 Ànd his lord said to him, Well done, servant, good and faithful, over a few things thou wast faithful, over many things I will set thee; enter into the joy of thy lord.

Matthew 25:22 Ànd he who also did receive the two talents having come, said, Sir, two talents thou didst deliver to me; lo, other two talents I did gain besides them.

Matthew 25:23 `His lord said to him, Well done, servant, good and faithful, over a few things thou wast faithful, over many things I will set thee; enter into the joy of thy lord.

Matthew 25:24 Ànd he also who hath received the one talent having come, said, Sir, I knew thee, that thou art a hard man, reaping where thou didst not sow, and gathering from whence thou didst not scatter;

Matthew 25:25 and having been afraid, having gone away, I hid thy talent in the earth; lo, thou hast thine own!

Matthew 25:26 Ànd his lord answering said to him, Evil servant, and slothful, thou hadst known that I reap where I did not sow, and I gather whence I did not scatter!

Matthew 25:27 it behoved thee then to put my money to the moneylenders, and having come I had received mine own with increase.

Matthew 25:28 `Take therefore from him the talent, and give to him having the ten talents,

Matthew 25:29 for to every one having shall be given, and he shall have overabundance, and from him who is not having, even that which he hath shall be taken from him;

Matthew 25:30 and the unprofitable servant cast ye forth to the outer darkness; there shall be the weeping and the gnashing of the teeth.

Matthew 25:31. Ànd whenever the Son of Man may come in his glory, and all the holy messengers with him, then he shall sit upon a throne of his glory;

Matthew 25:32 and gathered together before him shall be all the nations, and he shall separate them from one another, as the shepherd doth separate the sheep from the goats,

Matthew 25:33 and he shall set the sheep indeed on his right hand, and the goats on the left.

Matthew 25:34 `Then shall the king say to those on his right hand, Come ye, the blessed of my Father, inherit the reign that hath been prepared for you from the foundation of the world;

Matthew 25:35 for I did hunger, and ye gave me to eat; I did thirst, and ye gave me to drink; I was a stranger, and ye received me;

Matthew 25:36 naked, and ye put around me; I was infirm, and ye looked after me; in prison I was, and ye came unto me.

Matthew 25:37 `Then shall the righteous answer him, saying, Lord, when did we see thee hungering, and we nourished? or thirsting, and we gave to drink?

Matthew 25:38 and when did we see thee a stranger, and we received? or naked, and we put around?

Matthew 25:39 and when did we see thee infirm, or in prison, and we came unto thee?

Matthew 25:40 Ànd the king answering, shall say to them, Verily I say to you, Inasmuch as ye did [it] to one of these my brethren--the least--to me ye did [it].

Matthew 25:41 Then shall he say also to those on the left hand, Go ye from me, the cursed, to the fire, the age-during, that hath been prepared for the Devil and his messengers;

Matthew 25:42 for I did hunger, and ye gave me not to eat; I did thirst, and ye gave me not to drink;

Matthew 25:43 a stranger I was, and ye did not receive me; naked, and ye put not around me; infirm, and in prison, and ye did not look after me.

Matthew 25:44 `Then shall they answer, they also, saying, Lord, when did we see thee hungering, or thirsting, or a stranger, or naked, or infirm, or in prison, and we did not minister to thee?

Matthew 25:45 `Then shall he answer them, saying, Verily I say to you, Inasmuch as ye did [it] not to one of these, the least, ye did [it] not to me.

Matthew 25:46 And these shall go away to punishment age-during, but the righteous to life age-during.'

Matthew 26:1. And it came to pass, when Jesus finished all these words, he said to his disciples,

Matthew 26:2 `Ye have known that after two days the passover cometh, and the Son of Man is delivered up to be crucified.'

Matthew 26:3 Then were gathered together the chief priests, and the scribes, and the elders of the people, to the court of the chief priest who was called Caiaphas;

Matthew 26:4 and they consulted together that they might take Jesus by guile, and kill [him],

Matthew 26:5 and they said, `Not in the feast, that there may not be a tumult among the people.'

Matthew 26:6. And Jesus having been in Bethany, in the house of Simon the leper,

Matthew 26:7 there came to him a woman having an alabaster box of ointment, very precious, and she poured on his head as he is reclining (at meat).

Matthew 26:8 And having seen [it], his disciples were much displeased, saying, `To what purpose [is] this waste?

Matthew 26:9 for this ointment could have been sold for much, and given to the poor.'

Matthew 26:10 And Jesus having known, said to them, `Why do ye give trouble to the woman? for a good work she wrought for me;

Matthew 26:11 for the poor always ye have with you, and me ye have not always;

Matthew 26:12 for she having put this ointment on my body--for my burial she did [it].

Matthew 26:13 Verily I say to you, Wherever this good news may be proclaimed in the whole world, what

this [one] did shall also be spoken of--for a memorial of her.'

Matthew 26:14. Then one of the twelve, who is called Judas Iscariot, having gone unto the chief priests, said,

Matthew 26:15 `What are ye willing to give me, and I will deliver him up to you?' and they weighed out to him thirty silverlings,

Matthew 26:16 and from that time he was seeking a convenient season to deliver him up.

Matthew 26:17. And on the first [day] of the unleavened food came the disciples near to Jesus, saying to him, `Where wilt thou [that] we may prepare for thee to eat the passover?'

Matthew 26:18 and he said, `Go away to the city, unto such a one, and say to him, The Teacher saith, My time is nigh; near thee I keep the passover, with my disciples;'

Matthew 26:19 and the disciples did as Jesus appointed them, and prepared the passover.

Matthew 26:20 And evening having come, he was reclining (at meat) with the twelve,

Matthew 26:21 and while they are eating, he said, `Verily I say to you, that one of you shall deliver me up.'

Matthew 26:22 And being grieved exceedingly, they began to say to him, each of them, `Is it I, Sir?'

Matthew 26:23 And he answering said, `He who did dip with me the hand in the dish, he will deliver me up;

Matthew 26:24 the Son of Man doth indeed go, as it hath been written concerning him, but woe to that man through whom the Son of Man is delivered up! good it were for him if that man had not been born.'

Matthew 26:25 And Judas--he who delivered him up--answering said, `Is it I, Rabbi?' He saith to him, `Thou hast said.'

Matthew 26:26. And while they were eating, Jesus having taken the bread, and having blessed, did brake, and was giving to the disciples, and said, `Take, eat, this is my body;'

Matthew 26:27 and having taken the cup, and having given thanks, he gave to them, saying, `Drink ye of it--all;

Matthew 26:28 for this is my blood of the new covenant, that for many is being poured out--to remission of sins;

Matthew 26:29 and I say to you, that I may not drink henceforth on this produce of the vine, till that day when I may drink it with you new in the reign of my Father.'

Matthew 26:30 And having sung a hymn, they went forth to the mount of the Olives;

Matthew 26:31. then saith Jesus to them, `All ye shall be stumbled at me this night; for it hath been written, I will smite the shepherd, and the sheep of the flock shall be scattered abroad;

Matthew 26:32 but, after my having risen, I will go before you to Galilee.'

Matthew 26:33 And Peter answering said to him, `Even if all shall be stumbled at thee, I will never be stumbled.'

Matthew 26:34 Jesus said to him, `Verily I say to thee, that, this night, before cock-crowing, thrice thou wilt deny me.'

Matthew 26:35 Peter saith to him, `Even if it may be necessary for me to die with thee, I will not deny thee;' in like manner also said all the disciples.

Matthew 26:36. Then come with them doth Jesus to a place called Gethsemane, and he saith to the disciples, `Sit ye here, till having gone away, I shall pray yonder.'

Matthew 26:37 And having taken Peter, and the two sons of Zebedee, he began to be sorrowful, and to be very heavy;

Matthew 26:38 then saith he to them, `Exceedingly sorrowful is my soul--unto death; abide ye here, and watch with me.'

Matthew 26:39 And having gone forward a little, he fell on his face, praying, and saying, `My Father, if it be possible, let this cup pass from me; nevertheless, not as I will, but as Thou.'

Matthew 26:40 And he cometh unto the disciples, and findeth them sleeping, and he saith to Peter, `So! ye were not able one hour to watch with me!

Matthew 26:41 watch, and pray, that ye may not enter into temptation: the spirit indeed is forward, but the flesh weak.'

Matthew 26:42 Again, a second time, having gone away, he prayed, saying, `My Father, if this cup cannot pass away from me except I drink it, Thy will be done;'

Matthew 26:43 and having come, he findeth them again sleeping, for their eyes were heavy.

Matthew 26:44 And having left them, having gone away again, he prayed a third time, saying the same word;

Matthew 26:45 then cometh he unto his disciples, and saith to them, `Sleep on henceforth, and rest! lo, the hour hath come nigh, and the Son of Man is delivered up to the hands of sinners.

Matthew 26:46 Rise, let us go; lo, he hath come nigh who is delivering me up.'

Matthew 26:47. And while he is yet speaking, lo, Judas, one of the twelve did come, and with him a great multitude, with swords and sticks, from the chief priests and elders of the people.

Matthew 26:48 And he who did deliver him up did give them a sign, saying, `Whomsoever I will kiss, it is he: lay hold on him;'

Matthew 26:49 and immediately, having come to Jesus, he said, `Hail, Rabbi,' and kissed him;

Matthew 26:50 and Jesus said to him, `Comrade, for what art thou present?' Then having come near, they laid hands on Jesus, and took hold on him.

Matthew 26:51 And lo, one of those with Jesus, having stretched forth the hand, drew his sword, and having struck the servant of the chief priest, he took off his ear.

Matthew 26:52 Then saith Jesus to him, `Turn back thy sword to its place; for all who did take the sword, by the sword shall perish;

Matthew 26:53 dost thou think that I am not able now to call upon my Father, and He will place beside me more than twelve legions of messengers?

Matthew 26:54 how then may the Writings be fulfilled, that thus it behoveth to happen?'

Matthew 26:55 In that hour said Jesus to the multitudes, Às against a robber ye did come forth, with swords and sticks, to take me! daily with you I was sitting teaching in the temple, and ye did not lay hold on me;

Matthew 26:56 but all this hath come to pass, that the Writings of the prophets may be fulfilled;' then all the disciples, having left him, fled.

Matthew 26:57. And those laying hold on Jesus led [him] away unto Caiaphas the chief priest, where the scribes and the elders were gathered together,

Matthew 26:58 and Peter was following him afar off, unto the court of the chief priest, and having gone in within, he was sitting with the officers, to see the end.

Matthew 26:59 And the chief priests, and the elders, and all the council, were seeking false witness against Jesus, that they might put him to death,

Matthew 26:60 and they did not find; and many false witnesses having come near, they did not find; and at last two false witnesses having come near,

Matthew 26:61 said, `This one said, I am able to throw down the sanctuary of God, and after three days to build it.'

Matthew 26:62 And the chief priest having stood up, said to him, `Nothing thou dost answer! what do these witness against thee?

Matthew 26:63 and Jesus was silent. And the chief priest answering said to him, Ì adjure thee, by the living God, that thou mayest say to us, if thou art the Christ--the Son of God.'

Matthew 26:64 Jesus saith to him, `Thou hast said; nevertheless I say to you, hereafter ye shall see the Son of Man sitting on the right hand of the power, and coming upon the clouds, of the heaven.'

Matthew 26:65 Then the chief priest rent his garments, saying, -- `He hath spoken evil; what need have we yet of witnesses? lo, now ye heard his evil speaking;

Matthew 26:66 what think ye?' and they answering said, `He is worthy of death.'

Matthew 26:67 Then did they spit in his face and buffet him, and others did slap,

Matthew 26:68 saying, `Declare to us, O Christ, who he is that struck thee?'

Matthew 26:69. And Peter without was sitting in the court, and there came near to him a certain maid, saying, Ànd thou wast with Jesus of Galilee!'

Matthew 26:70 And he denied before all, saying, Ì have not known what thou sayest.'

Matthew 26:71 And he having gone forth to the porch, another female saw him, and saith to those there, Ànd this one was with Jesus of Nazareth;'

Matthew 26:72 and again did he deny with an oath--Ì have not known the man.'

Matthew 26:73 And after a little those standing near having come, said to Peter, `Truly thou also art of them, for even thy speech doth make thee manifest.'

Matthew 26:74 Then began he to anathematise, and to swear--Ì have not known the man;' and immediately did a cock crow,

Matthew 26:75 and Peter remembered the saying of Jesus, he having said to him--`Before cock-crowing, thrice thou wilt deny me;' and having gone without, he did weep bitterly.

Matthew 27:1. And morning having come, all the chief priests and the elders of the people took counsel against Jesus, so as to put him to death;

Matthew 27:2 and having bound him, they did lead away, and delivered him up to Pontius Pilate, the governor.

Matthew 27:3 Then Judas--he who delivered him up--having seen that he was condemned, having repented, brought back the thirty silverlings to the chief priests, and to the elders, saying,

Matthew 27:4 Ì did sin, having delivered up innocent blood;' and they said, `What--to us? thou shalt see!'

Matthew 27:5 and having cast down the silverlings in the sanctuary, he departed, and having gone away, he did strangle himself.

Matthew 27:6 And the chief priests having taken the silverlings, said, Ìt is not lawful to put them to the treasury, seeing it is the price of blood;'

Matthew 27:7 and having taken counsel, they bought with them the field of the potter, for the burial of strangers;

Matthew 27:8 therefore was that field called, `Field of blood,' unto this day.

Matthew 27:9 Then was fulfilled that spoken through Jeremiah the prophet, saying, Ànd I took the thirty silverlings, the price of him who hath been priced, whom they of the sons of Israel did price,

Matthew 27:10 and gave them for the field of the potter, as the Lord did appoint to me.'

Matthew 27:11. And Jesus stood before the governor, and the governor did question him, saying, Àrt thou the king of the Jews!' And Jesus said to him, `Thou sayest.'

Matthew 27:12 And in his being accused by the chief priests and the elders, he did not answer any thing,

Matthew 27:13 then saith Pilate to him, `Dost thou not hear how many things they witness against thee?'

Matthew 27:14 And he did not answer him, not even to one word, so that the governor did wonder greatly.

Matthew 27:15 And at the feast the governor had been accustomed to release one to the multitude, a prisoner, whom they willed,

Matthew 27:16 and they had then a noted prisoner, called Barabbas,

Matthew 27:17 they therefore having been gathered together, Pilate said to them, `Whom will ye I shall release to you? Barabbas or Jesus who is called Christ?'

Matthew 27:18 for he had known that because of envy they had delivered him up.

Matthew 27:19 And as he is sitting on the tribunal, his wife sent unto him, saying, `Nothing--to thee and to that righteous one, for many things did I suffer to-day in a dream because of him.'

Matthew 27:20 And the chief priests and the elders did persuade the multitudes that they might ask for themselves Barabbas, and might destroy Jesus;

Matthew 27:21 and the governor answering said to them, `Which of the two will ye [that] I shall release to you?' And they said, `Barabbas.'

Matthew 27:22 Pilate saith to them, `What then shall I do with Jesus who is called Christ?' They all say to him, `Let be crucified!'

Matthew 27:23 And the governor said, `Why, what evil did he?' and they were crying out the more, saying, `Let be crucified.'

Matthew 27:24 And Pilate having seen that it profiteth nothing, but rather a tumult is made, having taken water, he did wash the hands before the multitude, saying, Ì am innocent from the blood of this righteous one; ye--ye shall see;'

Matthew 27:25 and all the people answering said, `His blood [is] upon us, and upon our children!'

Matthew 27:26. Then did he release to them Barabbas, and having scourged Jesus, he delivered [him] up that he may be crucified;

Matthew 27:27 then the soldiers of the governor having taken Jesus to the Praetorium, did gather to him all the band;

Matthew 27:28 and having un-clothed him, they put around him a crimson cloak,

Matthew 27:29 and having plaited him a crown out of thorns they put [it] on his head, and a reed in his right hand, and having kneeled before him, they were mocking him, saying, `Hail, the king of the Jews.'

Matthew 27:30 And having spit on him, they took the reed, and were smiting on his head;

Matthew 27:31 and when they had mocked him, they took off from him the cloak, and put on him his own garments, and led him away to cru-cify [him].

Matthew 27:32 And coming forth, they found a man, a Cyrenian, by name Simon: him they impressed that he might bear his cross;

Matthew 27:33. and having come to a place called Golgotha, that is called Place of a Skull,

Matthew 27:34 they gave him to drink vinegar mixed with gall, and having tasted, he would not drink.

Matthew 27:35 And having cruci-fied him, they divided his garments, casting a lot, that it might be fulfilled that was spoken by the prophet, `They divided my garments to them-selves, and over my vesture they cast a lot;'

Matthew 27:36 and sitting down, they were watching him there,

Matthew 27:37 and they put up over his head, his accusation writ-ten, `This is Jesus, the king of the Jews.'

Matthew 27:38 Then crucified with him are two robbers, one on the right hand, and one on the left,

Matthew 27:39 and those passing by were speaking evil of him, wag-ging their heads,

Matthew 27:40 and saying, `Thou that art throwing down the sanctu-ary, and in three days building [it], save thyself; if Son thou art of God, come down from the cross.'

Matthew 27:41 And in like manner also the chief priests mocking, with the scribes and elders, said,

Matthew 27:42 Òthers he saved; himself he is not able to save! If he be King of Israel, let him come down now from the cross, and we will be-lieve him;

Matthew 27:43 he hath trusted on God, let Him now deliver him, if He wish him, because he said--Son of God I am;'

Matthew 27:44 with the same also the robbers, who were crucified with him, were reproaching him.

Matthew 27:45 And from the sixth hour darkness came over all the land unto the ninth hour,

Matthew 27:46 and about the ninth hour Jesus cried out with a great voice, saying, Èli, Eli, lama sabachthani?' that is, `My God, my God, why didst Thou forsake me?'

Matthew 27:47 And certain of those standing there having heard, said--Èlijah he doth call;'

Matthew 27:48 and immediately, one of them having run, and having taken a spunge, having filled [it] with vinegar, and having put [it] on a reed, was giving him to drink,

Matthew 27:49 but the rest said, `Let alone, let us see if Elijah doth come--about to save him.'

Matthew 27:50. And Jesus having again cried with a great voice, yielded the spirit;

Matthew 27:51 and lo, the vail of the sanctuary was rent in two from top unto bottom, and the earth did quake, and the rocks were rent,

Matthew 27:52 and the tombs were opened, and many bodies of the saints who have fallen asleep, arose,

Matthew 27:53 and having come forth out of the tombs after his rising, they went into the holy city, and appeared to many.

Matthew 27:54 And the centurion, and those with him watching Jesus, having seen the earthquake, and the things that were done, were exceedingly afraid, saying, `Truly this was God's Son.'

Matthew 27:55 And there were there many women beholding from afar, who did follow Jesus from Galilee, ministering to him,

Matthew 27:56 among whom was Mary the Magdalene, and Mary the mother of James and of Joses, and the mother of the sons of Zebedee.

Matthew 27:57. And evening having come, there came a rich man, from Arimathea, named Joseph, who also himself was discipled to Jesus,

Matthew 27:58 he having gone near to Pilate, asked for himself the body of Jesus; then Pilate commanded the body to be given back.

Matthew 27:59 And having taken the body, Joseph wrapped it in clean linen,

Matthew 27:60 and laid it in his new tomb, that he hewed in the rock, and having rolled a great stone to the door of the tomb, he went away;

Matthew 27:61 and there were there Mary the Magdalene, and the other Mary, sitting over-against the sepulchre.

Matthew 27:62 And on the morrow that is after the preparation, were gathered together the chief priests, and the Pharisees, unto Pilate,

Matthew 27:63 saying, `Sir, we have remembered that that deceiver said while yet living, After three days I do rise;

Matthew 27:64 command, then, the sepulchre to be made secure till the third day, lest his disciples, having come by night, may steal him away, and may say to the people, He rose from the dead, and the last deceit shall be worse than the first.'

Matthew 27:65 And Pilate said to them, `Ye have a watch, go away, make secure--as ye have known;'

Matthew 27:66 and they, having gone, did make the sepulchre secure, having sealed the stone, together with the watch.

Matthew 28:1. And on the eve of the sabbaths, at the dawn, toward the first of the sabbaths, came Mary the Magdalene, and the other Mary, to see the sepulchre,

Matthew 28:2 and lo, there came a great earthquake, for a messenger of the Lord, having come down out of heaven, having come, did roll away the stone from the door, and was sitting upon it,

Matthew 28:3 and his countenance was as lightning, and his clothing white as snow,

Matthew 28:4 and from the fear of him did the keepers shake, and they became as dead men.

Matthew 28:5 And the messenger answering said to the women, `Fear not ye, for I have known that Jesus, who hath been crucified, ye seek;

Matthew 28:6 he is not here, for he rose, as he said; come, see the place where the Lord was lying;

Matthew 28:7 and having gone quickly, say ye to his disciples, that he rose from the dead; and lo, he doth go before you to Galilee, there ye shall see him; lo, I have told you.'

Matthew 28:8 And having gone forth quickly from the tomb, with fear and great joy, they ran to tell to his disciples;

Matthew 28:9 and as they were going to tell to his disciples, then lo, Jesus met them, saying, `Hail!' and they having come near, laid hold of his feet, and did bow to him.

Matthew 28:10 Then saith Jesus to them, `Fear ye not, go away, tell to my brethren that they may go away to Galilee, and there they shall see me.'

Matthew 28:11. And while they are going on, lo, certain of the watch having come to the city, told to the chief priests all the things that happened,

Matthew 28:12 and having been gathered together with the elders, counsel also having taken, they gave much money to the soldiers,

Matthew 28:13 saying, `Say ye, that his disciples having come by night, stole him--we being asleep;

Matthew 28:14 and if this be heard by the governor, we will persuade

him, and you keep free from anxiety.'

Matthew 28:15 And they, having
received the money, did as they
were taught, and this account was
spread abroad among Jews till this
day.

Matthew 28:16. And the eleven disciples went to Galilee, to the mount
where Jesus appointed them,

Matthew 28:17 and having seen
him, they bowed to him, but some
did waver.

Matthew 28:18 And having come
near, Jesus spake to them, saying,
`Given to me was all authority in
heaven and on earth;

Matthew 28:19 having gone, then,
disciple all the nations, (baptizing
them--to the name of the Father, and
of the Son, and of the Holy Spirit,

Matthew 28:20 teaching them to
observe all, whatever I did command you,) and lo, I am with you all
the days--till the full end of the age.'

Mark

Mark 1:1. A beginning of the good news of Jesus Christ, Son of God.

Mark 1:2 As it hath been written in the prophets, `Lo, I send My messenger before thy face, who shall prepare thy way before thee,' --

Mark 1:3 À voice of one calling in the wilderness, Prepare ye the way of the Lord, straight make ye his paths,' --

Mark 1:4 John came baptizing in the wilderness, and proclaiming a baptism of reformation--to remission of sins,

Mark 1:5 and there were going forth to him all the region of Judea, and they of Jerusalem, and they were all baptized by him in the river Jordan, confessing their sins.

Mark 1:6 And John was clothed with camel's hair, and a girdle of skin around his loins, and eating locusts and honey of the field,

Mark 1:7 and he proclaimed, saying, `He doth come--who is mightier than I--after me, of whom I am not worthy--having stooped down--to loose the latchet of his sandals;

Mark 1:8 I indeed did baptize you with water, but he shall baptize you with the Holy Spirit.'

Mark 1:9. And it came to pass in those days, Jesus came from Nazareth of Galilee, and was baptized by John at the Jordan;

Mark 1:10 and immediately coming up from the water, he saw the heavens dividing, and the Spirit as a dove coming down upon him;

Mark 1:11 and a voice came out of the heavens, `Thou art My Son--the Beloved, in whom I did delight.'

Mark 1:12 And immediately doth the Spirit put him forth to the wilderness,

Mark 1:13 and he was there in the wilderness forty days, being tempted by the Adversary, and he was with the beasts, and the messengers were ministering to him.

Mark 1:14. And after the delivering up of John, Jesus came to Galilee, proclaiming the good news of the reign of God,

Mark 1:15 and saying--`Fulfilled hath been the time, and the reign of God hath come nigh, reform ye, and believe in the good news.'

Mark 1:16 And, walking by the sea of Galilee, he saw Simon, and Andrew his brother, casting a drag into the sea, for they were fishers,

Mark 1:17 and Jesus said to them, `Come ye after me, and I shall make you to become fishers of men;'

Mark 1:18 and immediately, having left their nets, they followed him.

Mark 1:19 And having gone on thence a little, he saw James of Zebedee, and John his brother, and they were in the boat refitting the nets,

Mark 1:20 and immediately he called them, and, having left their father Zebedee in the boat with the hired servants, they went away after him.

Mark 1:21 And they go on to Capernaum, and immediately, on the sabbaths, having gone into the synagogue, he was teaching,

Mark 1:22 and they were astonished at his teaching, for he was teaching them as having authority, and not as the scribes.

Mark 1:23. And there was in their synagogue a man with an unclean spirit, and he cried out,

Mark 1:24 saying, Àway! what--to us and to thee, Jesus the Nazarene? thou didst come to destroy us; I have known thee who thou art--the Holy One of God.'

Mark 1:25 And Jesus rebuked him, saying, `Be silenced, and come forth out of him,'

Mark 1:26 and the unclean spirit having torn him, and having cried with a great voice, came forth out of him,

Mark 1:27 and they were all amazed, so as to reason among themselves, saying, `What is this? what new teaching [is] this? that with authority also the unclean spirits he commandeth, and they obey him!'

Mark 1:28 And the fame of him went forth immediately to all the region, round about, of Galilee.

Mark 1:29. And immediately, having come forth out of the synagogue, they went to the house of Simon and Andrew, with James and John,

Mark 1:30 and the mother-in-law of Simon was lying fevered, and immediately they tell him about her,

Mark 1:31 and having come near, he raised her up, having laid hold of her hand, and the fever left her immediately, and she was ministering to them.

Mark 1:32 And evening having come, when the sun did set, they brought unto him all who were ill, and who were demoniacs,

Mark 1:33 and the whole city was gathered together near the door,

Mark 1:34 and he healed many who were ill of manifold diseases, and many demons he cast forth, and was not suffering the demons to speak, because they knew him.

Mark 1:35 And very early, it being yet night, having risen, he went forth, and went away to a desert place, and was there praying;

Mark 1:36 and Simon and those with him went in quest of him,

Mark 1:37 and having found him, they say to him, --`All do seek thee;'

Mark 1:38 and he saith to them, `We may go to the next towns, that there also I may preach, for for this I came forth.'

Mark 1:39 And he was preaching in their synagogues, in all Galilee, and is casting out the demons,

Mark 1:40. and there doth come to him a leper, calling on him, and kneeling to him, and saying to him--`If thou mayest will, thou art able to cleanse me.'

Mark 1:41 And Jesus having been moved with compassion, having stretched forth the hand, touched him, and saith to him, `I will; be thou cleansed;'

Mark 1:42 and he having spoken, immediately the leprosy went away from him, and he was cleansed.

Mark 1:43 And having sternly charged him, immediately he put him forth,

Mark 1:44 and saith to him, `See thou mayest say nothing to any one, but go away, thyself shew to the priest, and bring near for thy cleans-ing the things Moses directed, for a testimony to them.'

Mark 1:45 And he, having gone forth, began to proclaim much, and to spread abroad the thing, so that no more he was able openly to enter into the city, but he was without in desert places, and they were coming unto him from every quarter.

Mark 2:1. And again he entered into Capernaum, after [some] days, and it was heard that he is in the house,

Mark 2:2 and immediately many were gathered together, so that there was no more room, not even at the door, and he was speaking to them the word.

Mark 2:3 And they come unto him, bringing a paralytic, borne by four,

Mark 2:4 and not being able to come near to him because of the multitude, they uncovered the roof where he was, and, having broken [it] up, they let down the couch on which the paralytic was lying, **Mark 2:5** and Jesus having seen their faith, saith to the paralytic, `Child, thy sins have been forgiven thee.'

Mark 2:6 And there were certain of the scribes there sitting, and reason-ing in their hearts,

Mark 2:7 `Why doth this one thus speak evil words? who is able to for-give sins except one--God?'

Mark 2:8 And immediately Jesus, having known in his spirit that they thus reason in themselves, said to them, `Why these things reason ye in your hearts?

Mark 2:9 which is easier, to say to the paralytic, The sins have been forgiven to thee? or to say, Rise, and take up thy couch, and walk?

Mark 2:10 Ànd, that ye may know that the Son of Man hath authority on the earth to forgive sins--(he saith to the paralytic) --

Mark 2:11 I say to thee, Rise, and take up thy couch, and go away to thy house;'

Mark 2:12 and he rose immediately, and having taken up the couch, he went forth before all, so that all were astonished, and do glorify God, saying--`Never thus did we see.'

Mark 2:13. And he went forth again by the sea, and all the multitude was coming unto him, and he was teaching them,

Mark 2:14 and passing by, he saw Levi of Alpheus sitting at the tax-office, and saith to him, `Be following me,' and he, having risen, did follow him.

Mark 2:15 And it came to pass, in his reclining (at meat) in his house, that many tax-gatherers and sinners were reclining (at meat) with Jesus and his disciples, for there were many, and they followed him.

Mark 2:16 And the scribes and the Pharisees, having seen him eating with the tax-gatherers and sinners, said to his disciples, `Why--that with the tax-gatherers and sinners he doth eat and drink?'

Mark 2:17 And Jesus, having heard, saith to them, `They who are strong have no need of a physician, but they who are ill; I came not to call righteous men, but sinners to reformation.'

Mark 2:18. And the disciples of John and those of the Pharisees were fasting, and they come and say to him, `Wherefore do the disciples of John and those of the Pharisees fast, and thy disciples do not fast?'

Mark 2:19 And Jesus said to them, Àre the sons of the bride-chamber able, while the bridegroom is with them, to fast? so long time as they have the bridegroom with them they are not able to fast;

Mark 2:20 but days shall come when the bridegroom may be taken from them, and then they shall fast-- in those days.

Mark 2:21 Ànd no one a patch of undressed cloth doth sew on an old garment, and if not--the new filling it up doth take from the old and the rent doth become worse;

Mark 2:22 and no one doth put new wine into old skins, and if not--the new wine doth burst the skins, and the wine is poured out, and the skins will be destroyed; but new wine into new skins is to be put.'

Mark 2:23 And it came to pass--he is going along on the sabbaths through the corn-fields--and his disciples began to make a way, plucking the ears,

Mark 2:24 and the Pharisees said to him, `Lo, why do they on the sabbaths that which is not lawful?'

Mark 2:25 And he said to them, `Did ye never read what David did, when he had need and was hungry, he and those with him?

Mark 2:26 how he went into the house of God, (at Àbiathar the chief priest,') and the loaves of the presentation did eat, which it is not lawful to eat, except to the priests, and he gave also to those who were with him?'

Mark 2:27 And he said to them, `The sabbath for man was made, not man for the sabbath,

Mark 2:28 so that the son of man is lord also of the sabbath.'

Mark 3:1. And he entered again into the synagogue, and there was there a man having the hand withered,

Mark 3:2 and they were watching him, whether on the sabbaths he will heal him, that they might accuse him.

Mark 3:3 And he saith to the man having the hand withered, `Rise up in the midst.'

Mark 3:4 And he saith to them, `Is it lawful on the sabbaths to do good, or to do evil? life to save, or to kill?' but they were silent.

Mark 3:5 And having looked round upon them with anger, being grieved for the hardness of their heart, he saith to the man, `Stretch forth thy hand;' and he stretched forth, and his hand was restored whole as the other;

Mark 3:6 and the Pharisees having gone forth, immediately, with the Herodians, were taking counsel against him how they might destroy him.

Mark 3:7 And Jesus withdrew with his disciples unto the sea, and a great multitude from Galilee followed him, and from Judea,

Mark 3:8 and from Jerusalem, and from Idumea and beyond the Jordan; and they about Tyre and Sidon--a great multitude--having heard how great things he was doing, came unto him.

Mark 3:9 And he said to his disciples that a little boat may wait on him, because of the multitude, that they may not press upon him,

Mark 3:10 for he did heal many, so that they threw themselves on him, in order to touch him--as many as had plagues;

Mark 3:11 and the unclean spirits, when they were seeing him, were falling down before him, and were crying, saying--`Thou art the Son of God;'

Mark 3:12 and many times he was charging them that they might not make him manifest.

Mark 3:13. And he goeth up to the mountain, and doth call near whom he willed, and they went away to him;

Mark 3:14 and he appointed twelve, that they may be with him, and that he may send them forth to preach,

Mark 3:15 and to have power to heal the sicknesses, and to cast out the demons.

Mark 3:16 And he put on Simon the name Peter;

Mark 3:17 and James of Zebedee, and John the brother of James, and he put on them names--Boanerges, that is, `Sons of thunder;'

Mark 3:18 and Andrew, and Philip, and Bartholomew, and Matthew, and Thomas, and James of Alpheus, and Thaddeus, and Simon the Cananite,

Mark 3:19 and Judas Iscariot, who did also deliver him up; and they come into a house.

Mark 3:20 And come together again doth a multitude, so that they are not able even to eat bread;

Mark 3:21 and his friends having heard, went forth to lay hold on him, for they said that he was beside himself,

Mark 3:22. and the scribes who [are] from Jerusalem having come down, said--`He hath Beelzeboul,' and--`By the ruler of the demons he doth cast out the demons.'

Mark 3:23 And, having called them near, in similes he said to them, `How is the Adversary able to cast out the Adversary?

Mark 3:24 and if a kingdom against itself be divided, that kingdom cannot be made to stand;

Mark 3:25 and if a house against itself be divided, that house cannot be made to stand;

Mark 3:26 and if the Adversary did rise against himself, and hath been divided, he cannot be made to stand, but hath an end.

Mark 3:27 `No one is able the vessels of the strong man--having entered into his house--to spoil, if first he may not bind the strong man, and then his house he will spoil.

Mark 3:28 `Verily I say to you, that all the sins shall be forgiven to the sons of men, and evil speakings with which they might speak evil,

Mark 3:29 but whoever may speak evil in regard to the Holy Spirit hath not forgiveness--to the age, but is in danger of age-during judgment;'

Mark 3:30 because they said, `He hath an unclean spirit.'

Mark 3:31. Then come do his brethren and mother, and standing without, they sent unto him, calling him,

Mark 3:32 and a multitude was sitting about him, and they said to him, `Lo, thy mother and thy brethren without do seek thee.'

Mark 3:33 And he answered them, saying, `Who is my mother, or my brethren?'

Mark 3:34 And having looked round in a circle to those sitting about him, he saith, `Lo, my mother and my brethren!

Mark 3:35 for whoever may do the will of God, he is my brother, and my sister, and mother.'

Mark 4:1. And again he began to teach by the sea, and there was gathered unto him a great multitude, so that he, having gone into the boat, sat in the sea, and all the multitude was near the sea, on the land,

Mark 4:2 and he taught them many things in similes, and he said to them in his teaching:

Mark 4:3 `Hearken, lo, the sower went forth to sow;

Mark 4:4 and it came to pass, in the sowing, some fell by the way, and the fowls of the heaven did come and devour it;

Mark 4:5 and other fell upon the rocky ground, where it had not much earth, and immediately it sprang forth, because of not having depth of earth,

Mark 4:6 and the sun having risen, it was scorched, and because of not having root it did wither;

Mark 4:7 and other fell toward the thorns, and the thorns did come up, and choke it, and fruit it gave not;

Mark 4:8 and other fell to the good ground, and was giving fruit, coming up and increasing, and it bare, one thirty-fold, and one sixty, and one an hundred.'

Mark 4:9 And he said to them, `He who is having ears to hear--let him hear.'

Mark 4:10 And when he was alone, those about him, with the twelve, did ask him of the simile,

Mark 4:11 and he said to them, `To you it hath been given to know the secret of the reign of God, but to those who are without, in similes are all the things done;

Mark 4:12 that seeing they may see and not perceive, and hearing they may hear and not understand, lest they may turn, and the sins may be forgiven them.'

Mark 4:13 And he saith to them, `Have ye not known this simile? and how shall ye know all the similes?

Mark 4:14 He who is sowing doth sow the word;

Mark 4:15 and these are they by the way where the word is sown: and whenever they may hear, immediately cometh the Adversary, and he taketh away the word that hath been sown in their hearts.

Mark 4:16 Ànd these are they, in like manner, who on the rocky ground are sown: who, whenever they may hear the word, immediately with joy do receive it,

Mark 4:17 and have not root in themselves, but are temporary; afterward tribulation or persecution having come because of the word, immediately they are stumbled.

Mark 4:18 Ànd these are they who toward the thorns are sown: these are they who are hearing the word,

Mark 4:19 and the anxieties of this age, and the deceitfulness of the riches, and the desires concerning the other things, entering in, choke the word, and it becometh unfruitful.

Mark 4:20 Ànd these are they who on the good ground have been sown: who do hear the word, and receive, and do bear fruit, one thirty-fold, and one sixty, and one an hundred.'

Mark 4:21. And he said to them, `Doth the lamp come that under the measure it may be put, or under the couch--not that it may be put on the lamp-stand?

Mark 4:22 for there is not anything hid that may not be manifested, nor was anything kept hid but that it may come to light.

Mark 4:23 If any hath ears to hear--let him hear.'

Mark 4:24 And he said to them, `Take heed what ye hear; in what measure ye measure, it shall be measured to you; and to you who hear it shall be added;

Mark 4:25 for whoever may have, there shall be given to him, and whoever hath not, also that which he hath shall be taken from him.'

Mark 4:26 And he said, `Thus is the reign of God: as if a man may cast the seed on the earth,

Mark 4:27 and may sleep, and may rise night and day, and the seed spring up and grow, he hath not known how;

Mark 4:28 for of itself doth the earth bear fruit, first a blade, afterwards an ear, afterwards full corn in the ear;

Mark 4:29 and whenever the fruit may yield itself, immediately he doth send forth the sickle, because the harvest hath come.'

Mark 4:30 And he said, `To what may we liken the reign of God, or in what simile may we compare it?

Mark 4:31 As a grain of mustard, which, whenever it may be sown on the earth, is less than any of the seeds that are on the earth;

Mark 4:32 and whenever it may be sown, it cometh up, and doth become greater than any of the herbs, and doth make great branches, so that under its shade the fowls of the heaven are able to rest.'

Mark 4:33 And with many such similes he was speaking to them the word, as they were able to hear,

Mark 4:34 and without a simile he was not speaking to them, and by themselves, to his disciples he was expounding all.

Mark 4:35. And he saith to them on that day, evening having come, `We may pass over to the other side;'

Mark 4:36 and having let away the multitude, they take him up as he was in the boat, and other little boats also were with him.

Mark 4:37 And there cometh a great storm of wind, and the waves were beating on the boat, so that it is now being filled,

Mark 4:38 and he himself was upon the stern, upon the pillow sleeping, and they wake him up, and say to him, `Teacher, art thou not caring that we perish?'

Mark 4:39 And having waked up, he rebuked the wind, and said to the sea, `Peace, be stilled;' and the wind did lull, and there was a great calm:

Mark 4:40 and he said to them, `Why are ye so fearful? how have ye not faith?'

Mark 4:41 and they feared a great fear, and said one to another, `Who, then, is this, that even the wind and the sea do obey him?'

Mark 5:1. And they came to the other side of the sea, to the region of the Gadarenes,

Mark 5:2 and he having come forth out of the boat, immediately there met him out of the tombs a man with an unclean spirit,

Mark 5:3 who had his dwelling in the tombs, and not even with chains was any one able to bind him,

Mark 5:4 because that he many times with fetters and chains had been bound, and pulled in pieces by him had been the chains, and the fetters broken in pieces, and none was able to tame him,

Mark 5:5 and always, night and day, in the mountains, and in the tombs he was, crying and cutting himself with stones.

Mark 5:6 And, having seen Jesus from afar, he ran and bowed before him,

Mark 5:7 and having called with a loud voice, he said, `What--to me and to thee, Jesus, Son of God the

Most High? I adjure thee by God, mayest thou not afflict me!'

Mark 5:8 (for he said to him, `Come forth, spirit unclean, out of the man,')

Mark 5:9 and he was questioning him, `What [is] thy name?' and he answered, saying, `Legion [is] my name, because we are many;'

Mark 5:10 and he was calling on him much, that he may not send them out of the region.

Mark 5:11 And there was there, near the mountains, a great herd of swine feeding,

Mark 5:12 and all the demons did call upon him, saying, `Send us to the swine, that into them we may enter;'

Mark 5:13 and immediately Jesus gave them leave, and having come forth, the unclean spirits did enter into the swine, and the herd did rush down the steep place to the sea--and they were about two thousand--and they were choked in the sea.

Mark 5:14 And those feeding the swine did flee, and told in the city, and in the fields, and they came forth to see what it is that hath been done;

Mark 5:15 and they come unto Jesus, and see the demoniac, sitting, and clothed, and right-minded--him having had the legion--and they were afraid;

Mark 5:16 and those having seen [it], declared to them how it had come to pass to the demoniac, and about the swine;

Mark 5:17 and they began to call upon him to go away from their borders.

Mark 5:18 And he having gone into the boat, the demoniac was calling on him that he may be with him,

Mark 5:19 and Jesus did not suffer him, but saith to him, `Go away to thy house, unto thine own [friends], and tell them how great things the Lord did to thee, and dealt kindly with thee;

Mark 5:20 and he went away, and began to proclaim in the Decapolis how great things Jesus did to him, and all were wondering.

Mark 5:21. And Jesus having passed over in the boat again to the other side, there was gathered a great multitude to him, and he was near the sea,

Mark 5:22 and lo, there doth come one of the chiefs of the synagogue, by name Jairus, and having seen him, he doth fall at his feet,

Mark 5:23 and he was calling upon him much, saying--`My little daughter is at the last extremity--that having come, thou mayest lay on her [thy] hands, so that she may be saved, and she shall live;'

Mark 5:24 and he went away with him. And there was following him a great multitude, and they were thronging him,

Mark 5:25 and a certain woman, having an issue of blood twelve years,

Mark 5:26 and many things having suffered under many physicians, and having spent all that she had, and having profited nothing, but rather having come to the worse,

Mark 5:27 having heard about Jesus, having come in the multitude behind, she touched his garment,

Mark 5:28 for she said--Ìf even his garments I may touch, I shall be saved;'

Mark 5:29 and immediately was the fountain of her blood dried up, and she knew in the body that she hath been healed of the plague.

Mark 5:30 And immediately Jesus having known in himself that out of him power had gone forth, having turned about in the multitude, said, `Who did touch my garments?'

Mark 5:31 and his disciples said to him, `Thou seest the multitude thronging thee, and thou sayest, `Who did touch me!'

Mark 5:32 And he was looking round to see her who did this,

Mark 5:33 and the woman, having been afraid, and trembling, knowing what was done on her, came, and fell down before him, and told him all the truth,

Mark 5:34 and he said to her, `Daughter, thy faith hath saved thee; go away in peace, and be whole from thy plague.'

Mark 5:35. As he is yet speaking, there come from the chief of the synagogue's [house, certain], saying--`Thy daughter did die, why still dost thou harass the Teacher?'

Mark 5:36 And Jesus immediately, having heard the word that is spoken, saith to the chief of the synagogue, `Be not afraid, only believe.'

Mark 5:37 And he did not suffer any one to follow with him, except Peter, and James, and John the brother of James;

Mark 5:38 and he cometh to the house of the chief of the synagogue, and seeth a tumult, much weeping and wailing;

Mark 5:39 and having gone in he saith to them, `Why do ye make a tumult, and weep? the child did not die, but doth sleep;

Mark 5:40 and they were laughing at him. And he, having put all forth, doth take the father of the child, and the mother, and those with him, and goeth in where the child is lying,

Mark 5:41 and, having taken the hand of the child, he saith to her, `Talitha cumi;' which is, being interpreted, `Damsel (I say to thee), arise.'

Mark 5:42 And immediately the damsel arose, and was walking, for she was twelve years [old]; and they were amazed with a great amazement,

Mark 5:43 and he charged them much, that no one may know this thing, and he said that there be given to her to eat.

Mark 6:1. And he went forth thence, and came to his own country, and his disciples do follow him,

Mark 6:2 and sabbath having come, he began in the synagogue to teach, and many hearing were astonished, saying, `Whence hath this one these things? and what the wisdom that was given to him, that also such mighty works through his hands are done?

Mark 6:3 Is not this the carpenter, the son of Mary, and brother of James, and Joses, and Judas, and Simon? and are not his sisters here with us?' --and they were being stumbled at him.

Mark 6:4 And Jesus said to them--À prophet is not without honour, except in his own country, and among his kindred, and in his own house;'

Mark 6:5 and he was not able there any mighty work to do, except on a few infirm people having put hands he did heal [them];

Mark 6:6 and he wondered because of their unbelief. And he was going round the villages, in a circle, teaching,

Mark 6:7. and he doth call near the twelve, and he began to send them forth two by two, and he was giving them power over the unclean spirits,

Mark 6:8 and he commanded them that they may take nothing for the way, except a staff only--no scrip, no bread, no brass in the girdle,

Mark 6:9 but having been shod with sandals, and ye may not put on two coats.

Mark 6:10 And he said to them, `Whenever ye may enter into a house, there remain till ye may depart thence,

Mark 6:11 and as many as may not receive you, nor hear you, going out thence, shake off the dust that is under your feet for a testimony to them; verily I say to you, It shall be more tolerable for Sodom or Gomorrah in a day of judgment than for that city.'

Mark 6:12 And having gone forth they were preaching that [men] might reform,

Mark 6:13 and many demons they were casting out, and they were anointing with oil many infirm, and they were healing [them].

Mark 6:14. And the king Herod heard, (for his name became public,) and he said--`John the Baptist out of the dead was raised, and because of this the mighty powers are working in him.'

Mark 6:15 Others said--`It is Elijah,' and others said--`It is a prophet, or as one of the prophets.'

Mark 6:16 And Herod having heard, said--`He whom I did behead--John--this is he; he was raised out of the dead.'

Mark 6:17 For Herod himself, having sent forth, did lay hold on John, and bound him in the prison, because of Herodias the wife of Philip his brother, because he married her,

Mark 6:18 for John said to Herod--`It is not lawful to thee to have the wife of thy brother;'

Mark 6:19 and Herodias was having a quarrel with him, and was willing to kill him, and was not able,

Mark 6:20 for Herod was fearing John, knowing him a man righteous and holy, and was keeping watch over him, and having heard him, was doing many things, and hearing him gladly.

Mark 6:21 And a seasonable day having come, when Herod on his birthday was making a supper to his great men, and to the chiefs of thousands, and to the first men of Galilee,

Mark 6:22 and the daughter of that Herodias having come in, and having danced, and having pleased Herod

and those reclining (at meat) with him, the king said to the damsel, `Ask of me whatever thou wilt, and I will give to thee,'

Mark 6:23 and he sware to her--`Whatever thou mayest ask me, I will give to thee--unto the half of my kingdom.'

Mark 6:24 And she, having gone forth, said to her mother, `What shall I ask for myself?' and she said, `The head of John the Baptist;'

Mark 6:25 and having come in immediately with haste unto the king, she asked, saying, `I will that thou mayest give me presently, upon a plate, the head of John the Baptist.'

Mark 6:26 And the king--made very sorrowful--because of the oaths and of those reclining (at meat) with him, would not put her away,

Mark 6:27 and immediately the king having sent a guardsman, did command his head to be brought,

Mark 6:28 and he having gone, beheaded him in the prison, and brought his head upon a plate, and did give it to the damsel, and the damsel did give it to her mother;

Mark 6:29 and having heard, his disciples came and took up his corpse, and laid it in the tomb.

Mark 6:30. And the apostles are gathered together unto Jesus, and they told him all, and how many things they did, and how many things they taught,

Mark 6:31 and he said to them, `Come ye yourselves apart to a desert place, and rest a little,' for those coming and those going were many, and not even to eat had they opportunity,

Mark 6:32 and they went away to a desert place, in the boat, by themselves.

Mark 6:33 And the multitudes saw them going away, and many recognised him, and by land from all the cities they ran thither, and went before them, and came together to him,

Mark 6:34 and having come forth, Jesus saw a great multitude, and was moved with compassion on them, that they were as sheep not having a shepherd, and he began to teach many things.

Mark 6:35 And now the hour being advanced, his disciples having come near to him, say, --`The place is desolate, and the hour is now advanced,

Mark 6:36 let them away, that, having gone away to the surrounding fields and villages, they may buy to themselves loaves, for what they may eat they have not.'

Mark 6:37 And he answering said to them, `Give ye them to eat,' and they say to him, `Having gone away, may we buy two hundred denaries'

worth of loaves, and give to them to eat?'

Mark 6:38 And he saith to them, `How many loaves have ye? go and see;' and having known, they say, `Five, and two fishes.'

Mark 6:39 And he commanded them to make all recline in companies upon the green grass,

Mark 6:40 and they sat down in squares, by hundreds, and by fifties.

Mark 6:41 And having taken the five loaves and the two fishes, having looked up to the heaven, he blessed, and brake the loaves, and was giving to his disciples, that they may set before them, and the two fishes divided he to all,

Mark 6:42 and they did all eat, and were filled,

Mark 6:43 and they took up of broken pieces twelve hand-baskets full, and of the fishes,

Mark 6:44 and those eating of the loaves were about five thousand men.

Mark 6:45. And immediately he constrained his disciples to go into the boat, and to go before to the other side, unto Bethsaida, till he may let the multitude away,

Mark 6:46 and having taken leave of them, he went away to the mountain to pray.

Mark 6:47 And evening having come, the boat was in the midst of the sea, and he alone upon the land;

Mark 6:48 and he saw them harassed in the rowing, for the wind was against them, and about the fourth watch of the night he doth come to them walking on the sea, and wished to pass by them.

Mark 6:49 And they having seen him walking on the sea, thought [it] to be an apparition, and cried out,

Mark 6:50 for they all saw him, and were troubled, and immediately he spake with them, and saith to them, `Take courage, I am [he], be not afraid.'

Mark 6:51 And he went up unto them to the boat, and the wind lulled, and greatly out of measure were they amazed in themselves, and were wondering,

Mark 6:52 for they understood not concerning the loaves, for their heart hath been hard.

Mark 6:53 And having passed over, they came upon the land of Gennesaret, and drew to the shore,

Mark 6:54 and they having come forth out of the boat, immediately having recognised him,

Mark 6:55 having run about through all that region round about, they began upon the couches to carry about those ill, where they were hearing that he is,

Mark 6:56 and wherever he was going, to villages, or cities, or fields, in the market-places they were laying the infirm, and were calling upon him, that they may touch if it were but the fringe of his garment, and as many as were touching him were saved.

Mark 7:1. And gathered together unto him are the Pharisees, and certain of the scribes, having come from Jerusalem,

Mark 7:2 and having seen certain of his disciples with defiled hands--that is, unwashed--eating bread, they found fault;

Mark 7:3 for the Pharisees, and all the Jews, if they do not wash the hands to the wrist, do not eat, holding the tradition of the elders,

Mark 7:4 and, [coming] from the market-place, if they do not baptize themselves, they do not eat; and many other things there are that they received to hold, baptisms of cups, and pots, and brazen vessels, and couches.

Mark 7:5 Then question him do the Pharisees and the scribes, `Wherefore do thy disciples not walk according to the tradition of the elders, but with unwashed hands do eat the bread?'

Mark 7:6 and he answering said to them--`Well did Isaiah prophesy concerning you, hypocrites, as it hath been written, This people with the lips doth honour Me, and their heart is far from Me;

Mark 7:7 and in vain do they worship Me, teaching teachings, commands of men;

Mark 7:8 for, having put away the command of God, ye hold the tradition of men, baptisms of pots and cups; and many other such like things ye do.'

Mark 7:9 And he said to them, `Well do ye put away the command of God that your tradition ye may keep;

Mark 7:10 for Moses said, Honour thy father and thy mother; and, He who is speaking evil of father or mother--let him die the death;

Mark 7:11 and ye say, If a man may say to father or to mother, Korban (that is, a gift), [is] whatever thou mayest be profited out of mine,

Mark 7:12 and no more do ye suffer him to do anything for his father or for his mother,

Mark 7:13 setting aside the word of God for your tradition that ye delivered; and many such like things ye do.'

Mark 7:14 And having called near all the multitude, he said to them, `Hearken to me, ye all, and understand;

Mark 7:15 there is nothing from without the man entering into him that is able to defile him, but the

things coming out from him, those are the things defiling the man.

Mark 7:16 If any hath ears to hear-- let him hear.'

Mark 7:17 And when he entered into a house from the multitude, his disciples were questioning him about the simile,

Mark 7:18 and he saith to them, `So also ye are without understanding! Do ye not perceive that nothing from without entering into the man is able to defile him?

Mark 7:19 because it doth not enter into his heart, but into the belly, and into the drain it doth go out, purifying all the meats.'

Mark 7:20 And he said--`That which is coming out from the man, that doth defile the man;

Mark 7:21 for from within, out of the heart of men, the evil reasonings do come forth, adulteries, whoredoms, murders,

Mark 7:22 thefts, covetous desires, wickedness, deceit, arrogance, an evil eye, evil speaking, pride, foolishness;

Mark 7:23 all these evils do come forth from within, and they defile the man.'

Mark 7:24. And from thence having risen, he went away to the borders of Tyre and Sidon, and having entered into the house, he wished none to know, and he was not able to be hid,

Mark 7:25 for a woman having heard about him, whose little daughter had an unclean spirit, having come, fell at his feet, --

Mark 7:26 and the woman was a Greek, a Syro-Phenician by nation-- and was asking him, that the demon he may cast forth out of her daughter.

Mark 7:27 And Jesus said to her, `Suffer first the children to be filled, for it is not good to take the children's bread, and to cast [it] to the little dogs.'

Mark 7:28 And she answered and saith to him, `Yes, sir; for the little dogs also under the table do eat of the children's crumbs.'

Mark 7:29 And he said to her, `Because of this word go; the demon hath gone forth out of thy daughter;'

Mark 7:30 and having come away to her house, she found the demon gone forth, and the daughter laid upon the couch.

Mark 7:31. And again, having gone forth from the coasts of Tyre and Sidon, he came unto the sea of Galilee, through the midst of the coasts of Decapolis,

Mark 7:32 and they bring to him a deaf, stuttering man, and they call on him that he may put the hand on him.

Mark 7:33 And having taken him away from the multitude by himself, he put his fingers to his ears, and having spit, he touched his tongue,

Mark 7:34 and having looked to the heaven, he sighed, and saith to him, Èphphatha,' that is, `Be thou opened;'

Mark 7:35 and immediately were his ears opened, and the string of his tongue was loosed, and he was speaking plain.

Mark 7:36 And he charged them that they may tell no one, but the more he was charging them, the more abundantly they were proclaiming [it],

Mark 7:37 and they were being beyond measure astonished, saying, `Well hath he done all things; both the deaf he doth make to hear, and the dumb to speak.'

Mark 8:1. In those days the multitude being very great, and not having what they may eat, Jesus having called near his disciples, saith to them,

Mark 8:2 Ì have compassion upon the multitude, because now three days they do continue with me, and they have not what they may eat;

Mark 8:3 and if I shall let them away fasting to their home, they will faint in the way, for certain of them are come from far.'

Mark 8:4 And his disciples answered him, `Whence shall any one be able these here to feed with bread in a wilderness?'

Mark 8:5 And he was questioning them, `How many loaves have ye?' and they said, `Seven.'

Mark 8:6 And he commanded the multitude to sit down upon the ground, and having taken the seven loaves, having given thanks, he brake, and was giving to his disciples that they may set before [them]; and they did set before the multitude.

Mark 8:7 And they had a few small fishes, and having blessed, he said to set them also before [them];

Mark 8:8 and they did eat and were filled, and they took up that which was over of broken pieces--seven baskets;

Mark 8:9 and those eating were about four thousand. And he let them away,

Mark 8:10. and immediately having entered into the boat with his disciples, he came to the parts of Dalmanutha,

Mark 8:11 and the Pharisees came forth, and began to dispute with him, seeking from him a sign from the heaven, tempting him;

Mark 8:12 and having sighed deeply in his spirit, he saith, `Why doth this generation seek after a sign?

Verily I say to you, no sign shall be given to this generation.'

Mark 8:13 And having left them, having entered again into the boat, he went away to the other side;

Mark 8:14 and they forgot to take loaves, and except one loaf they had nothing with them in the boat,

Mark 8:15 and he was charging them, saying, `Take heed, beware of the leaven of the Pharisees, and of the leaven of Herod,'

Mark 8:16 and they were reasoning with one another, saying--`Because we have no loaves.'

Mark 8:17 And Jesus having known, saith to them, `Why do ye reason, because ye have no loaves? do ye not yet perceive, nor understand, yet have ye your heart hardened?

Mark 8:18 Having eyes, do ye not see? and having ears, do ye not hear? and do ye not remember?

Mark 8:19 When the five loaves I did brake to the five thousand, how many hand-baskets full of broken pieces took ye up?' they say to him, `Twelve.'

Mark 8:20 Ànd when the seven to the four thousand, how many hand-baskets full of broken pieces took ye up?' and they said, `Seven.'

Mark 8:21 And he said to them, `How do ye not understand?'

Mark 8:22. And he cometh to Bethsaida, and they bring to him one blind, and call upon him that he may touch him,

Mark 8:23 and having taken the hand of the blind man, he led him forth without the village, and having spit on his eyes, having put [his] hands on him, he was questioning him if he doth behold anything:

Mark 8:24 and he, having looked up, said, Ì behold men, as I see trees, walking.'

Mark 8:25 Afterwards again he put [his] hands on his eyes, and made him look up, and he was restored, and discerned all things clearly,

Mark 8:26 and he sent him away to his house, saying, `Neither to the village mayest thou go, nor tell [it] to any in the village.'

Mark 8:27. And Jesus went forth, and his disciples, to the villages of Caesarea Philippi, and in the way he was questioning his disciples, saying to them, `Who do men say me to be?'

Mark 8:28 And they answered, `John the Baptist, and others Elijah, but others one of the prophets.'

Mark 8:29 And he saith to them, Ànd ye--who do ye say me to be?' and Peter answering saith to him, `Thou art the Christ.'

Mark 8:30 And he strictly charged them that they may tell no one about it,

Mark 8:31 and began to teach them, that it behoveth the Son of Man to suffer many things, and to be rejected by the elders, and chief priests, and scribes, and to be killed, and after three days to rise again;

Mark 8:32 and openly he was speaking the word. And Peter having taken him aside, began to rebuke him,

Mark 8:33 and he, having turned, and having looked on his disciples, rebuked Peter, saying, `Get behind me, Adversary, because thou dost not mind the things of God, but the things of men.'

Mark 8:34 And having called near the multitude, with his disciples, he said to them, `Whoever doth will to come after me--let him disown himself, and take up his cross, and follow me;

Mark 8:35 for whoever may will to save his life shall lose it; and whoever may lose his life for my sake and for the good news' sake, he shall save it;

Mark 8:36 for what shall it profit a man, if he may gain the whole world, and forfeit his life?

Mark 8:37 Or what shall a man give as an exchange for his life?

Mark 8:38 for whoever may be ashamed of me, and of my words, in this adulterous and sinful generation, the Son of Man also shall be ashamed of him, when he may come in the glory of his Father, with the holy messengers.'

Mark 9:1. And he said to them, `Verily I say to you, That there are certain of those standing here, who may not taste of death till they see the reign of God having come in power.'

Mark 9:2 And after six days doth Jesus take Peter, and James, and John, and bringeth them up to a high mount by themselves, alone, and he was transfigured before them,

Mark 9:3 and his garments became glittering, white exceedingly, as snow, so as a fuller upon the earth is not able to whiten [them].

Mark 9:4 And there appeared to them Elijah with Moses, and they were talking with Jesus.

Mark 9:5 And Peter answering saith to Jesus, `Rabbi, it is good to us to be here; and we may make three booths, for thee one, and for Moses one, and for Elijah one:'

Mark 9:6 for he was not knowing what he might say, for they were greatly afraid.

Mark 9:7 And there came a cloud overshadowing them, and there came a voice out of the cloud, saying, `This is My Son--the Beloved, hear ye him;'

Mark 9:8 and suddenly, having looked around, they saw no one any more, but Jesus only with themselves.

Mark 9:9 And as they are coming down from the mount, he charged them that they may declare to no one the things that they saw, except when the Son of Man may rise out of the dead;

Mark 9:10 and the thing they kept to themselves, questioning together what the rising out of the dead is.

Mark 9:11 And they were questioning him, saying, that the scribes say that Elijah it behoveth to come first.

Mark 9:12 And he answering said to them, Èlijah indeed, having come first, doth restore all things; and how hath it been written concerning the Son of Man, that many things he may suffer, and be set at nought?

Mark 9:13 But I say to you, That also Elijah hath come, and they did to him what they willed, as it hath been written of him.'

Mark 9:14. And having come unto the disciples, he saw a great multitude about them, and scribes questioning with them,

Mark 9:15 and immediately, all the multitude having seen him, were amazed, and running near, were saluting him.

Mark 9:16 And he questioned the scribes, `What dispute ye with them?'

Mark 9:17 and one out of the multitude answering said, `Teacher, I brought my son unto thee, having a dumb spirit;

Mark 9:18 and wherever it doth seize him, it doth tear him, and he foameth, and gnasheth his teeth, and pineth away; and I spake to thy disciples that they may cast it out, and they were not able.'

Mark 9:19 And he answering him, said, Ò generation unbelieving, till when shall I be with you? till when shall I suffer you? bring him unto me;'

Mark 9:20 and they brought him unto him, and he having seen him, immediately the spirit tare him, and he, having fallen upon the earth, was wallowing--foaming.

Mark 9:21 And he questioned his father, `How long time is it since this came to him?' and he said, `From childhood,

Mark 9:22 and many times also it cast him into fire, and into water, that it might destroy him; but if thou art able to do anything, help us, having compassion on us.'

Mark 9:23 And Jesus said to him, Ìf thou art able to believe! all things are possible to the one that is believing;'

Mark 9:24 and immediately the father of the child, having cried out,

with tears said, Ì believe, sir; be helping mine unbelief.'

Mark 9:25 Jesus having seen that a multitude doth run together, rebuked the unclean spirit, saying to it, `Spirit--dumb and deaf--I charge thee, come forth out of him, and no more thou mayest enter into him;'

Mark 9:26 and having cried, and rent him much, it came forth, and he became as dead, so that many said that he was dead,

Mark 9:27 but Jesus, having taken him by the hand, lifted him up, and he arose.

Mark 9:28 And he having come into the house, his disciples were questioning him by himself--`Why were we not able to cast it forth?'

Mark 9:29 And he said to them, `This kind is able to come forth with nothing except with prayer and fasting.'

Mark 9:30. And having gone forth thence, they were passing through Galilee, and he did not wish that any may know,

Mark 9:31 for he was teaching his disciples, and he said to them, `The Son of Man is being delivered to the hands of men, and they shall kill him, and having been killed the third day he shall rise,'

Mark 9:32 but they were not understanding the saying, and they were afraid to question him.

Mark 9:33 And he came to Capernaum, and being in the house, he was questioning them, `What were ye reasoning in the way among yourselves?'

Mark 9:34 and they were silent, for with one another they did reason in the way who is greater;

Mark 9:35 and having sat down he called the twelve, and he saith to them, Ìf any doth will to be first, he shall be last of all, and minister of all.'

Mark 9:36 And having taken a child, he set him in the midst of them, and having taken him in his arms, said to them,

Mark 9:37 `Whoever may receive one of such children in my name, doth receive me, and whoever may receive me, doth not receive me, but Him who sent me.'

Mark 9:38 And John did answer him, saying, `Teacher, we saw a certain one in thy name casting out demons, who doth not follow us, and we forbade him, because he doth not follow us.'

Mark 9:39 And Jesus said, `Forbid him not, for there is no one who shall do a mighty work in my name, and shall be able readily to speak evil of me:

Mark 9:40 for he who is not against us is for us;

Mark 9:41. for whoever may give you to drink a cup of water in my name, because ye are Christ's, verily I say to you, he may not lose his reward;

Mark 9:42 and whoever may cause to stumble one of the little ones believing in me, better is it for him if a millstone is hanged about his neck, and he hath been cast into the sea.

Mark 9:43 Ànd if thy hand may cause thee to stumble, cut it off; it is better for thee maimed to enter into the life, than having the two hands, to go away to the gehenna, to the fire--the unquenchable--

Mark 9:44 where there worm is not dying, and the fire is not being quenched.

Mark 9:45 Ànd if thy foot may cause thee to stumble, cut it off; it is better for thee to enter into the life lame, than having the two feet to be cast to the gehenna, to the fire--the unquenchable--

Mark 9:46 where there worm is not dying, and the fire is not being quenched.

Mark 9:47 And if thine eye may cause thee to stumble, cast it out; it is better for thee one-eyed to enter into the reign of God, than having two eyes, to be cast to the gehenna of the fire--

Mark 9:48 where their worm is not dying, and the fire is not being quenched;

Mark 9:49 for every one with fire shall be salted, and every sacrifice with salt shall be salted.

Mark 9:50 The salt [is] good, but if the salt may become saltless, in what will ye season [it]? Have in yourselves salt, and have peace in one another.'

Mark 10:1. And having risen thence, he doth come to the coasts of Judea, through the other side of the Jordan, and again do multitudes come together unto him, and, as he had been accustomed, again he was teaching them.

Mark 10:2 And the Pharisees, having come near, questioned him, if it is lawful for a husband to put away a wife, tempting him,

Mark 10:3 and he answering said to them, `What did Moses command you?'

Mark 10:4 and they said, `Moses suffered to write a bill of divorce, and to put away.'

Mark 10:5 And Jesus answering said to them, `For the stiffness of your heart he wrote you this command,

Mark 10:6 but from the beginning of the creation, a male and a female God did make them;

Mark 10:7 on this account shall a man leave his father and mother, and shall cleave unto his wife,

Mark 10:8 and they shall be--the two--for one flesh; so that they are no more two, but one flesh;

Mark 10:9 what therefore God did join together, let not man put asunder.'

Mark 10:10 And in the house again his disciples of the same thing questioned him,

Mark 10:11 and he saith to them, `Whoever may put away his wife, and may marry another, doth commit adultery against her;

Mark 10:12 and if a woman may put away her husband, and is married to another, she committeth adultery.'

Mark 10:13. And they were bringing to him children, that he might touch them, and the disciples were rebuking those bringing them,

Mark 10:14 and Jesus having seen, was much displeased, and he said to them, `Suffer the children to come unto me, and forbid them not, for of such is the reign of God;

Mark 10:15 verily I say to you, whoever may not receive the reign of God, as a child--he may not enter into it;'

Mark 10:16 and having taken them in his arms, having put [his] hands upon them, he was blessing them.

Mark 10:17. And as he is going forth into the way, one having run and having kneeled to him, was questioning him, `Good teacher, what may I do, that life age-during I may inherit?'

Mark 10:18 And Jesus said to him, `Why me dost thou call good? no one [is] good except One--God;

Mark 10:19 the commands thou hast known: Thou mayest not commit adultery, Thou mayest do no murder, Thou mayest not steal, Thou mayest not bear false witness, Thou mayest not defraud, Honour thy father and mother.'

Mark 10:20 And he answering said to him, `Teacher, all these did I keep from my youth.'

Mark 10:21 And Jesus having looked upon him, did love him, and said to him, Òne thing thou dost lack; go away, whatever thou hast--sell, and give to the poor, and thou shalt have treasure in heaven, and come, be following me, having taken up the cross.'

Mark 10:22 And he--gloomy at the word--went away sorrowing, for he was having many possessions.

Mark 10:23 And Jesus having looked round, saith to his disciples, `How hardly shall they who have riches enter into the reign of God!'

Mark 10:24 And the disciples were astonished at his words, and Jesus again answering saith to them, `Children, how hard is it to those trusting on the riches to enter into the reign of God!

Mark 10:25 It is easier for a camel through the eye of the needle to enter, than for a rich man to enter into the reign of God.'

Mark 10:26 And they were astonished beyond measure, saying unto themselves, Ànd who is able to be saved?'

Mark 10:27 And Jesus, having looked upon them, saith, `With men it is impossible, but not with God; for all things are possible with God.'

Mark 10:28 And Peter began to say to him, `Lo, we left all, and we followed thee.'

Mark 10:29 And Jesus answering said, `Verily I say to you, there is no one who left house, or brothers, or sisters, or father, or mother, or wife, or children, or fields, for my sake, and for the good news',

Mark 10:30 who may not receive an hundredfold now in this time, houses, and brothers, and sisters, and mothers, and children, and fields, with persecutions, and in the age that is coming, life age-during;

Mark 10:31 and many first shall be last, and the last first.'

Mark 10:32. And they were in the way going up to Jerusalem, and Jesus was going before them, and they were amazed, and following they were afraid. And having again taken the twelve, he began to tell them the things about to happen to him,

Mark 10:33 --`Lo, we go up to Jerusalem, and the Son of Man shall be delivered to the chief priests, and to the scribes, and they shall condemn him to death, and shall deliver him to the nations,

Mark 10:34 and they shall mock him, and scourge him, and spit on him, and kill him, and the third day he shall rise again.'

Mark 10:35 And there come near to him James and John, the sons of Zebedee, saying, `Teacher, we wish that whatever we may ask for ourselves, thou mayest do for us;'

Mark 10:36 and he said to them, `What do ye wish me to do for you?'

Mark 10:37 and they said to him, `Grant to us that, one on thy right hand and one on thy left, we may sit in thy glory;'

Mark 10:38 and Jesus said to them, `Ye have not known what ye ask; are ye able to drink of the cup that I drink of, and with the baptism that I am baptized with--to be baptized?'

Mark 10:39 And they said to him, `We are able;' and Jesus said to them, Òf the cup indeed that I drink of, ye shall drink, and with the baptism that I am baptized with, ye shall be baptized;

Mark 10:40 but to sit on my right and on my left, is not mine to give, but--to those for whom it hath been prepared.'

Mark 10:41 And the ten having heard, began to be much displeased at James and John,

Mark 10:42 but Jesus having called them near, saith to them, `Ye have known that they who are considered to rule the nations do exercise lordship over them, and their great ones do exercise authority upon them;

Mark 10:43 but not so shall it be among you; but whoever may will to become great among you, he shall be your minister,

Mark 10:44 and whoever of you may will to become first, he shall be servant of all;

Mark 10:45 for even the Son of Man came not to be ministered to, but to minister, and to give his life a ransom for many.'

Mark 10:46. And they come to Jericho, and as he is going forth from Jericho, with his disciples and a great multitude, a son of Timaeus--Bartimaeus the blind--was sitting beside the way begging,

Mark 10:47 and having heard that it is Jesus the Nazarene, he began to cry out, and to say, `The Son of David--Jesus! deal kindly with me;'

Mark 10:48 and many were rebuking him, that he might keep silent, but the more abundantly he cried out, `Son of David, deal kindly with me.'

Mark 10:49 And Jesus having stood, he commanded him to be called, and they call the blind man, saying to him, `Take courage, rise, he doth call thee;'

Mark 10:50 and he, having cast away his garment, having risen, did come unto Jesus.

Mark 10:51 And answering, Jesus saith to him, `What wilt thou I may do to thee?' and the blind man said to him, `Rabboni, that I may see again;'

Mark 10:52 and Jesus said to him, `Go, thy faith hath saved thee:' and immediately he saw again, and was following Jesus in the way.

Mark 11:1. And when they come nigh to Jerusalem, to Bethphage, and Bethany, unto the mount of the Olives, he sendeth forth two of his disciples,

Mark 11:2 and saith to them, `Go away to the village that is over-against you, and immediately, entering into it, ye shall find a colt tied, on

which no one of men hath sat, having loosed it, bring [it]:

Mark 11:3 and if any one may say to you, Why do ye this? say ye that the lord hath need of it, and immediately he will send it hither.'

Mark 11:4 And they went away, and found the colt tied at the door without, by the two ways, and they loose it,

Mark 11:5 and certain of those standing there said to them, `What do ye--loosing the colt?'

Mark 11:6 and they said to them as Jesus commanded, and they suffered them.

Mark 11:7 And they brought the colt unto Jesus, and did cast upon it their garments, and he sat upon it,

Mark 11:8 and many did spread their garments in the way, and others were cutting down branches from the trees, and were strewing in the way.

Mark 11:9 And those going before and those following were crying out, saying, `Hosanna! Blessed [is] he who is coming in the name of the Lord;

Mark 11:10 blessed is the coming reign, in the name of the Lord, of our father David; Hosanna in the highest.'

Mark 11:11 And Jesus entered into Jerusalem, and into the temple, and having looked round on all things, it being now evening, he went forth to Bethany with the twelve.

Mark 11:12. And on the morrow, they having come forth from Bethany, he hungered,

Mark 11:13 and having seen a fig-tree afar off having leaves, he came, if perhaps he shall find anything in it, and having come to it, he found nothing except leaves, for it was not a time of figs,

Mark 11:14 and Jesus answering said to it, `No more from thee--to the age--may any eat fruit;' and his disciples were hearing.

Mark 11:15 And they come to Jerusalem, and Jesus having gone into the temple, began to cast forth those selling and buying in the temple, and the tables of the money-changers and the seats of those selling the doves, he overthrew,

Mark 11:16 and he did not suffer that any might bear a vessel through the temple,

Mark 11:17 and he was teaching, saying to them, `Hath it not been written--My house a house of prayer shall be called for all the nations, and ye did make it a den of robbers?'

Mark 11:18 And the scribes and the chief priests heard, and they were seeking how they shall destroy him, for they were afraid of him, because all the multitude was astonished at his teaching;

Mark 11:19 and when evening came, he was going forth without the city.

Mark 11:20 And in the morning, passing by, they saw the fig-tree having been dried up from the roots,

Mark 11:21 and Peter having remembered saith to him, `Rabbi, lo, the fig-tree that thou didst curse is dried up.'

Mark 11:22 And Jesus answering saith to them, `Have faith of God;

Mark 11:23 for verily I say to you, that whoever may say to this mount, Be taken up, and be cast into the sea, and may not doubt in his heart, but may believe that the things that he saith do come to pass, it shall be to him whatever he may say.

Mark 11:24 Because of this I say to you, all whatever--praying--ye do ask, believe that ye receive, and it shall be to you.

Mark 11:25 And whenever ye may stand praying, forgive, if ye have anything against any one, that your Father also who is in the heavens may forgive you your trespasses;

Mark 11:26 and, if ye do not forgive, neither will your Father who is in the heavens forgive your trespasses.'

Mark 11:27. And they come again to Jerusalem, and in the temple, as he is walking, there come unto him the chief priests, and the scribes, and the elders,

Mark 11:28 and they say to him, `By what authority dost thou these things? and who gave thee this authority that these things thou mayest do?'

Mark 11:29 And Jesus answering said to them, Ì will question you--I also--one word; and answer me, and I will tell you by what authority I do these things;

Mark 11:30 the baptism of John-- from heaven was it? or from men? answer me.'

Mark 11:31 And they were reasoning with themselves, saying, Ìf we may say, From heaven, he will say, Wherefore, then, did ye not believe him?

Mark 11:32 But if we may say, From men,' --they were fearing the people, for all were holding John that he was indeed a prophet;

Mark 11:33 and answering they say to Jesus, `We have not known;' and Jesus answering saith to them, `Neither do I tell you by what authority I do these things.'

Mark 12:1. And he began to speak to them in similes: À man planted a vineyard, and put a hedge around, and digged an under-wine-vat, and built a tower, and gave it out to husbandmen, and went abroad;

Mark 12:2 and he sent unto the husbandmen at the due time a servant, that from the husbandmen he may receive from the fruit of the vineyard,

Mark 12:3 and they, having taken him, did severely beat [him], and did send him away empty.

Mark 12:4 Ànd again he sent unto them another servant, and at that one having cast stones, they wounded [him] in the head, and sent away--dishonoured.

Mark 12:5 Ànd again he sent another, and that one they killed; and many others, some beating, and some killing.

Mark 12:6 `Having yet therefore one son--his beloved--he sent also him unto them last, saying--They will reverence my son;

Mark 12:7 and those husbandmen said among themselves--This is the heir, come, we may kill him, and ours shall be the inheritance;

Mark 12:8 and having taken him, they did kill, and cast [him] forth without the vineyard.

Mark 12:9 `What therefore shall the lord of the vineyard do? he will come and destroy the husbandmen, and will give the vineyard to others.

Mark 12:10 And this Writing did ye not read: A stone that the builders rejected, it did become the head of a corner:

Mark 12:11 from the Lord was this, and it is wonderful in our eyes.'

Mark 12:12 And they were seeking to lay hold on him, and they feared the multitude, for they knew that against them he spake the simile, and having left him, they went away;

Mark 12:13. and they send unto him certain of the Pharisees and of the Herodians, that they may ensnare him in discourse,

Mark 12:14 and they having come, say to him, `Teacher, we have known that thou art true, and thou art not caring for any one, for thou dost not look to the face of men, but in truth the way of God dost teach; is it lawful to give tribute to Caesar or not? may we give, or may we not give?'

Mark 12:15 And he, knowing their hypocrisy, said to them, `Why me do ye tempt? bring me a denary, that I may see;'

Mark 12:16 and they brought, and he saith to them, `Whose [is] this image, and the inscription?' and they said to him, `Caesar's;'

Mark 12:17 and Jesus answering said to them, `Give back the things of Caesar to Caesar, and the things of God to God;' and they did wonder at him.

Mark 12:18. And the Sadducees come unto him, who say there is not a rising again, and they questioned him, saying,

Mark 12:19 `Teacher, Moses wrote to us, that if any one's brother may die, and may leave a wife, and may leave no children, that his brother may take his wife, and raise up seed to his brother.

Mark 12:20 `There were then seven brothers, and the first took a wife, and dying, he left no seed;

Mark 12:21 and the second took her, and died, neither left he seed, and the third in like manner,

Mark 12:22 and the seven took her, and left no seed, last of all died also the woman;

Mark 12:23 in the rising again, then, whenever they may rise, of which of them shall she be wife--for the seven had her as wife?'

Mark 12:24 And Jesus answering said to them, `Do ye not because of this go astray, not knowing the Writings, nor the power of God?

Mark 12:25 for when they may rise out of the dead, they neither marry nor are they given in marriage, but are as messengers who are in the heavens.

Mark 12:26 Ànd concerning the dead, that they rise: have ye not read in the Book of Moses (at The Bush), how God spake to him, saying, I [am]

the God of Abraham, and the God of Isaac, and the God of Jacob;

Mark 12:27 he is not the God of dead men, but a God of living men; ye then go greatly astray.'

Mark 12:28. And one of the scribes having come near, having heard them disputing, knowing that he answered them well, questioned him, `Which is the first command of all?'

Mark 12:29 and Jesus answered him--`The first of all the commands [is], Hear, O Israel, the Lord is our God, the Lord is one;

Mark 12:30 and thou shalt love the Lord thy God out of all thy heart, and out of thy soul, and out of all thine understanding, and out of all thy strength--this [is] the first command;

Mark 12:31 and the second [is] like [it], this, Thou shalt love thy neighbour as thyself; --greater than these there is no other command.'

Mark 12:32 And the scribe said to him, `Well, Teacher, in truth thou hast spoken that there is one God, and there is none other but He;

Mark 12:33 and to love Him out of all the heart, and out of all the understanding, and out of all the soul, and out of all the strength, and to love one's neighbour as one's self, is more than all the whole burnt-offerings and the sacrifices.'

Mark 12:34 And Jesus, having seen him that he answered with understanding, said to him, `Thou art not far from the reign of God;' and no one any more durst question him.

Mark 12:35. And Jesus answering said, teaching in the temple, `How say the scribes that the Christ is son of David?

Mark 12:36 for David himself said in the Holy Spirit, The Lord said to my lord, Sit thou on My right hand, till I place thine enemies--thy footstool;

Mark 12:37 therefore David himself saith of him Lord, and whence is he his son?' And the great multitude were hearing him gladly,

Mark 12:38 and he was saying to them in his teaching, `Beware of the scribes, who will in long robes to walk, and love salutations in the market-places,

Mark 12:39 and first seats in the synagogues, and first couches in suppers,

Mark 12:40 who are devouring the widows' houses, and for a pretence are making long prayers; these shall receive more abundant judgment.'

Mark 12:41. And Jesus having sat down over-against the treasury, was beholding how the multitude do put brass into the treasury, and many rich were putting in much,

Mark 12:42 and having come, a poor widow did put in two mites, which are a farthing.

Mark 12:43 And having called near his disciples, he saith to them, `Verily I say to you, that this poor widow hath put in more than all those putting into the treasury;

Mark 12:44 for all, out of their abundance, put in, but she, out of her want, all that she had put in--all her living.'

Mark 13:1. And as he is going forth out of the temple, one of his disciples saith to him, `Teacher, see! what stones! and what buildings!'

Mark 13:2 and Jesus answering said to him, `Seest thou these great buildings? there may not be left a stone upon a stone, that may not be thrown down.'

Mark 13:3 And as he is sitting at the mount of the Olives, over-against the temple, Peter, and James, and John, and Andrew, were questioning him by himself,

Mark 13:4 `Tell us when these things shall be? and what [is] the sign when all these may be about to be fulfilled?'

Mark 13:5. And Jesus answering them, began to say, `Take heed lest any one may lead you astray,

Mark 13:6 for many shall come in my name, saying--I am [he], and many they shall lead astray;

Mark 13:7 and when ye may hear of wars and reports of wars, be not troubled, for these behove to be, but the end [is] not yet;

Mark 13:8 for nation shall rise against nation, and kingdom against kingdom, and there shall be earthquakes in divers places, and there shall be famines and troubles; beginnings of sorrows [are] these.

Mark 13:9 And take ye heed to yourselves, for they shall deliver you up to sanhedrims, and to synagogues, ye shall be beaten, and before governors and kings ye shall be set for my sake, for a testimony to them;

Mark 13:10 and to all the nations it behoveth first that the good news be proclaimed.

Mark 13:11 And when they may lead you, delivering up, be not anxious beforehand what ye may speak, nor premeditate, but whatever may be given to you in that hour, that speak ye, for it is not ye who are speaking, but the Holy Spirit.

Mark 13:12 And brother shall deliver up brother to death, and father child, and children shall rise up against parents, and shall put them to death,

Mark 13:13 and ye shall be hated by all because of my name, but he who hath endured to the end--he shall be saved.

Mark 13:14. And when ye may see the abomination of the desolation, that was spoken of by Daniel the prophet, standing where it ought not, (whoever is reading let him understand), then those in Judea, let them flee to the mountains;

Mark 13:15 and he upon the house-top, let him not come down to the house, nor come in to take anything out of his house;

Mark 13:16 and he who is in the field, let him not turn to the things behind, to take up his garment.

Mark 13:17 And woe to those with child, and to those giving suck, in those days;

Mark 13:18 and pray ye that your flight may not be in winter,

Mark 13:19 for those days shall be tribulation, such as hath not been from the beginning of the creation that God created, till now, and may not be;

Mark 13:20 and if the Lord did not shorten the days, no flesh had been saved; but because of the chosen, whom He did choose to Himself, He did shorten the days.

Mark 13:21 And then, if any may say to you, Lo, here [is] the Christ, or, Lo, there, ye may not believe;

Mark 13:22 for there shall rise false Christs and false prophets, and they shall give signs and wonders, to seduce, if possible, also the chosen;

Mark 13:23 and ye, take heed; lo, I have foretold you all things.

Mark 13:24. `But in those days, after that tribulation, the sun shall be darkened, and the moon shall not give her light,

Mark 13:25 and the stars of the heaven shall be falling, and the powers that are in the heavens shall be shaken.

Mark 13:26 And then they shall see the Son of Man coming in clouds with much power and glory,

Mark 13:27 and then he shall send his messengers, and gather together his chosen from the four winds, from the end of the earth unto the end of heaven.

Mark 13:28. And from the fig-tree learn ye the simile: when the branch may already become tender, and may put forth the leaves, ye know that nigh is the summer;

Mark 13:29 so ye, also, when these ye may see coming to pass, ye know that it is nigh, at the doors.

Mark 13:30 Verily I say to you, that this generation may not pass away till all these things may come to pass;

Mark 13:31 the heaven and the earth shall pass away, but my words shall not pass away.

Mark 13:32 And concerning that day and the hour no one hath known--not even the messengers who are in the heaven, not even the Son--except the Father.

Mark 13:33 Take heed, watch and pray, for ye have not known when the time is;

Mark 13:34 as a man who is gone abroad, having left his house, and given to his servants the authority, and to each one his work, did command also the porter that he may watch;

Mark 13:35 watch ye, therefore, for ye have not known when the lord of the house doth come, at even, or at midnight, or at cock-crowing, or at the morning;

Mark 13:36 lest, having come suddenly, he may find you sleeping;

Mark 13:37 and what I say to you, I say to all, Watch.'

Mark 14:1. And the passover and the unleavened food were after two days, and the chief priests and the scribes were seeking how, by guile, having taken hold of him, they might kill him;

Mark 14:2 and they said, `Not in the feast, lest there shall be a tumult of the people.'

Mark 14:3 And he, being in Bethany, in the house of Simon the leper, at his reclining (at meat), there came a woman having an alabaster box of ointment, of spikenard, very precious, and having broken the alabaster box, did pour on his head;

Mark 14:4 and there were certain much displeased within themselves, and saying, `For what hath this waste of the ointment been made?

Mark 14:5 for this could have been sold for more than three hundred denaries, and given to the poor;' and they were murmuring at her.

Mark 14:6 And Jesus said, `Let her alone; why are ye giving her trouble? a good work she wrought on me;

Mark 14:7 for the poor always ye have with you, and whenever ye may will ye are able to do them good, but me ye have not always;

Mark 14:8 what she could she did, she anticipated to anoint my body for the embalming.

Mark 14:9 Verily I say to you, wherever this good news may be proclaimed in the whole world, what also this woman did shall be spoken of--for a memorial of her.'

Mark 14:10 And Judas the Iscariot, one of the twelve, went away unto the chief priests that he might deliver him up to them,

Mark 14:11 and having heard, they were glad, and promised to give him money, and he was seeking how, conveniently, he might deliver him up.

Mark 14:12. And the first day of the unleavened food, when they were killing the passover, his disciples say to him, `Where wilt thou, [that,] having gone, we may prepare, that thou mayest eat the passover?'

Mark 14:13 And he sendeth forth two of his disciples, and saith to them, `Go ye away to the city, and there shall meet you a man bearing a pitcher of water, follow him;

Mark 14:14 and wherever he may go in, say ye to the master of the house--The Teacher saith, Where is the guest-chamber, where the passover, with my disciples, I may eat?

Mark 14:15 and he will shew you a large upper room, furnished, prepared--there make ready for us.'

Mark 14:16 And his disciples went forth, and came to the city, and found as he said to them, and they made ready the passover.

Mark 14:17 And evening having come, he cometh with the twelve,

Mark 14:18 and as they are reclining, and eating, Jesus said, `Verily I say to you--one of you, who is eating with me--shall deliver me up.'

Mark 14:19 And they began to be sorrowful, and to say to him, one by one, Ìs it I?' and another, Ìs it I?'

Mark 14:20 And he answering said to them, Òne of the twelve who is dipping with me in the dish;

Mark 14:21 the Son of Man doth indeed go, as it hath been written concerning him, but woe to that man through whom the Son of Man is delivered up; good were it to him if that man had not been born.'

Mark 14:22 And as they are eating, Jesus having taken bread, having blessed, brake, and gave to them, and said, `Take, eat; this is my body.'

Mark 14:23 And having taken the cup, having given thanks, he gave to them, and they drank of it--all;

Mark 14:24 and he said to them, `This is my blood of the new covenant, which for many is being poured out;

Mark 14:25 verily I say to you, that no more may I drink of the produce of the vine till that day when I may drink it new in the reign of God.'

Mark 14:26 And having sung an hymn, they went forth to the mount of the Olives,

Mark 14:27 and Jesus saith to them--Àll ye shall be stumbled at me this night, because it hath been written, I will smite the shepherd, and the sheep shall be scattered abroad,

Mark 14:28 but after my having risen I will go before you to Galilee.'

Mark 14:29 And Peter said to him, Ànd if all shall be stumbled, yet not I;'

Mark 14:30 And Jesus said to him, `Verily I say to thee, that to-day, this night, before a cock shall crow twice, thrice thou shalt deny me.'

Mark 14:31 And he spake the more vehemently, Ìf it may be necessary for me to die with thee--I will in no wise deny thee;' and in like manner also said they all.

Mark 14:32. And they come to a spot, the name of which [is] Gethsemane, and he saith to his disciples, `Sit ye here till I may pray;'

Mark 14:33 and he taketh Peter, and James, and John with him, and began to be amazed, and to be very heavy,

Mark 14:34 and he saith to them, Èxceeding sorrowful is my soul--to death; remain here, and watch.'

Mark 14:35 And having gone forward a little, he fell upon the earth, and was praying, that, if it be possible the hour may pass from him,

Mark 14:36 and he said, Àbba, Father; all things are possible to Thee; make this cup pass from me; but, not what I will, but what Thou.'

Mark 14:37 And he cometh, and findeth them sleeping, and saith to Peter, `Simon, thou dost sleep! thou wast not able to watch one hour!

Mark 14:38 Watch ye and pray, that ye may not enter into temptation; the spirit indeed is forward, but the flesh weak.'

Mark 14:39 And again having gone away, he prayed, the same word saying;

Mark 14:40 and having returned, he found them again sleeping, for their eyes were heavy, and they had not known what they might answer him.

Mark 14:41 And he cometh the third time, and saith to them, `Sleep on henceforth, and rest--it is over; the hour did come; lo, the Son of Man is delivered up to the hands of the sinful;

Mark 14:42 rise, we may go, lo, he who is delivering me up hath come nigh.'

Mark 14:43. And immediately--while he is yet speaking--cometh near Judas, one of the twelve, and with him a great multitude, with swords and sticks, from the chief priests, and the scribes, and the elders;

Mark 14:44 and he who is delivering him up had given a token to them, saying, `Whomsoever I shall kiss, he it is, lay hold on him, and lead him away safely,'

Mark 14:45 and having come, immediately, having gone near him, he saith, `Rabbi, Rabbi,' and kissed him.

Mark 14:46 And they laid on him their hands, and kept hold on him;

Mark 14:47 and a certain one of those standing by, having drawn the sword, struck the servant of the chief priest, and took off his ear.

Mark 14:48 And Jesus answering said to them, Às against a robber ye came out, with swords and sticks, to take me!

Mark 14:49 daily I was with you in the temple teaching, and ye did not lay hold on me--but that the Writings may be fulfilled.'

Mark 14:50 And having left him they all fled;

Mark 14:51 and a certain young man was following him, having put a linen cloth about [his] naked body, and the young men lay hold on him,

Mark 14:52 and he, having left the linen cloth, did flee from them naked.

Mark 14:53. And they led away Jesus unto the chief priest, and come together to him do all the chief priests, and the elders, and the scribes;

Mark 14:54 and Peter afar off did follow him, to the inside of the hall of the chief priest, and he was sitting with the officers, and warming himself near the fire.

Mark 14:55 And the chief priests and all the sanhedrim were seeking against Jesus testimony--to put him to death, and they were not finding,

Mark 14:56 for many were bearing false testimony against him, and their testimonies were not alike.

Mark 14:57 And certain having risen up, were bearing false testimony against him, saying--

Mark 14:58 `We heard him saying--I will throw down this sanctuary made with hands, and by three days, another made without hands I will build;'

Mark 14:59 and neither so was their testimony alike.

Mark 14:60 And the chief priest, having risen up in the midst, questioned Jesus, saying, `Thou dost not answer anything! what do these testify against thee?'

Mark 14:61 and he was keeping silent, and did not answer anything. Again the chief priest was questioning him, and saith to him, Àrt thou the Christ--the Son of the Blessed?'

Mark 14:62 and Jesus said, Ì am; and ye shall see the Son of Man sitting on the right hand of the power, and coming with the clouds, of the heaven.'

Mark 14:63 And the chief priest, having rent his garments, saith, `What need have we yet of witnesses?

Mark 14:64 Ye heard the evil speaking, what appeareth to you?' and they all condemned him to be worthy of death,

Mark 14:65 and certain began to spit on him, and to cover his face, and to buffet him, and to say to him, `Prophesy;' and the officers were striking him with their palms.

Mark 14:66. And Peter being in the hall beneath, there doth come one of the maids of the chief priest,

Mark 14:67 and having seen Peter warming himself, having looked on him, she said, `And thou wast with Jesus of Nazareth!'

Mark 14:68 and he denied, saying, `I have not known [him], neither do I understand what thou sayest;' and he went forth without to the porch, and a cock crew.

Mark 14:69 And the maid having seen him again, began to say to those standing near--`This is of them;'

Mark 14:70 and he was again denying. And after a little again, those standing near said to Peter, `Truly thou art of them, for thou also art a Galilean, and thy speech is alike;'

Mark 14:71 and he began to anathematize, and to swear--`I have not known this man of whom ye speak;'

Mark 14:72 and a second time a cock crew, and Peter remembered the saying that Jesus said to him--`Before a cock crow twice, thou mayest deny me thrice;' and having thought thereon--he was weeping.

Mark 15:1. And immediately, in the morning, the chief priests having made a consultation, with the elders, and scribes, and the whole sanhedrim, having bound Jesus, did lead away, and delivered [him] to Pilate;

Mark 15:2 and Pilate questioned him, `Art thou the king of the Jews?' and he answering said to him, `Thou dost say [it].'

Mark 15:3 And the chief priests were accusing him of many things, [but he answered nothing.]

Mark 15:4 And Pilate again questioned him, saying, `Thou dost not answer anything! lo, how many things they do testify against thee!'

Mark 15:5 and Jesus did no more answer anything, so that Pilate wondered.

Mark 15:6 And at every feast he was releasing to them one prisoner, whomsoever they were asking;

Mark 15:7 and there was [one] named Barabbas, bound with those making insurrection with him, who had in the insurrection committed murder.

Mark 15:8 And the multitude having cried out, began to ask for themselves as he was always doing to them,

Mark 15:9 and Pilate answered them, saying, `Will ye [that] I shall release to you the king of the Jews?'

Mark 15:10 for he knew that because of envy the chief priests had delivered him up;

Mark 15:11 and the chief priests did move the multitude, that he might rather release Barabbas to them.

Mark 15:12 And Pilate answering, again said to them, `What, then, will ye [that] I shall do to him whom ye call king of the Jews?'

Mark 15:13 and they again cried out, `Crucify him.'

Mark 15:14 And Pilate said to them, `Why--what evil did he?' and they cried out the more vehemently, `Crucify him;'

Mark 15:15. and Pilate, wishing to content the multitude, released to them Barabbas, and delivered up Jesus--having scourged [him] --that he might be crucified.

Mark 15:16 And the soldiers led him away into the hall, which is Praetorium, and call together the whole band,

Mark 15:17 and clothe him with purple, and having plaited a crown of thorns, they put [it] on him,

Mark 15:18 and began to salute him, `Hail, King of the Jews.'

Mark 15:19 And they were smiting him on the head with a reed, and were spitting on him, and having bent the knee, were bowing to him,

Mark 15:20 and when they [had] mocked him, they took the purple from off him, and clothed him in his own garments, and they led him forth, that they may crucify him.

Mark 15:21 And they impress a certain one passing by--Simon, a Cyrenian, coming from the field, the father of Alexander and Rufus--that he may bear his cross,

Mark 15:22. and they bring him to the place Golgotha, which is, being interpreted, `Place of a skull;'

Mark 15:23 and they were giving him to drink wine mingled with myrrh, and he did not receive.

Mark 15:24 And having crucified him, they were dividing his garments, casting a lot upon them, what each may take;

Mark 15:25 and it was the third hour, and they crucified him;

Mark 15:26 and the inscription of his accusation was written above-- `The King of the Jews.'

Mark 15:27 And with him they crucify two robbers, one on the right hand, and one on his left,

Mark 15:28 and the Writing was fulfilled that is saying, `And with lawless ones he was numbered.'

Mark 15:29 And those passing by were speaking evil of him, shaking their heads, and saying, Àh, the thrower down of the sanctuary, and in three days the builder!

Mark 15:30 save thyself, and come down from the cross!'

Mark 15:31 And in like manner also the chief priests, mocking with one another, with the scribes, said, Òthers he saved; himself he is not able to save.

Mark 15:32 The Christ! the king of Israel--let him come down now from the cross, that we may see and believe;' and those crucified with him were reproaching him.

Mark 15:33. And the sixth hour having come, darkness came over the whole land till the ninth hour,

Mark 15:34 and at the ninth hour Jesus cried with a great voice, saying, Èloi, Eloi, lamma sabachthani?' which is, being interpreted, `My God, my God, why didst Thou forsake me?'

Mark 15:35 And certain of those standing by, having heard, said, `Lo, Elijah he doth call;'

Mark 15:36 and one having run, and having filled a spunge with vinegar, having put [it] also on a reed, was giving him to drink, saying, `Let alone, let us see if Elijah doth come to take him down.'

Mark 15:37 And Jesus having uttered a loud cry, yielded the spirit,

Mark 15:38 and the veil of the sanctuary was rent in two, from top to bottom,

Mark 15:39 and the centurion who was standing over-against him, having seen that, having so cried out, he yielded the spirit, said, `Truly this man was Son of God.'

Mark 15:40 And there were also women afar off beholding, among whom was also Mary the Magdalene, and Mary of James the less, and of Joses, and Salome,

Mark 15:41 (who also, when he was in Galilee, were following him, and were ministering to him,) and many other women who came up with him to Jerusalem.

Mark 15:42. And now evening having come, seeing it was the preparation, that is, the fore-sabbath,

Mark 15:43 Joseph of Arimathea, an honourable counsellor, who also himself was waiting for the reign of God, came, boldly entered in unto Pilate, and asked the body of Jesus.

Mark 15:44 And Pilate wondered if he were already dead, and having called near the centurion, did question him if he were long dead,

Mark 15:45 and having known [it] from the centurion, he granted the body to Joseph.

Mark 15:46 And he, having brought fine linen, and having taken him down, wrapped him in the linen, and laid him in a sepulchre that had been hewn out of a rock, and he rolled a stone unto the door of the sepulchre,

Mark 15:47 and Mary the Magdalene, and Mary of Joses, were beholding where he is laid.

Mark 16:1. And the sabbath having past, Mary the Magdalene, and Mary of James, and Salome, bought spices, that having come, they may anoint him,

Mark 16:2 and early in the morning of the first of the sabbaths, they come unto the sepulchre, at the rising of the sun,

Mark 16:3 and they said among themselves, `Who shall roll away for us the stone out of the door of the sepulchre?'

Mark 16:4 And having looked, they see that the stone hath been rolled away--for it was very great,

Mark 16:5 and having entered into the sepulchre, they saw a young man sitting on the right hand, arrayed in a long white robe, and they were amazed.

Mark 16:6 And he saith to them, `Be not amazed, ye seek Jesus the Nazarene, the crucified: he did rise--he is not here; lo, the place where they laid him!

Mark 16:7 and go, say to his disciples, and Peter, that he doth go before you to Galilee; there ye shall see him, as he said to you.'

Mark 16:8 And, having come forth quickly, they fled from the sepulchre, and trembling and amazement had seized them, and to no one said they anything, for they were afraid.

Mark 16:9. And he, having risen in the morning of the first of the sabbaths, did appear first to Mary the Magdalene, out of whom he had cast seven demons;

Mark 16:10 she having gone, told those who had been with him, mourning and weeping;

Mark 16:11 and they, having heard that he is alive, and was seen by her, did not believe.

Mark 16:12 And after these things, to two of them, as they are going into a field, walking, he was manifested in another form,

Mark 16:13 and they having gone, told to the rest; not even them did they believe.

Mark 16:14. Afterwards, as they are reclining (at meat), he was manifested to the eleven, and did reproach their unbelief and stiffness of heart, because they believed not those having seen him being raised;

Mark 16:15 and he said to them, `Having gone to all the world, proclaim the good news to all the creation;

Mark 16:16 he who hath believed, and hath been baptized, shall be

saved; and he who hath not believed, shall be condemned.

Mark 16:17 Ànd signs shall accom-
pany those believing these things; in
my name demons they shall cast out;
with new tongues they shall speak;

Mark 16:18 serpents they shall take
up; and if any deadly thing they may
drink, it shall not hurt them; on the
ailing they shall lay hands, and they
shall be well.'

Mark 16:19. The Lord, then, indeed,
after speaking to them, was received
up to the heaven, and sat on the
right hand of God;

Mark 16:20 and they, having gone
forth, did preach everywhere, the
Lord working with [them], and con-
firming the word, through the signs
following. Amen.

Luke

Luke 1:1. Seeing that many did take in hand to set in order a narration of the matters that have been fully assured among us,

Luke 1:2 as they did deliver to us, who from the beginning became eye-witnesses, and officers of the Word, --

Luke 1:3 it seemed good also to me, having followed from the first after all things exactly, to write to thee in order, most noble Theophilus,

Luke 1:4 that thou mayest know the certainty of the things wherein thou wast instructed.

Luke 1:5. There was in the days of Herod, the king of Judea, a certain priest, by name Zacharias, of the course of Abijah, and his wife of the daughters of Aaron, and her name Elisabeth;

Luke 1:6 and they were both righteous before God, going on in all the commands and righteousnesses of the Lord blameless,

Luke 1:7 and they had no child, because that Elisabeth was barren, and both were advanced in their days.

Luke 1:8 And it came to pass, in his acting as priest, in the order of his course before God,

Luke 1:9 according to the custom of the priesthood, his lot was to make perfume, having gone into the sanctuary of the Lord,

Luke 1:10 and all the multitude of the people were praying without, at the hour of the perfume.

Luke 1:11 And there appeared to him a messenger of the Lord standing on the right side of the altar of the perfume,

Luke 1:12 and Zacharias, having seen, was troubled, and fear fell on him;

Luke 1:13 and the messenger said unto him, `Fear not, Zacharias, for thy supplication was heard, and thy wife Elisabeth shall bear a son to thee, and thou shalt call his name John,

Luke 1:14 and there shall be joy to thee, and gladness, and many at his birth shall joy,

Luke 1:15 for he shall be great before the Lord, and wine and strong drink he may not drink, and of the Holy Spirit he shall be full, even from his mother's womb;

Luke 1:16 and many of the sons of Israel he shall turn to the Lord their God,

Luke 1:17 and he shall go before Him, in the spirit and power of Elijah, to turn hearts of fathers unto children, and disobedient ones to the wisdom of righteous ones, to make ready for the Lord, a people prepared.'

Luke 1:18 And Zacharias said unto the messenger, `Whereby shall I know this? for I am aged, and my wife is advanced in her days?'

Luke 1:19 And the messenger answering said to him, Ì am Gabriel, who have been standing near before God, and I was sent to speak unto thee, and to proclaim these good news to thee,

Luke 1:20 and lo, thou shalt be silent, and not able to speak, till the day that these things shall come to pass, because thou didst not believe my words, that shall be fulfilled in their season.'

Luke 1:21 And the people were waiting for Zacharias, and wondering at his tarrying in the sanctuary,

Luke 1:22 and having come out, he was not able to speak to them, and they perceived that a vision he had seen in the sanctuary, and he was beckoning to them, and did remain dumb.

Luke 1:23 And it came to pass, when the days of his service were fulfilled, he went away to his house,

Luke 1:24 and after those days, his wife Elisabeth conceived, and hid herself five months, saying--

Luke 1:25 `Thus hath the Lord done to me, in days in which He looked upon [me], to take away my reproach among men.'

Luke 1:26. And in the sixth month was the messenger Gabriel sent by God, to a city of Galilee, the name of which [is] Nazareth,

Luke 1:27 to a virgin, betrothed to a man, whose name [is] Joseph, of the house of David, and the name of the virgin [is] Mary.

Luke 1:28 And the messenger having come in unto her, said, `Hail, favoured one, the Lord [is] with thee; blessed [art] thou among women;'

Luke 1:29 and she, having seen, was troubled at his word, and was reasoning of what kind this salutation may be.

Luke 1:30 And the messenger said to her, `Fear not, Mary, for thou hast found favour with God;

Luke 1:31 and lo, thou shalt conceive in the womb, and shalt bring forth a son, and call his name Jesus;

Luke 1:32 he shall be great, and Son of the Highest he shall be called, and the Lord God shall give him the throne of David his father,

Luke 1:33 and he shall reign over the house of Jacob to the ages; and of his reign there shall be no end.'

Luke 1:34 And Mary said unto the messenger, `How shall this be, seeing a husband I do not know?'

Luke 1:35 And the messenger answering said to her, `The Holy Spirit shall come upon thee, and the power of the Highest shall overshadow thee, therefore also the holy-begotten thing shall be called Son of God;

Luke 1:36 and lo, Elisabeth, thy kinswoman, she also hath conceived a son in her old age, and this is the sixth month to her who was called barren;

Luke 1:37 because nothing shall be impossible with God.'

Luke 1:38 And Mary said, `Lo, the maid-servant of the Lord; let it be to me according to thy saying,' and the messenger went away from her.

Luke 1:39. And Mary having arisen in those days, went to the hill-country, with haste, to a city of Judea,

Luke 1:40 and entered into the house of Zacharias, and saluted Elisabeth.

Luke 1:41 And it came to pass, when Elisabeth heard the salutation of Mary, the babe did leap in her womb; and Elisabeth was filled with the Holy Spirit,

Luke 1:42 and spake out with a loud voice, and said, `Blessed [art] thou among women, and blessed [is] the fruit of thy womb;

Luke 1:43 and whence [is] this to me, that the mother of my Lord might come unto me?

Luke 1:44 for, lo, when the voice of thy salutation came to my ears, leap in gladness did the babe in my womb;

Luke 1:45 and happy [is] she who did believe, for there shall be a completion to the things spoken to her from the Lord.'

Luke 1:46 And Mary said, `My soul doth magnify the Lord,

Luke 1:47 And my spirit was glad on God my Saviour,

Luke 1:48 Because He looked on the lowliness of His maid-servant, For, lo, henceforth call me happy shall all the generations,

Luke 1:49 For He who is mighty did to me great things, And holy [is] His name,

Luke 1:50 And His kindness [is] to generations of generations, To those fearing Him,

Luke 1:51 He did powerfully with His arm, He scattered abroad the proud in the thought of their heart,

Luke 1:52 He brought down the mighty from thrones, And He exalted the lowly,

Luke 1:53 The hungry He did fill with good, And the rich He sent away empty,

Luke 1:54 He received again Israel His servant, To remember kindness,

Luke 1:55 As He spake unto our fathers, To Abraham and to his seed-- to the age.'

Luke 1:56 And Mary remained with her about three months, and turned back to her house.

Luke 1:57. And to Elisabeth was the time fulfilled for her bringing forth, and she bare a son,

Luke 1:58 and the neighbours and her kindred heard that the Lord was making His kindness great with her, and they were rejoicing with her.

Luke 1:59 And it came to pass, on the eighth day, they came to circumcise the child, and they were calling him by the name of his father, Zacharias,

Luke 1:60 and his mother answering said, `No, but he shall be called John.'

Luke 1:61 And they said unto her-- `There is none among thy kindred who is called by this name,'

Luke 1:62 and they were making signs to his father, what he would wish him to be called,

Luke 1:63 and having asked for a tablet, he wrote, saying, `John is his name;' and they did all wonder;

Luke 1:64 and his mouth was opened presently, and his tongue, and he was speaking, praising God.

Luke 1:65 And fear came upon all those dwelling around them, and in all the hill-country of Judea were all these sayings spoken of,

Luke 1:66 and all who heard did lay them up in their hearts, saying, `What then shall this child be?' and the hand of the Lord was with him.

Luke 1:67. And Zacharias his father was filled with the Holy Spirit, and did prophesy, saying,

Luke 1:68 `Blessed [is] the Lord, the God of Israel, Because He did look upon, And wrought redemption for His people,

Luke 1:69 And did raise an horn of salvation to us, In the house of David His servant,

Luke 1:70 As He spake by the mouth of His holy prophets, Which have been from the age;

Luke 1:71 Salvation from our enemies, And out of the hand of all hating us,

Luke 1:72 To do kindness with our fathers, And to be mindful of His holy covenant,

Luke 1:73 An oath that He sware to Abraham our father,

Luke 1:74 To give to us, without fear, Out of the hand of our enemies having been delivered,

Luke 1:75 To serve Him, in holiness and righteousness Before Him, all the days of our life.

Luke 1:76 And thou, child, Prophet of the Highest Shalt thou be called; For thou shalt go before the face of the Lord, To prepare His ways.

Luke 1:77 To give knowledge of salvation to His people In remission of their sins,

Luke 1:78 Through the tender mercies of our God, In which the rising from on high did look upon us,

Luke 1:79 To give light to those sitting in darkness and death-shade, To guide our feet to a way of peace.'

Luke 1:80 And the child grew, and was strengthened in spirit, and he was in the deserts till the day of his shewing unto Israel.

Luke 2:1. And it came to pass in those days, there went forth a decree from Caesar Augustus, that all the world be enrolled--

Luke 2:2 this enrolment first came to pass when Cyrenius was governor of Syria--

Luke 2:3 and all were going to be enrolled, each to his proper city,

Luke 2:4 and Joseph also went up from Galilee, out of the city of Nazareth, to Judea, to the city of David, that is called Bethlehem, because of his being of the house and family of David,

Luke 2:5 to enrol himself with Mary his betrothed wife, being with child.

Luke 2:6 And it came to pass, in their being there, the days were fulfilled for her bringing forth,

Luke 2:7 and she brought forth her son--the first-born, and wrapped him up, and laid him down in the manger, because there was not for them a place in the guest-chamber.

Luke 2:8. And there were shepherds in the same region, lodging in the field, and keeping the night-watches over their flock,

Luke 2:9 and lo, a messenger of the Lord stood over them, and the glory of the Lord shone around them, and they feared a great fear.

Luke 2:10 And the messenger said to them, `Fear not, for lo, I bring you good news of great joy, that shall be to all the people--

Luke 2:11 because there was born to you to-day a Saviour--who is Christ the Lord--in the city of David,

Luke 2:12 and this [is] to you the sign: Ye shall find a babe wrapped up, lying in the manger.'

Luke 2:13 And suddenly there came with the messenger a multitude of the heavenly host, praising God, and saying,

Luke 2:14 `Glory in the highest to God, and upon earth peace, among men--good will.'

Luke 2:15 And it came to pass, when the messengers were gone away from them to the heavens, that the men, the shepherds, said unto one another, `We may go over indeed unto Bethlehem, and see this thing that hath come to pass, that the Lord did make knownto us.'

Luke 2:16 And they came, having hasted, and found both Mary, and Joseph, and the babe lying in the manger,

Luke 2:17 and having seen, they made known abroad concerning the saying spoken to them concerning the child.

Luke 2:18 And all who heard, did wonder concerning the things spoken by the shepherds unto them;

Luke 2:19 and Mary was preserving all these things, pondering in her heart;

Luke 2:20 and the shepherds turned back, glorifying and praising God, for all those things they heard and saw, as it was spoken unto them.

Luke 2:21. And when eight days were fulfilled to circumcise the child, then was his name called Jesus, having been so called by the messenger before his being conceived in the womb.

Luke 2:22 And when the days of their purification were fulfilled, according to the law of Moses, they brought him up to Jerusalem, to present to the Lord,

Luke 2:23 as it hath been written in the Law of the Lord, --Èvery male opening a womb shall be called holy to the Lord,'

Luke 2:24 and to give a sacrifice, according to that said in the Law of the Lord, À pair of turtle-doves, or two young pigeons.'

Luke 2:25. And lo, there was a man in Jerusalem, whose name [is] Simeon, and this man is righteous and devout, looking for the comforting of Israel, and the Holy Spirit was upon him,

Luke 2:26 and it hath been divinely told him by the Holy Spirit--not to see death before he may see the Christ of the Lord.

Luke 2:27 And he came in the Spirit to the temple, and in the parents bringing in the child Jesus, for their doing according to the custom of the law regarding him,

Luke 2:28 then he took him in his arms, and blessed God, and he said,

Luke 2:29 `Now Thou dost send away Thy servant, Lord, according to Thy word, in peace,

Luke 2:30 because mine eyes did see Thy salvation,

Luke 2:31 which Thou didst prepare before the face of all the peoples,

Luke 2:32 a light to the uncovering of nations, and the glory of Thy people Israel.'

Luke 2:33 And Joseph and his mother were wondering at the things spoken concerning him,

Luke 2:34 and Simeon blessed them, and said unto Mary his mother, `Lo, this [one] is set for the falling and rising again of many in Israel, and for a sign spoken against--

Luke 2:35 (and also thine own soul shall a sword pass through) --that the reasonings of many hearts may be revealed.'

Luke 2:36 And there was Anna, a prophetess, daughter of Phanuel, of the tribe of Asher, she was much advanced in days, having lived with an husband seven years from her virginity,

Luke 2:37 and she [is] a widow of about eighty-four years, who did depart not from the temple, with fasts and supplications serving, night and day,

Luke 2:38 and she, at that hour, having come in, was confessing, likewise, to the Lord, and was speaking concerning him, to all those looking for redemption in Jerusalem.

Luke 2:39 And when they finished all things, according to the Law of the Lord, they turned back to Galilee, to their city Nazareth;

Luke 2:40 and the child grew and was strengthened in spirit, being filled with wisdom, and the grace of God was upon him.

Luke 2:41. And his parents were going yearly to Jerusalem, at the feast of the passover,

Luke 2:42 and when he became twelve years old, they having gone up to Jerusalem, according to the custom of the feast,

Luke 2:43 and having finished the days, in their returning the child Jesus remained behind in Jerusalem, and Joseph and his mother did not know,

Luke 2:44 and, having supposed him to be in the company, they went a day's journey, and were seeking him among the kindred and among the acquaintances,

Luke 2:45 and not having found him, they turned back to Jerusalem seeking him.

Luke 2:46 And it came to pass, after three days, they found him in the temple, sitting in the midst of the teachers, both hearing them and questioning them,

Luke 2:47 and all those hearing him were astonished at his understanding and answers.

Luke 2:48 And, having seen him, they were amazed, and his mother said unto him, `Child, why didst thou thus to us? lo, thy father and I, sorrowing, were seeking thee.'

Luke 2:49 And he said unto them, `Why [is it] that ye were seeking me? did ye not know that in the things of my Father it behoveth me to be?'

Luke 2:50 and they did not understand the saying that he spake to them,

Luke 2:51 and he went down with them, and came to Nazareth, and he was subject to them, and his mother was keeping all these sayings in her heart,

Luke 2:52 and Jesus was advancing in wisdom, and in stature, and in favour with God and men.

Luke 3:1. And in the fifteenth year of the government of Tiberius Caesar--Pontius Pilate being governor of Judea, and Herod tetrarch of Galilee, and Philip his brother, tetrarch of Ituraea and of the region of Trachonitis, and Lysanias tetrarch of Abilene--

Luke 3:2 Annas and Caiaphas being chief priests--there came a word of God unto John the son of Zacharias, in the wilderness,

Luke 3:3 and he came to all the region round the Jordan, proclaiming a baptism of reformation--to remission of sins,

Luke 3:4 as it hath been written in the scroll of the words of Isaiah the prophet, saying, À voice of one crying in the wilderness, Prepare ye the way of the Lord, straight make ye His paths;

Luke 3:5 every valley shall be filled, and every mountain and hill shall be made low, and the crooked shall become straightness, and the rough become smooth ways;

Luke 3:6 and all flesh shall see the salvation of God.'

Luke 3:7 Then said he to the multitudes coming forth to be baptised by him, `Brood of vipers! who did prompt you to flee from the coming wrath?

Luke 3:8 make, therefore, fruits worthy of the reformation, and begin not to say within yourselves, We have a father--Abraham; for I say to you, that God is able out of these stones to raise children to Abraham;

Luke 3:9 and already also the axe unto the root of the trees is laid, every tree, therefore, not making good fruit is cut down, and to fire it is cast.'

Luke 3:10 And the multitudes were questioning him, saying, `What, then, shall we do?'

Luke 3:11 and he answering saith to them, `He having two coats--let him impart to him having none, and he having victuals--in like manner let him do.'

Luke 3:12 And there came also tax-gatherers to be baptised, and they said unto him, `Teacher, what shall we do?'

Luke 3:13 and he said unto them, Èxact no more than that directed you.'

Luke 3:14 And questioning him also were those warring, saying, Ànd we, what shall we do?' and he said unto them, `Do violence to no one, nor accuse falsely, and be content with your wages.'

Luke 3:15. And the people are looking forward, and all are reasoning in their hearts concerning John, whether or not he may be the Christ;

Luke 3:16 John answered, saying to all, Ì indeed with water do baptise you, but he cometh who is mightier than I, of whom I am not worthy to loose the latchet of his sandals--he

shall baptise you with the Holy Spirit and with fire;

Luke 3:17 whose winnowing shovel [is] in his hand, and he will thoroughly cleanse his floor, and will gather the wheat to his storehouse, and the chaff he will burn with fire unquenchable.'

Luke 3:18 And, therefore, indeed with many other things, exhorting, he was proclaiming good news to the people,

Luke 3:19 and Herod the tetrarch, being reproved by him concerning Herodias the wife of Philip his brother, and concerning all the evils that Herod did,

Luke 3:20 added also this to all, that he shut up John in the prison.

Luke 3:21. And it came to pass, in all the people being baptised, Jesus also being baptised, and praying, the heaven was opened,

Luke 3:22 and the Holy Spirit came down in a bodily appearance, as if a dove, upon him, and a voice came out of heaven, saying, `Thou art My Son--the Beloved, in thee I did delight.'

Luke 3:23 And Jesus himself was beginning to be about thirty years of age, being, as was supposed, son of Joseph,

Luke 3:24 the [son] of Eli, the [son] of Matthat, the [son] of Levi, the

[son] of Melchi, the [son] of Janna, the [son] of Joseph,

Luke 3:25 the [son] of Mattathias, the [son] of Amos, the [son] of Naum, the [son] of Esli,

Luke 3:26 the [son] of Naggai, the [son] of Maath, the [son] of Mattathias, the [son] of Semei, the [son] of Joseph, the [son] of Juda,

Luke 3:27 the [son] of Joanna, the [son] of Rhesa, the [son] of Zerubbabel, the [son] of Shealtiel,

Luke 3:28 the [son] of Neri, the [son] of Melchi, the [son] of Addi, the [son] of Cosam, the [son] of Elmodam, the [son] of Er,

Luke 3:29 the [son] of Jose, the [son] of Eliezer, the [son] of Jorim, the [son] of Matthat,

Luke 3:30 the [son] of Levi, the [son] of Simeon, the [son] of Juda, the [son] of Joseph, the [son] of Jonan, the [son] of Eliakim,

Luke 3:31 the [son] of Melea, the [son] of Mainan, the [son] of Mattatha, the [son] of Nathan,

Luke 3:32 the [son] of David, the [son] of Jesse, the [son] of Obed, the [son] of Booz, the [son] of Salmon, the [son] of Nahshon,

Luke 3:33 the [son] of Amminadab, the [son] of Aram, the [son] of Esrom, the [son] of Pharez,

Luke 3:34 the [son] of Judah, the [son] of Jacob, the [son] of Isaac, the [son] of Abraham, the [son] of Terah, the [son] of Nahor,

Luke 3:35 the [son] of Serug, the [son] of Reu, the [son] of Peleg, the [son] of Eber,

Luke 3:36 the [son] of Salah, the [son] of Cainan, the [son] of Arphaxad, the [son] of Shem, the [son] of Noah, the [son] of Lamech,

Luke 3:37 the [son] of Methuselah, the [son] of Enoch, the [son] of Jared, the [son] of Mahalaleel,

Luke 3:38 the [son] of Cainan, the [son] of Enos, the [son] of Seth, the [son] of Adam, the [son] of God.

Luke 4:1. And Jesus, full of the Holy Spirit, turned back from the Jordan, and was brought in the Spirit to the wilderness,

Luke 4:2 forty days being tempted by the Devil, and he did not eat anything in those days, and they having been ended, he afterward hungered,

Luke 4:3 and the Devil said to him, Ìf Son thou art of God, speak to this stone that it may become bread.'

Luke 4:4 And Jesus answered him, saying, Ìt hath been written, that, not on bread only shall man live, but on every saying of God.'

Luke 4:5 And the Devil having brought him up to an high mountain, shewed to him all the kingdoms of the world in a moment of time,

Luke 4:6 and the Devil said to him, `To thee I will give all this authority, and their glory, because to me it hath been delivered, and to whomsoever I will, I do give it;

Luke 4:7 thou, then, if thou mayest bow before me--all shall be thine.'

Luke 4:8 And Jesus answering him said, `Get thee behind me, Adversary, for it hath been written, Thou shalt bow before the Lord thy God, and Him only thou shalt serve.'

Luke 4:9 And he brought him to Jerusalem, and set him on the pinnacle of the temple, and said to him, Ìf the Son thou art of God, cast thyself down hence,

Luke 4:10 for it hath been written-- To His messengers He will give charge concerning thee, to guard over thee,

Luke 4:11 and--On hands they shall bear thee up, lest at any time thou mayest dash against a stone thy foot.'

Luke 4:12 And Jesus answering said to him--Ìt hath been said, Thou shalt not tempt the Lord thy God.'

Luke 4:13 And having ended all temptation, the Devil departed from him till a convenient season.

Luke 4:14. And Jesus turned back in the power of the Spirit to Galilee,

and a fame went forth through all the region round about concerning him,

Luke 4:15 and he was teaching in their synagogues, being glorified by all.

Luke 4:16 And he came to Nazareth, where he hath been brought up, and he went in, according to his custom, on the sabbath-day, to the synagogue, and stood up to read;

Luke 4:17 and there was given over to him a roll of Isaiah the prophet, and having unfolded the roll, he found the place where it hath been written:

Luke 4:18 `The Spirit of the Lord [is] upon me, Because He did anoint me; To proclaim good news to the poor, Sent me to heal the broken of heart, To proclaim to captives deliverance, And to blind receiving of sight, To send away the bruised with deliverance,

Luke 4:19 To proclaim the acceptable year of the Lord.'

Luke 4:20 And having folded the roll, having given [it] back to the officer, he sat down, and the eyes of all in the synagogue were gazing on him.

Luke 4:21 And he began to say unto them--`To-day hath this writing been fulfilled in your ears;'

Luke 4:22 and all were bearing testimony to him, and were wondering at the gracious words that are coming forth out of his mouth, and they said, `Is not this the son of Joseph?'

Luke 4:23 And he said unto them, `Certainly ye will say to me this simile, Physician, heal thyself; as great things as we heard done in Capernaum, do also here in thy country;'

Luke 4:24 and he said, `Verily I say to you--No prophet is accepted in his own country;

Luke 4:25 and of a truth I say to you, Many widows were in the days of Elijah, in Israel, when the heaven was shut for three years and six months, when great famine came on all the land,

Luke 4:26 and unto none of them was Elijah sent, but--to Sarepta of Sidon, unto a woman, a widow;

Luke 4:27 and many lepers were in the time of Elisha the prophet, in Israel, and none of them was cleansed, but--Naaman the Syrian.'

Luke 4:28 And all in the synagogue were filled with wrath, hearing these things,

Luke 4:29 and having risen, they put him forth without the city, and brought him unto the brow of the hill on which their city had been built--to cast him down headlong,

Luke 4:30 and he, having gone through the midst of them, went away.

Luke 4:31. And he came down to Capernaum, a city of Galilee, and was teaching them on the sabbaths,

Luke 4:32 and they were astonished at his teaching, because his word was with authority.

Luke 4:33 And in the synagogue was a man, having a spirit of an unclean demon, and he cried out with a great voice,

Luke 4:34 saying, `Away, what--to us and to thee, Jesus, O Nazarene? thou didst come to destroy us; I have known thee who thou art--the Holy One of God.'

Luke 4:35 And Jesus did rebuke him, saying, `Be silenced, and come forth out of him;' and the demon having cast him into the midst, came forth from him, having hurt him nought;

Luke 4:36 and amazement came upon all, and they were speaking together, with one another, saying, `What [is] this word, that with authority and power he doth command the unclean spirits, and they come forth?'

Luke 4:37 and there was going forth a fame concerning him to every place of the region round about.

Luke 4:38 And having risen out of the synagogue, he entered into the house of Simon, and the mother-in-law of Simon was pressed with a great fever, and they did ask him about her,

Luke 4:39 and having stood over her, he rebuked the fever, and it left her, and presently, having risen, she was ministering to them.

Luke 4:40 And at the setting of the sun, all, as many as had any ailing with manifold sicknesses, brought them unto him, and he on each one of them [his] hands having put, did heal them.

Luke 4:41 And demons also were coming forth from many, crying out and saying--`Thou art the Christ, the Son of God;' and rebuking, he did not suffer them to speak, because they knew him to be the Christ.

Luke 4:42 And day having come, having gone forth, he went on to a desert place, and the multitudes were seeking him, and they came unto him, and were staying him--not to go on from them,

Luke 4:43 and he said unto them-- `Also to the other cities it behoveth me to proclaim good news of the reign of God, because for this I have been sent;'

Luke 4:44 and he was preaching in the synagogues of Galilee.

Luke 5:1. And it came to pass, in the multitude pressing on him to hear the word of God, that he was standing beside the lake of Gennesaret,

Luke 5:2 and he saw two boats standing beside the lake, and the fishers, having gone away from them, were washing the nets,

Luke 5:3 and having entered into one of the boats, that was Simon's, he asked him to put back a little from the land, and having sat down, was teaching the multitudes out of the boat.

Luke 5:4 And when he left off speaking, he said unto Simon, `Put back to the deep, and let down your nets for a draught;'

Luke 5:5 and Simon answering said to him, `Master, through the whole night, having laboured, we have taken nothing, but at thy saying I will let down the net.'

Luke 5:6 And having done this, they enclosed a great multitude of fishes, and their net was breaking,

Luke 5:7 and they beckoned to the partners, who [are] in the other boat, having come, to help them; and they came, and filled both the boats, so that they were sinking.

Luke 5:8 And Simon Peter having seen, fell down at the knees of Jesus, saying, `Depart from me, because I am a sinful man, O lord;'

Luke 5:9 for astonishment seized him, and all those with him, at the draught of the fishes that they took,

Luke 5:10 and in like manner also James and John, sons of Zebedee, who were partners with Simon; and Jesus said unto Simon, `Fear not, henceforth thou shalt be catching men;'

Luke 5:11 and they, having brought the boats upon the land, having left all, did follow him.

Luke 5:12. And it came to pass, in his being in one of the cities, that lo, a man full of leprosy, and having seen Jesus, having fallen on [his] face, he besought him, saying, `Sir, if thou mayest will, thou art able to cleanse me;'

Luke 5:13 and having stretched forth [his] hand, he touched him, having said, İ will; be thou cleansed;' and immediately the leprosy went away from him.

Luke 5:14 And he charged him to tell no one, `But, having gone away, shew thyself to the priest, and bring near for thy cleansing according as Moses directed, for a testimony to them;'

Luke 5:15 but the more was the report going abroad concerning him, and great multitudes were coming together to hear, and to be healed by him of their infirmities,

Luke 5:16 and he was withdrawing himself in the desert places and was praying.

Luke 5:17. And it came to pass, on one of the days, that he was teaching, and there were sitting by Pharisees and teachers of the Law, who were come out of every village of Galilee, and Judea, and Jerusalem, and the power of the Lord was--to heal them.

Luke 5:18 And lo, men bearing upon a couch a man, who hath been struck with palsy, and they were seeking to bring him in, and to place before him,

Luke 5:19 and not having found by what way they may bring him in because of the multitude, having gone up on the house-top, through the tiles they let him down, with the little couch, into the midst before Jesus,

Luke 5:20 and he having seen their faith, said to him, `Man, thy sins have been forgiven thee.'

Luke 5:21 And the scribes and the Pharisees began to reason, saying, `Who is this that doth speak evil words? who is able to forgive sins, except God only?'

Luke 5:22 And Jesus having known their reasonings, answering, said unto them, `What reason ye in your hearts?

Luke 5:23 which is easier--to say, Thy sins have been forgiven thee? or to say, Arise, and walk?

Luke 5:24 And that ye may know that the Son of Man hath authority upon the earth to forgive sins--(he said to the one struck with palsy) --I say to thee, Arise, and having taken up thy little couch, be going on to thy house.'

Luke 5:25 And presently having risen before them, having taken up [that] on which he was lying, he went away to his house, glorifying God,

Luke 5:26 and astonishment took all, and they were glorifying God, and were filled with fear, saying-- `We saw strange things to-day.'

Luke 5:27. And after these things he went forth, and beheld a tax-gatherer, by name Levi, sitting at the tax-office, and said to him, `Be following me;'

Luke 5:28 and he, having left all, having arisen, did follow him.

Luke 5:29 And Levi made a great entertainment to him in his house, and there was a great multitude of tax-gatherers and others who were with them reclining (at meat),

Luke 5:30 and the scribes and the Pharisees among them were murmuring at his disciples, saying, `Wherefore with tax-gatherers and sinners do ye eat and drink?'

Luke 5:31 And Jesus answering said unto them, `They who are well have no need of a physician, but they that are ill:

Luke 5:32 I came not to call righteous men, but sinners, to reformation.'

Luke 5:33 And they said unto him, `Wherefore do the disciples of John fast often, and make supplications-- in like manner also those of the Pharisees--but thine do eat and drink?'

Luke 5:34 And he said unto them, Àre ye able to make the sons of the bride-chamber--in the bridegroom being with them--to fast?

Luke 5:35 but days will come, and, when the bridegroom may be taken away from them, then they shall fast in those days.'

Luke 5:36 And he spake also a simile unto them--`No one a patch of new clothing doth put on old clothing, and if otherwise, the new also doth make a rent, and with the old the patch doth not agree, that [is] from the new.

Luke 5:37 Ànd no one doth put new wine into old skins, and if otherwise, the new wine will burst the skins, and itself will be poured out, and the skins will be destroyed;

Luke 5:38 but new wine into new skins is to be put, and both are preserved together;

Luke 5:39 and no one having drunk old [wine], doth immediately wish new, for he saith, The old is better.'

Luke 6:1. And it came to pass, on the second-first sabbath, as he is going through the corn fields, that his disciples were plucking the ears, and were eating, rubbing with the hands,

Luke 6:2 and certain of the Pharisees said to them, `Why do ye that which is not lawful to do on the sabbaths?'

Luke 6:3 And Jesus answering said unto them, `Did ye not read even this that David did, when he hungered, himself and those who are with him,

Luke 6:4 how he went into the house of God, and the loaves of the presentation did take, and did eat, and gave also to those with him, which it is not lawful to eat, except only to the priests?'

Luke 6:5 and he said to them, --`The Son of Man is lord also of the sabbath.'

Luke 6:6 And it came to pass also, on another sabbath, that he goeth into the synagogue, and teacheth, and there was there a man, and his right hand was withered,

Luke 6:7 and the scribes and the Pharisees were watching him, if on the sabbath he will heal, that they might find an accusation against him.

Luke 6:8 And he himself had known their reasonings, and said to the man having the withered hand, `Rise, and stand in the midst;' and he having risen, stood.

Luke 6:9 Then said Jesus unto them, Ì will question you something: Is it lawful on the sabbaths to do good, or to do evil? life to save or to kill?'

Luke 6:10 And having looked round on them all, he said to the man, `Stretch forth thy hand;' and he did so, and his hand was restored whole as the other;

Luke 6:11 and they were filled with madness, and were speaking with one another what they might do to Jesus.

Luke 6:12. And it came to pass in those days, he went forth to the mountain to pray, and was passing the night in the prayer of God,

Luke 6:13 and when it became day, he called near his disciples, and having chosen from them twelve, whom also he named apostles,

Luke 6:14 (Simon, whom also he named Peter, and Andrew his brother, James and John, Philip and Bartholomew,

Luke 6:15 Matthew and Thomas, James of Alphaeus, and Simon called Zelotes,

Luke 6:16 Judas of James, and Judas Iscariot, who also became betrayer;)

Luke 6:17 and having come down with them, he stood upon a level spot, and a crowd of his disciples, and a great multitude of the people from all Judea, and Jerusalem, and the maritime Tyre and Sidon, who came to hear him, and to be healed of their sicknesses,

Luke 6:18 and those harassed by unclean spirits, and they were healed,

Luke 6:19 and all the multitude were seeking to touch him, because power from him was going forth, and he was healing all.

Luke 6:20. And he, having lifted up his eyes to his disciples, said: `Happy the poor--because yours is the reign of God.

Luke 6:21 `Happy those hungering now--because ye shall be filled. `Happy those weeping now--because ye shall laugh.

Luke 6:22 `Happy are ye when men shall hate you, and when they shall separate you, and shall reproach, and shall cast forth your name as evil, for the Son of Man's sake--

Luke 6:23 rejoice in that day, and leap, for lo, your reward [is] great in the heaven, for according to these things were their fathers doing to the prophets.

Luke 6:24 `But woe to you--the rich, because ye have got your comfort.

Luke 6:25 `Woe to you who have been filled--because ye shall hunger. `Woe to you who are laughing now--because ye shall mourn and weep.

Luke 6:26 `Woe to you when all men shall speak well of you--for ac-

cording to these things were their fathers doing to false prophets.

Luke 6:27. `But I say to you who are hearing, Love your enemies, do good to those hating you,

Luke 6:28 bless those cursing you, and pray for those accusing you falsely;

Luke 6:29 and to him smiting thee upon the cheek, give also the other, and from him taking away from thee the mantle, also the coat thou mayest not keep back.

Luke 6:30 And to every one who is asking of thee, be giving; and from him who is taking away thy goods, be not asking again;

Luke 6:31 and as ye wish that men may do to you, do ye also to them in like manner;

Luke 6:32 and--if ye love those loving you, what grace have ye? for also the sinful love those loving them;

Luke 6:33 and if ye do good to those doing good to you, what grace have ye? for also the sinful do the same;

Luke 6:34 and if ye lend [to those] of whom ye hope to receive back, what grace have ye? for also the sinful lend to sinners--that they may receive again as much.

Luke 6:35 `But love your enemies, and do good, and lend, hoping for nothing again, and your reward will be great, and ye shall be sons of the

Highest, because He is kind unto the ungracious and evil;

Luke 6:36 be ye therefore merciful, as also your Father is merciful.

Luke 6:37. Ànd judge not, and ye may not be judged; condemn not, and ye may not be condemned; release, and ye shall be released.

Luke 6:38 `Give, and it shall be given to you; good measure, pressed, and shaken, and running over, they shall give into your bosom; for with that measure with which ye measure, it shall be measured to you again.'

Luke 6:39 And he spake a simile to them, Ìs blind able to lead blind? shall they not both fall into a pit?

Luke 6:40 A disciple is not above his teacher, but every one perfected shall be as his teacher.

Luke 6:41 Ànd why dost thou behold the mote that is in thy brother's eye, and the beam that [is] in thine own eye dost not consider?

Luke 6:42 or how art thou able to say to thy brother, Brother, suffer, I may take out the mote that [is] in thine eye--thyself the beam in thine own eye not beholding? Hypocrite, take first the beam out of thine own eye, and then thou shalt see clearly to take out the mote that [is] in thy brother's eye.

Luke 6:43 `For there is not a good tree making bad fruit, nor a bad tree making good fruit;

Luke 6:44 for each tree from its own fruit is known, for not from thorns do they gather figs, nor from a bramble do they crop a grape.

Luke 6:45 `The good man out of the good treasure of his heart doth bring forth that which [is] good; and the evil man out of the evil treasure of his heart doth bring forth that which [is] evil; for out of the abounding of the heart doth his mouth speak.

Luke 6:46 Ànd why do ye call me, Lord, Lord, and do not what I say?

Luke 6:47 Every one who is coming unto me, and is hearing my words, and is doing them, I will shew you to whom he is like;

Luke 6:48 he is like to a man building a house, who did dig, and deepen, and laid a foundation upon the rock, and a flood having come, the stream broke forth on that house, and was not able to shake it, for it had been founded upon the rock.

Luke 6:49 Ànd he who heard and did not, is like to a man having builded a house upon the earth, without a foundation, against which the stream brake forth, and immediately it fell, and the ruin of that house became great.'

Luke 7:1. And when he completed all his sayings in the ears of the people, he went into Capernaum;

Luke 7:2 and a certain centurion's servant being ill, was about to die, who was much valued by him,

Luke 7:3 and having heard about Jesus, he sent unto him elders of the Jews, beseeching him, that having come he might thoroughly save his servant.

Luke 7:4 And they, having come near unto Jesus, were calling upon him earnestly, saying--`He is worthy to whom thou shalt do this,

Luke 7:5 for he doth love our nation, and the synagogue he did build to us.'

Luke 7:6 And Jesus was going on with them, and now when he is not far distant from the house the centurion sent unto him friends, saying to him, `Sir, be not troubled, for I am not worthy that under my roof thou mayest enter;

Luke 7:7 wherefore not even myself thought I worthy to come unto thee, but say in a word, and my lad shall be healed;

Luke 7:8 for I also am a man placed under authority, having under myself soldiers, and I say to this [one], Go, and he goeth; and to another, Be coming, and he cometh; and to my servant, Do this, and he doth [it].'

Luke 7:9 And having heard these things Jesus wondered at him, and having turned to the multitude following him, he said, `I say to you, not even in Israel so much faith did I find;'

Luke 7:10 and those sent, having turned back to the house, found the ailing servant in health.

Luke 7:11. And it came to pass, on the morrow, he was going on to a city called Nain, and there were going with him many of his disciples, and a great multitude,

Luke 7:12 and as he came nigh to the gate of the city, then, lo, one dead was being carried forth, an only son of his mother, and she a widow, and a great multitude of the city was with her.

Luke 7:13 And the Lord having seen her, was moved with compassion towards her, and said to her, `Be not weeping;'

Luke 7:14 and having come near, he touched the bier, and those bearing [it] stood still, and he said, `Young man, to thee I say, Arise;'

Luke 7:15 and the dead sat up, and began to speak, and he gave him to his mother;

Luke 7:16 and fear took hold of all, and they were glorifying God, saying--`A great prophet hath risen among us,' and--`God did look upon His people.'

Luke 7:17 And the account of this went forth in all Judea about him, and in all the region around.

Luke 7:18 And the disciples of John told him about all these things,

Luke 7:19. and John having called near a certain two of his disciples, sent unto Jesus, saying, Àrt thou he who is coming, or for another do we look?'

Luke 7:20 And having come near to him, the men said, `John the Baptist sent us unto thee, saying, Art thou he who is coming, or for another do we look?'

Luke 7:21 And in that hour he cured many from sicknesses, and plagues, and evil spirits, and to many blind he granted sight.

Luke 7:22 And Jesus answering said to them, `Having gone on, report to John what ye saw and heard, that blind men do see again, lame do walk, lepers are cleansed, deaf do hear, dead are raised, poor have good news proclaimed;

Luke 7:23 and happy is he whoever may not be stumbled in me.'

Luke 7:24 And the messengers of John having gone away, he began to say unto the multitudes concerning John: `What have ye gone forth to the wilderness to look on? a reed by the wind shaken?

Luke 7:25 but what have ye gone forth to see? a man in soft garments clothed? lo, they in splendid apparellings, and living in luxury, are in the houses of kings!

Luke 7:26 `But what have ye gone forth to see? a prophet? Yes, I say to you, and much more than a prophet:

Luke 7:27 this is he concerning whom it hath been written, Lo, I send my messenger before thy face, who shall prepare thy way before thee;

Luke 7:28 for I say to you, a greater prophet, among those born of women, than John the Baptist there is not; but the least in the reign of God is greater than he.'

Luke 7:29 And all the people having heard, and the tax-gatherers, declared God righteous, having been baptized with the baptism of John,

Luke 7:30 but the Pharisees, and the lawyers, the counsel of God did put away for themselves, not having been baptized by him.

Luke 7:31 And the Lord said, `To what, then, shall I liken the men of this generation? and to what are they like?

Luke 7:32 they are like to children, to those sitting in a market-place, and calling one to another, and saying, We piped to you, and ye did not dance, we mourned to you, and ye did not weep!

Luke 7:33 `For John the Baptist came neither eating bread nor drinking wine, and ye say, He hath a demon;

Luke 7:34 the Son of Man came eating and drinking, and ye say, Lo, a man, a glutton, and a wine drinker, a friend of tax-gatherers and sinners;

Luke 7:35 and the wisdom was justified from all her children.'

Luke 7:36. And a certain one of the Pharisees was asking him that he might eat with him, and having gone into the house of the Pharisee he reclined (at meat),

Luke 7:37 and lo, a woman in the city, who was a sinner, having known that he reclineth (at meat) in the house of the Pharisee, having provided an alabaster box of ointment,

Luke 7:38 and having stood behind, beside his feet, weeping, she began to wet his feet with the tears, and with the hairs of her head she was wiping, and was kissing his feet, and was anointing with the ointment.

Luke 7:39 And the Pharisee who did call him, having seen, spake within himself, saying, `This one, if he were a prophet, would have known who and of what kind [is] the woman who doth touch him, that she is a sinner.'

Luke 7:40 And Jesus answering said unto him, `Simon, I have something to say to thee;' and he saith, `Teacher, say on.'

Luke 7:41 `Two debtors were to a certain creditor; the one was owing five hundred denaries, and the other fifty;

Luke 7:42 and they not having [wherewith] to give back, he forgave both; which then of them, say thou, will love him more?'

Luke 7:43 And Simon answering said, `I suppose that to whom he forgave the more;' and he said to him, `Rightly thou didst judge.'

Luke 7:44 And having turned unto the woman, he said to Simon, `Seest thou this woman? I entered into thy house; water for my feet thou didst not give, but this woman with tears did wet my feet, and with the hairs of her head did wipe;

Luke 7:45 a kiss to me thou didst not give, but this woman, from what [time] I came in, did not cease kissing my feet;

Luke 7:46 with oil my head thou didst not anoint, but this woman with ointment did anoint my feet;

Luke 7:47 therefore I say to thee, her many sins have been forgiven, because she did love much; but to whom little is forgiven, little he doth love.'

Luke 7:48 And he said to her, `Thy sins have been forgiven;'

Luke 7:49 and those reclining with him (at meat) began to say within themselves, `Who is this, who also doth forgive sins?'

Luke 7:50 and he said unto the woman, `Thy faith have saved thee, be going on to peace.'

Luke 8:1. And it came to pass thereafter, that he was going through every city and village, preaching and proclaiming good news of the reign of God, and the twelve [are] with him,

Luke 8:2 and certain women, who were healed of evil spirits and infirmities, Mary who is called Magdalene, from whom seven demons had gone forth,

Luke 8:3 and Joanna wife of Chuza, steward of Herod, and Susanna, and many others, who were ministering to him from their substance.

Luke 8:4. And a great multitude having gathered, and those who from city and city were coming unto him, he spake by a simile:

Luke 8:5 `The sower went forth to sow his seed, and in his sowing some indeed fell beside the way, and it was trodden down, and the fowls of the heaven did devour it.

Luke 8:6 And other fell upon the rock, and having sprung up, it did wither, through not having moisture.

Luke 8:7 And other fell amidst the thorns, and the thorns having sprung up with it, did choke it.

Luke 8:8 And other fell upon the good ground, and having sprung up, it made fruit an hundred fold.' These things saying, he was calling, `He having ears to hear--let him hear.'

Luke 8:9 And his disciples were questioning him, saying, `What may this simile be?'

Luke 8:10 And he said, `To you it hath been given to know the secrets of the reign of God, and to the rest in similes; that seeing they may not see, and hearing they may not understand.

Luke 8:11 And this is the simile: The seed is the word of God,

Luke 8:12 and those beside the way are those hearing, then cometh the Devil, and taketh up the word from their heart, lest having believed, they may be saved.

Luke 8:13 And those upon the rock: They who, when they may hear, with joy do receive the word, and these have no root, who for a time believe, and in time of temptation fall away.

Luke 8:14 And that which fell to the thorns: These are they who have heard, and going forth, through anxieties, and riches, and pleasures of life, are choked, and bear not to completion.

Luke 8:15 And that in the good ground: These are they, who in an upright and good heart, having heard the word, do retain [it], and bear fruit in continuance.

Luke 8:16 Ànd no one having lighted a lamp doth cover it with a vessel, or under a couch doth put [it]; but upon a lamp-stand he doth put [it], that those coming in may see the light,

Luke 8:17 for nothing is secret, that shall not become manifest, nor hid, that shall not be known, and become manifest.

Luke 8:18 `See, therefore, how ye hear, for whoever may have, there shall be given to him, and whoever may not have, also what he seemeth to have, shall be taken from him.'

Luke 8:19 And there came unto him his mother and brethren, and they were not able to get to him because of the multitude,

Luke 8:20 and it was told him, saying, `Thy mother and thy brethren do stand without, wishing to see thee;'

Luke 8:21 and he answering said unto them, `My mother and my brethren! they are those who the word of God are hearing, and doing.'

Luke 8:22. And it came to pass, on one of the days, that he himself went into a boat with his disciples, and he said unto them, `We may go over to the other side of the lake;' and they set forth,

Luke 8:23 and as they are sailing he fell deeply asleep, and there came down a storm of wind to the lake, and they were filling, and were in peril.

Luke 8:24 And having come near, they awoke him, saying, `Master, master, we perish;' and he, having arisen, rebuked the wind and the raging of the water, and they ceased, and there came a calm,

Luke 8:25 and he said to them, `Where is your faith?' and they being afraid did wonder, saying unto one another, `Who, then, is this, that even the winds he doth command, and the water, and they obey him?'

Luke 8:26 And they sailed down to the region of the Gadarenes, that is over-against Galilee,

Luke 8:27 and he having gone forth upon the land, there met him a certain man, out of the city, who had demons for a long time, and with a garment was not clothed, and in a house was not abiding, but in the tombs,

Luke 8:28 and having seen Jesus, and having cried out, he fell before him, and with a loud voice, said, `What--to me and to thee, Jesus, Son of God Most High? I beseech thee, mayest thou not afflict me!'

Luke 8:29 For he commanded the unclean spirit to come forth from the man, for many times it had caught him, and he was being bound with chains and fetters--guarded, and breaking asunder the bonds he was driven by the demons to the deserts.

Luke 8:30 And Jesus questioned him, saying, `What is thy name?' and he said, `Legion,' (because many demons were entered into him,)

Luke 8:31 and he was calling on him, that he may not command them to go away to the abyss,

Luke 8:32 and there was there a herd of many swine feeding in the mountain, and they were calling on him, that he might suffer them to enter into these, and he suffered them,

Luke 8:33 and the demons having gone forth from the man, did enter into the swine, and the herd rushed down the steep to the lake, and were choked.

Luke 8:34 And those feeding [them], having seen what was come to pass, fled, and having gone, told [it] to the city, and to the fields;

Luke 8:35 and they came forth to see what was come to pass, and they came unto Jesus, and found the man sitting, out of whom the demons had gone forth, clothed, and right-minded, at the feet of Jesus, and they were afraid;

Luke 8:36 and those also having seen [it], told them how the demoniac was saved.

Luke 8:37 And the whole multitude of the region of the Gadarenes round about asked him to go away from them, because with great fear they were pressed, and he having entered into the boat, did turn back.

Luke 8:38 And the man from whom the demons had gone forth was beseeching of him to be with him, and Jesus sent him away, saying,

Luke 8:39 `Turn back to thy house, and tell how great things God did to thee;' and he went away through all the city proclaiming how great things Jesus did to him.

Luke 8:40. And it came to pass, in the turning back of Jesus, the multitude received him, for they were all looking for him,

Luke 8:41 and lo, there came a man, whose name [is] Jairus, and he was a chief of the synagogue, and having fallen at the feet of Jesus, was calling on him to come to his house;

Luke 8:42 because he had an only daughter about twelve years [old], and she was dying. And in his going away, the multitudes were thronging him,

Luke 8:43 and a woman, having an issue of blood for twelve years, who, having spent on physicians all her living, was not able to be healed by any,

Luke 8:44 having come near behind, touched the fringe of his garment, and presently the issue of her blood stood.

Luke 8:45 And Jesus said, `Who [is] it that touched me?' and all denying, Peter and those with him said, `Master, the multitudes press thee, and throng [thee], and thou dost say, Who [is] it that touched me!'

Luke 8:46 And Jesus said, `Some one did touch me, for I knew power having gone forth from me.'

Luke 8:47 And the woman, having seen that she was not hid, trembling, came, and having fallen before him, for what cause she touched him declared to him before all the people, and how she was healed presently;

Luke 8:48 and he said to her, `Take courage, daughter, thy faith hath saved thee, be going on to peace.'

Luke 8:49 While he is yet speaking, there doth come a certain one from the chief of the synagogue's [house], saying to him--`Thy daughter hath died, harass not the Teacher;'

Luke 8:50 and Jesus having heard, answered him, saying, `Be not afraid, only believe, and she shall be saved.'

Luke 8:51 And having come to the house, he suffered no one to go in, except Peter, and James, and John, and the father of the child, and the mother;

Luke 8:52 and they were all weeping, and beating themselves for her,

and he said, `Weep not, she did not die, but doth sleep;

Luke 8:53 and they were deriding him, knowing that she did die;

Luke 8:54 and he having put all forth without, and having taken hold of her hand, called, saying, `Child, arise;'

Luke 8:55 and her spirit came back, and she arose presently, and he directed that there be given to her to eat;

Luke 8:56 and her parents were amazed, but he charged them to say to no one what was come to pass.

Luke 9:1. And having called together his twelve disciples, he gave them power and authority over all the demons, and to cure sicknesses,

Luke 9:2 and he sent them to proclaim the reign of God, and to heal the ailing.

Luke 9:3 And he said unto them, `Take nothing for the way, neither staff, nor scrip, nor bread, nor money; neither have two coats each;

Luke 9:4 and into whatever house ye may enter, there remain, and thence depart;

Luke 9:5 and as many as may not receive you, going forth from that city, even the dust from your feet shake off, for a testimony against them.'

Luke 9:6 And going forth they were going through the several villages, proclaiming good news, and healing everywhere.

Luke 9:7 And Herod the tetrarch heard of all the things being done by him, and was perplexed, because it was said by certain, that John hath been raised out of the dead;

Luke 9:8 and by certain, that Elijah did appear, and by others, that a prophet, one of the ancients, was risen;

Luke 9:9 and Herod said, `John I did behead, but who is this concerning whom I hear such things?' and he was seeking to see him.

Luke 9:10. And the apostles having turned back, declared to him how great things they did, and having taken them, he withdrew by himself to a desert place of a city called Bethsaida,

Luke 9:11 and the multitudes having known did follow him, and having received them, he was speaking to them concerning the reign of God, and those having need of service he cured.

Luke 9:12 And the day began to decline, and the twelve having come near, said to him, `Let away the multitude, that having gone to the villages and the fields round about, they may lodge and may find provision, because here we are in a desert place.'

Luke 9:13 And he said unto them, `Give ye them to eat;' and they said, `We have no more than five loaves, and two fishes: except, having gone, we may buy for all this people victuals;'

Luke 9:14 for they were about five thousand men. And he said unto his disciples, `Cause them to recline in companies, in each fifty;'

Luke 9:15 and they did so, and made all to recline;

Luke 9:16 and having taken the five loaves, and the two fishes, having looked up to the heaven, he blessed them, and brake, and was giving to the disciples to set before the multitude;

Luke 9:17 and they did eat, and were all filled, and there was taken up what was over to them of broken pieces, twelve baskets.

Luke 9:18. And it came to pass, as he is praying alone, the disciples were with him, and he questioned them, saying, `Who do the multitudes say me to be?'

Luke 9:19 And they answering said, `John the Baptist; and others, Elijah; and others, that a prophet, one of the ancients, was risen;'

Luke 9:20 and he said to them, `And ye--who do ye say me to be?' and Peter answering said, `The Christ of God.'

Luke 9:21 And having charged them, he commanded [them] to say this to no one,

Luke 9:22 saying--Ìt behoveth the Son of Man to suffer many things, and to be rejected by the elders, and chief priests, and scribes, and to be killed, and the third day to be raised.'

Luke 9:23 And he said unto all, Ìf any one doth will to come after me, let him disown himself, and take up his cross daily, and follow me;

Luke 9:24 for whoever may will to save his life, shall lose it, and whoever may lose his life for my sake, he shall save it;

Luke 9:25 for what is a man profited, having gained the whole world, and having lost or having forfeited himself?

Luke 9:26 `For whoever may be ashamed of me, and of my words, of this one shall the Son of Man be ashamed, when he may come in his glory, and the Father's, and the holy messengers';

Luke 9:27 and I say to you, truly, there are certain of those here standing, who shall not taste of death till they may see the reign of God.'

Luke 9:28. And it came to pass, after these words, as it were eight days, that having taken Peter, and John, and James, he went up to the mountain to pray,

Luke 9:29 and it came to pass, in his praying, the appearance of his face became altered, and his garment white--sparkling.

Luke 9:30 And lo, two men were speaking together with him, who were Moses and Elijah,

Luke 9:31 who having appeared in glory, spake of his outgoing that he was about to fulfil in Jerusalem,

Luke 9:32 but Peter and those with him were heavy with sleep, and having waked, they saw his glory, and the two men standing with him.

Luke 9:33 And it came to pass, in their parting from him, Peter said unto Jesus, `Master, it is good to us to be here; and we may make three booths, one for thee, and one for Moses, and one for Elijah,' not knowing what he saith:

Luke 9:34 and as he was speaking these things, there came a cloud, and overshadowed them, and they feared in their entering into the cloud,

Luke 9:35 and a voice came out of the cloud saying, `This is My Son-- the Beloved; hear ye him;'

Luke 9:36 and when the voice was past, Jesus was found alone; and they were silent, and declared to no one in those days anything of what they have seen.

Luke 9:37. And it came to pass on the next day, they having come down from the mount, there met him a great multitude,

Luke 9:38 and lo, a man from the multitude cried out, saying, `Teacher, I beseech thee, look upon my son, because he is my only begotten;

Luke 9:39 and lo, a spirit doth take him, and suddenly he doth cry out, and it teareth him, with foaming, and it hardly departeth from him, bruising him,

Luke 9:40 and I besought thy disciples that they might cast it out, and they were not able.'

Luke 9:41 And Jesus answering said, Ò generation, unstedfast and perverse, till when shall I be with you, and suffer you? bring near hither thy son;'

Luke 9:42 and as he is yet coming near, the demon rent him, and tore [him] sore, and Jesus rebuked the unclean spirit, and healed the youth, and gave him back to his father.

Luke 9:43. And they were all amazed at the greatness of God, and while all are wondering at all things that Jesus did, he said unto his disciples,

Luke 9:44 `Lay ye to your ears these words, for the Son of Man is about to be delivered up to the hands of men.'

Luke 9:45 And they were not knowing this saying, and it was veiled from them, that they might not perceive it, and they were afraid to ask him about this saying.

Luke 9:46 And there entered a reasoning among them, this, Who may be greater of them?

Luke 9:47 and Jesus having seen the reasoning of their heart, having taken hold of a child, set him beside himself,

Luke 9:48 and said to them, `Whoever may receive this child in my name, doth receive me, and whoever may receive me, doth receive Him who sent me, for he who is least among you all--he shall be great.'

Luke 9:49 And John answering said, `Master, we saw a certain one in thy name casting forth the demons, and we forbade him, because he doth not follow with us;'

Luke 9:50 and Jesus said unto him, `Forbid not, for he who is not against us, is for us.'

Luke 9:51. And it came to pass, in the completing of the days of his being taken up, that he fixed his face to go on to Jerusalem,

Luke 9:52 and he sent messengers before his face, and having gone on, they went into a village of Samaritans, to make ready for him,

Luke 9:53 and they did not receive him, because his face was going on to Jerusalem.

Luke 9:54 And his disciples James and John having seen, said, `Sir, wilt thou [that] we may command fire to come down from the heaven, and to consume them, as also Elijah did?'

Luke 9:55 and having turned, he rebuked them, and said, `Ye have not known of what spirit ye are;

Luke 9:56 for the Son of Man did not come to destroy men's lives, but to save;' and they went on to another village.

Luke 9:57. And it came to pass, as they are going on in the way, a certain one said unto him, Ì will follow thee wherever thou mayest go, sir;'

Luke 9:58 and Jesus said to him, `The foxes have holes, and the fowls of the heaven places of rest, but the Son of Man hath not where he may recline the head.'

Luke 9:59 And he said unto another, `Be following me;' and he said, `Sir, permit me, having gone away, first to bury my father;'

Luke 9:60 and Jesus said to him, `Suffer the dead to bury their own dead, and thou, having gone away, publish the reign of God.'

Luke 9:61 And another also said, Ì will follow thee, sir, but first permit me to take leave of those in my house;'

Luke 9:62 and Jesus said unto him, `No one having put his hand on a plough, and looking back, is fit for the reign of God.'

Luke 10:1. And after these things, the Lord did appoint also other seventy, and sent them by twos before his face, to every city and place whither he himself was about to come,

Luke 10:2 then said he unto them, `The harvest indeed [is] abundant, but the workmen few; beseech ye then the Lord of the harvest, that He may put forth workmen to His harvest.

Luke 10:3 `Go away; lo, I send you forth as lambs in the midst of wolves;

Luke 10:4 carry no bag, no scrip, nor sandals; and salute no one on the way;

Luke 10:5 and into whatever house ye do enter, first say, Peace to this house;

Luke 10:6 and if indeed there may be there the son of peace, rest on it shall your peace; and if not so, upon you it shall turn back.

Luke 10:7 Ànd in that house remain, eating and drinking the things they have, for worthy [is] the workman of his hire; go not from house to house,

Luke 10:8 and into whatever city ye enter, and they may receive you, eat the things set before you,

Luke 10:9 and heal the ailing in it, and say to them, The reign of God hath come nigh to you.

Luke 10:10 Ànd into whatever city ye do enter, and they may not receive you, having gone forth to its broad places, say,

Luke 10:11 And the dust that hath cleaved to us, from your city, we do wipe off against you, but this know ye, that the reign of God hath come nigh to you;

Luke 10:12 and I say to you, that for Sodom in that day it shall be more tolerable than for that city.

Luke 10:13 `Woe to thee, Chorazin; woe to thee, Bethsaida; for if in Tyre and Sidon had been done the mighty works that were done in you, long ago, sitting in sackcloth and ashes, they had reformed;

Luke 10:14 but for Tyre and Sidon it shall be more tolerable in the judgment than for you.

Luke 10:15 Ànd thou, Capernaum, which unto the heaven wast exalted, unto hades thou shalt be brought down.

Luke 10:16 `He who is hearing you, doth hear me; and he who is putting you away, doth put me away; and he who is putting me away, doth put away Him who sent me.'

Luke 10:17. And the seventy turned back with joy, saying, `Sir, and the demons are being subjected to us in thy name;'

Luke 10:18 and he said to them, Ì was beholding the Adversary, as lightning from the heaven having fallen;

Luke 10:19 lo, I give to you the authority to tread upon serpents and scorpions, and on all the power of the enemy, and nothing by any means shall hurt you;

Luke 10:20 but, in this rejoice not, that the spirits are subjected to you, but rejoice rather that your names were written in the heavens.'

Luke 10:21 In that hour was Jesus glad in the Spirit, and said, Ì do confess to thee, Father, Lord of the heaven and of the earth, that Thou didst hide these things from wise men and understanding, and didst reveal them to babes; yes, Father, because soit became good pleasure before Thee.

Luke 10:22 Àll things were delivered up to me by my Father, and no one doth know who the Son is, except the Father, and who the Father is, except the Son, and he to whom the Son may wish to reveal [Him].'

Luke 10:23 And having turned unto the disciples, he said, by themselves, `Happy the eyes that are perceiving what ye perceive;

Luke 10:24 for I say to you, that many prophets and kings did wish to see what ye perceive, and did not see, and to hear what ye hear, and did not hear.'

Luke 10:25. And lo, a certain lawyer stood up, trying him, and saying, `Teacher, what having done, life age-during shall I inherit?'

Luke 10:26 And he said unto him, Ìn the law what hath been written? how dost thou read?'

Luke 10:27 And he answering said, `Thou shalt love the Lord thy God out of all thy heart, and out of all thy soul, and out of all thy strength, and out of all thy understanding, and thy neighbour as thyself.'

Luke 10:28 And he said to him, `Rightly thou didst answer; this do, and thou shalt live.'

Luke 10:29 And he, willing to declare himself righteous, said unto Jesus, Ànd who is my neighbour?'

Luke 10:30 and Jesus having taken up [the word], said, À certain man was going down from Jerusalem to Jericho, and fell among robbers, and having stripped him and inflicted blows, they went away, leaving [him] half dead.

Luke 10:31 Ànd by a coincidence a certain priest was going down in that way, and having seen him, he passed over on the opposite side;

Luke 10:32 and in like manner also, a Levite, having been about the place, having come and seen, passed over on the opposite side.

Luke 10:33 `But a certain Samaritan, journeying, came along him, and having seen him, he was moved with compassion,

Luke 10:34 and having come near, he bound up his wounds, pouring on oil and wine, and having lifted him up on his own beast, he brought him to an inn, and was careful of him;

Luke 10:35 and on the morrow, going forth, taking out two denaries, he gave to the innkeeper, and said to him, Be careful of him, and whatever thou mayest spend more, I, in my coming again, will give back to thee.

Luke 10:36 `Who, then, of these three, seemeth to thee to have become neighbour of him who fell among the robbers?'

Luke 10:37 and he said, `He who did the kindness with him,' then Jesus said to him, `Be going on, and thou be doing in like manner.'

Luke 10:38. And it came to pass, in their going on, that he entered into a certain village, and a certain woman, by name Martha, did receive him into her house,

Luke 10:39 and she had also a sister, called Mary, who also, having seated herself beside the feet of Jesus, was hearing the word,

Luke 10:40 and Martha was distracted about much serving, and having stood by him, she said, `Sir, dost thou not care that my sister left me alone to serve? say then to her, that she may partake along with me.'

Luke 10:41 And Jesus answering said to her, `Martha, Martha, thou art anxious and disquieted about many things,

Luke 10:42 but of one thing there is need, and Mary the good part did choose, that shall not be taken away from her.'

Luke 11:1. And it came to pass, in his being in a certain place praying, as he ceased, a certain one of his disciples said unto him, `Sir, teach us to pray, as also John taught his disciples.'

Luke 11:2 And he said to them, `When ye may pray, say ye: Our Father who art in the heavens; hallowed be Thy name: Thy reign come; Thy will come to pass, as in heaven also on earth;

Luke 11:3 our appointed bread be giving us daily;

Luke 11:4 and forgive us our sins, for also we ourselves forgive every one indebted to us; and mayest Thou not bring us into temptation; but do Thou deliver us from the evil.'

Luke 11:5 And he said unto them, `Who of you shall have a friend, and shall go on unto him at midnight,

and may say to him, Friend, lend me three loaves,

Luke 11:6 seeing a friend of mine came out of the way unto me, and I have not what I shall set before him,

Luke 11:7 and he from within answering may say, Do not give me trouble, already the door hath been shut, and my children with me are in the bed, I am not able, having risen, to give to thee.

Luke 11:8 Ì say to you, even if he will not give to him, having risen, because of his being his friend, yet because of his importunity, having risen, he will give him as many as he doth need;

Luke 11:9 and I say to you, Ask, and it shall be given to you; seek, and ye shall find; knock, and it shall be opened to you;

Luke 11:10 for every one who is asking doth receive; and he who is seeking doth find; and to him who is knocking it shall be opened.

Luke 11:11 Ànd of which of you-- the father--if the son shall ask a loaf, a stone will he present to him? and if a fish, will he instead of a fish, a serpent present to him?

Luke 11:12 and if he may ask an egg, will he present to him a scorpion?

Luke 11:13 If, then, ye, being evil, have known good gifts to be giving to your children, how much more shall the Father who is from heaven give the Holy Spirit to those asking Him!'

Luke 11:14. And he was casting forth a demon, and it was dumb, and it came to pass, the demon having gone forth, the dumb man spake, and the multitudes wondered,

Luke 11:15 and certain of them said, `By Beelzeboul, ruler of the demons, he doth cast forth the demons;'

Luke 11:16 and others, tempting, a sign out of heaven from him were asking.

Luke 11:17 And he, knowing their thoughts, said to them, `Every kingdom having been divided against itself is desolated; and house against house doth fall;

Luke 11:18 and if also the Adversary against himself was divided, how shall his kingdom be made to stand? for ye say, by Beelzeboul is my casting forth the demons.

Luke 11:19 `But if I by Beelzeboul cast forth the demons--your sons, by whom do they cast forth? because of this your judges they shall be;

Luke 11:20 but if by the finger of God I cast forth the demons, then come unawares upon you did the reign of God.

Luke 11:21 `When the strong man armed may keep his hall, in peace are his goods;

Luke 11:22 but when the stronger than he, having come upon [him], may overcome him, his whole-armour he doth take away in which he had trusted, and his spoils he distributeth;

Luke 11:23 he who is not with me is against me, and he who is not gathering with me doth scatter.

Luke 11:24 `When the unclean spirit may go forth from the man it walketh through waterless places seeking rest, and not finding, it saith, I will turn back to my house whence I came forth;

Luke 11:25 and having come, it findeth [it] swept and adorned;

Luke 11:26 then doth it go, and take to it seven other spirits more evil than itself, and having entered, they dwell there, and the last of that man becometh worst than the first.'

Luke 11:27. And it came to pass, in his saying these things, a certain woman having lifted up the voice out of the multitude, said to him, `Happy the womb that carried thee, and the paps that thou didst suck!'

Luke 11:28 And he said, `Yea, rather, happy those hearing the word of God, and keeping [it]!'

Luke 11:29. And the multitudes crowding together upon him, he began to say, `This generation is evil, a sign it doth seek after, and a sign shall not be given to it, except the sign of Jonah the prophet,

Luke 11:30 for as Jonah became a sign to the Ninevites, so also shall the Son of Man be to this generation.

Luke 11:31 À queen of the south shall rise up in the judgment with the men of this generation, and shall condemn them, because she came from the ends of the earth to hear the wisdom of Solomon; and lo, greater than Solomon here!

Luke 11:32 `Men of Nineveh shall stand up in the judgment with this generation, and shall condemn it, because they reformed at the proclamation of Jonah; and lo, greater than Jonah here!

Luke 11:33 Ànd no one having lighted a lamp, doth put [it] in a secret place, nor under the measure, but on the lamp-stand, that those coming in may behold the light.

Luke 11:34 `The lamp of the body is the eye, when then thine eye may be simple, thy whole body also is lightened; and when it may be evil, thy body also is darkened;

Luke 11:35 take heed, then, lest the light that [is] in thee be darkness;

Luke 11:36 if then thy whole body is lightened, not having any part darkened, the whole shall be lightened, as when the lamp by the brightness may give thee light.'

Luke 11:37. And in [his] speaking, a certain Pharisee was asking him that he might dine with him, and having gone in, he reclined (at meat),

Luke 11:38 and the Pharisee having seen, did wonder that he did not first baptize himself before the dinner.

Luke 11:39 And the Lord said unto him, `Now do ye, the Pharisees, the outside of the cup and of the plate make clean, but your inward part is full of rapine and wickedness;

Luke 11:40 unthinking! did not He who made the outside also the inside make?

Luke 11:41 But what ye have give ye [as] alms, and, lo, all things are clean to you.

Luke 11:42 `But woe to you, the Pharisees, because ye tithe the mint, and the rue, and every herb, and ye pass by the judgment, and the love of God; these things it behoveth to do, and those not to be neglecting.

Luke 11:43 `Woe to you, the Pharisees, because ye love the first seats in the synagogues, and the salutations in the market-places.

Luke 11:44 `Woe to you, scribes and Pharisees, hypocrites, because ye are as the unseen tombs, and the men walking above have not known.'

Luke 11:45 And one of the lawyers answering, saith to him, `Teacher, these things saying, us also thou dost insult;'

Luke 11:46 and he said, Ànd to you, the lawyers, woe! because ye burden men with burdens grievous to be borne, and ye yourselves with one of your fingers do not touch the burdens.

Luke 11:47 `Woe to you, because ye build the tombs of the prophets, and your fathers killed them.

Luke 11:48 Then do ye testify, and are well pleased with the works of your fathers, because they indeed killed them, and ye do build their tombs;

Luke 11:49 because of this also the wisdom of God said: I will send to them prophets, and apostles, and some of them they shall kill and persecute,

Luke 11:50 that the blood of all the prophets, that is being poured forth from the foundation of the world, may be required from this generation;

Luke 11:51 from the blood of Abel unto the blood of Zacharias, who perished between the altar and the house; yes, I say to you, It shall be required from this generation.

Luke 11:52 `Woe to you, the lawyers, because ye took away the key of the knowledge; yourselves ye did not enter; and those coming in, ye did hinder.'

Luke 11:53 And in his speaking these things unto them, the scribes and the Pharisees began fearfully to urge and to press him to speak about many things,

Luke 11:54 laying wait for him, and seeking to catch something out of his mouth, that they might accuse him.

Luke 12:1. At which time the myriads of the multitude having been gathered together, so as to tread upon one another, he began to say unto his disciples, first, `Take heed to yourselves of the leaven of the Pharisees, which is hypocrisy;

Luke 12:2 and there is nothing covered, that shall not be revealed; and hid, that shall not be known;

Luke 12:3 because whatever in the darkness ye said, in the light shall be heard: and what to the ear ye spake in the inner-chambers, shall be proclaimed upon the house-tops.

Luke 12:4 Ànd I say to you, my friends, be not afraid of those killing the body, and after these things are not having anything over to do;

Luke 12:5 but I will show to you, whom ye may fear; Fear him who, after the killing, is having authority to cast to the gehenna; yes, I say to you, Fear ye Him.

Luke 12:6 Àre not five sparrows sold for two assars? and one of them is not forgotten before God,

Luke 12:7 but even the hairs of your head have been all numbered; therefore fear ye not, than many sparrows ye are of more value.

Luke 12:8 Ànd I say to you, Every one--whoever may confess with me before men, the Son of Man also shall confess with him before the messengers of God,

Luke 12:9 and he who hath denied me before men, shall be denied before the messengers of God,

Luke 12:10 and every one whoever shall say a word to the Son of Man, it shall be forgiven to him, but to him who to the Holy Spirit did speak evil, it shall not be forgiven.

Luke 12:11 Ànd when they bring you before the synagogues, and the rulers, and the authorities, be not anxious how or what ye may reply, or what ye may say,

Luke 12:12 for the Holy Spirit shall teach you in that hour what it behoveth [you] to say.'

Luke 12:13 . And a certain one said to him, out of the multitude, `Teacher, say to my brother to divide with me the inheritance.'

Luke 12:14 And he said to him, `Man, who set me a judge or a divider over you?'

Luke 12:15 And he said unto them, Òbserve, and beware of the covetousness, because not in the abundance of one's goods is his life.'

Luke 12:16 And he spake a simile unto them, saying, Òf a certain rich man the field brought forth well;

Luke 12:17 and he was reasoning within himself, saying, What shall I do, because I have not where I shall gather together my fruits?

Luke 12:18 and he said, This I will do, I will take down my storehouses, and greater ones I will build, and I will gather together there all my products and my good things,

Luke 12:19 and I will say to my soul, Soul, thou hast many good things laid up for many years, be resting, eat, drink, be merry.

Luke 12:20 Ànd God said to him, Unthinking one! this night thy soul they shall require from thee, and what things thou didst prepare--to whom shall they be?

Luke 12:21 so [is] he who is treasuring up to himself, and is not rich toward God.'

Luke 12:22 . And he said unto his disciples, `Because of this, to you I say, Be not anxious for your life, what ye may eat; nor for the body, what ye may put on;

Luke 12:23 the life is more than the nourishment, and the body than the clothing.

Luke 12:24 `Consider the ravens, that they sow not, nor reap, to which there is no barn nor storehouse, and

God doth nourish them; how much better are ye than the fowls?

Luke 12:25 and who of you, being anxious, is able to add to his age one cubit?

Luke 12:26 If, then, ye are not able for the least--why for the rest are ye anxious?

Luke 12:27 `Consider the lilies, how do they grow? they labour not, nor do they spin, and I say to you, not even Solomon in all his glory was arrayed as one of these;

Luke 12:28 and if the herbage in the field, that to-day is, and to-morrow into an oven is cast, God doth so clothe, how much more you--ye of little faith?

Luke 12:29 And ye--seek not what ye may eat, or what ye may drink, and be not in suspense,

Luke 12:30 for all these things do the nations of the world seek after, and your Father hath known that ye have need of these things;

Luke 12:31 but, seek ye the reign of God, and all these things shall be added to you.

Luke 12:32 `Fear not, little flock, because your Father did delight to give you the reign;

Luke 12:33 sell your goods, and give alms, make to yourselves bags that become not old, a treasure unfailing in the heavens, where thief doth not come near, nor moth destroy;

Luke 12:34 for where your treasure is, there also your heart will be.

Luke 12:35 `Let your loins be girded, and the lamps burning,

Luke 12:36 and ye like to men waiting for their lord, when he shall return out of the wedding feasts, that he having come and knocked, immediately they may open to him.

Luke 12:37 `Happy those servants, whom the lord, having come, shall find watching; verily I say to you, that he will gird himself, and will cause them to recline (at meat), and having come near, will minister to them;

Luke 12:38 and if he may come in the second watch, and in the third watch he may come, and may find [it] so, happy are those servants.

Luke 12:39 And this know, that if the master of the house had known what hour the thief doth come, he would have watched, and would not have suffered his house to be broken through;

Luke 12:40 and ye, then, become ye ready, because at the hour ye think not, the Son of Man doth come.'

Luke 12:41. And Peter said to him, `Sir, unto us this simile dost thou speak, or also unto all?'

Luke 12:42 And the Lord said, `Who, then, is the faithful and prudent steward whom the lord shall set over his household, to give in season the wheat measure?

Luke 12:43 Happy that servant, whom his lord, having come, shall find doing so;

Luke 12:44 truly I say to you, that over all his goods he will set him.

Luke 12:45 And if that servant may say in his heart, My lord doth delay to come, and may begin to beat the men-servants and the maid-servants, to eat also, and to drink, and to be drunken;

Luke 12:46 the lord of that servant will come in a day in which he doth not look for [him], and in an hour that he doth not know, and will cut him off, and his portion with the unfaithful he will appoint.

Luke 12:47 And that servant, who having known his lord's will, and not having prepared, nor having gone according to his will, shall be beaten with many stripes,

Luke 12:48 and he who, not having known, and having done things worthy of stripes, shall be beaten with few; and to every one to whom much was given, much shall be required from him; and to whom they did commit much, more abundantly they will ask of him.

Luke 12:49 `Fire I came to cast to the earth, and what will I if already it was kindled?

Luke 12:50 but I have a baptism to be baptized with, and how am I pressed till it may be completed!

Luke 12:51 `Think ye that peace I came to give in the earth? no, I say to you, but rather division;

Luke 12:52 for there shall be henceforth five in one house divided-- three against two, and two against three;

Luke 12:53 a father shall be divided against a son, and a son against a father, a mother against a daughter, and a daughter against a mother, a mother-in-law against her daughter-in-law, and a daughter-in-law against her mother-in-law.'

Luke 12:54. And he said also to the multitudes, `When ye may see the cloud rising from the west, immediately ye say, A shower doth come, and it is so;

Luke 12:55 and when--a south wind blowing, ye say, that there will be heat, and it is;

Luke 12:56 hypocrites! the face of the earth and of the heaven ye have known to make proof of, but this time--how do ye not make proof of [it]?

Luke 12:57 And why, also, of yourselves, judge ye not what is righteous?

Luke 12:58 for, as thou art going away with thy opponent to the ruler, in the way give diligence to be released from him, lest he may drag thee unto the judge, and the judge may deliver thee to the officer, and the officer may cast thee into prison;

Luke 12:59 I say to thee, thou mayest not come forth thence till even the last mite thou mayest give back.'

Luke 13:1. And there were present certain at that time, telling him about the Galileans, whose blood Pilate did mingle with their sacrifices;

Luke 13:2 and Jesus answering said to them, `Think ye that these Galileans became sinners beyond all the Galileans, because they have suffered such things?

Luke 13:3 No--I say to you, but, if ye may not reform, all ye even so shall perish.

Luke 13:4 Òr those eighteen, on whom the tower in Siloam fell, and killed them; think ye that these became debtors beyond all men who are dwelling in Jerusalem?

Luke 13:5 No--I say to you, but, if ye may not reform, all ye in like manner shall perish.'

Luke 13:6. And he spake this simile: À certain one had a fig-tree planted in his vineyard, and he came seeking fruit in it, and he did not find;

Luke 13:7 and he said unto the vine-dresser, Lo, three years I come seeking fruit in this fig-tree, and do not find, cut it off, why also the ground doth it render useless?

Luke 13:8 Ànd he answering saith to him, Sir, suffer it also this year, till that I may dig about it, and cast in dung;

Luke 13:9 and if indeed it may bear fruit--;and if not so, thereafter thou shalt cut it off.'

Luke 13:10. And he was teaching in one of the synagogues on the sabbath,

Luke 13:11 and lo, there was a woman having a spirit of infirmity eighteen years, and she was bowed together, and not able to bend back at all,

Luke 13:12 and Jesus having seen her, did call [her] near, and said to her, `Woman, thou hast been loosed from thy infirmity;'

Luke 13:13 and he laid on her [his] hands, and presently she was set upright, and was glorifying God.

Luke 13:14 And the chief of the synagogue answering--much displeased that on the sabbath Jesus healed--said to the multitude, `Six days there are in which it behoveth [us] to be working; in these, then, coming, be healed, and not on the sabbath-day.'

Luke 13:15 Then the Lord answered him and said, `Hypocrite, doth not each of you on the sabbath loose his ox or ass from the stall, and having led away, doth water [it]?

Luke 13:16 and this one, being a daughter of Abraham, whom the Adversary bound, lo, eighteen years, did it not behove to be loosed from this bond on the sabbath-day?'

Luke 13:17 And he saying these things, all who were opposed to him were being ashamed, and all the multitude were rejoicing over all the glorious things that are being done by him.

Luke 13:18. And he said, `To what is the reign of God like? and to what shall I liken it?

Luke 13:19 It is like to a grain of mustard, which a man having taken, did cast into his garden, and it increased, and came to a great tree, and the fowls of the heavens did rest in its branches.'

Luke 13:20 And again he said, `To what shall I liken the reign of God?

Luke 13:21 It is like leaven, which a woman, having taken, did hide in three measures of meal, till that all was leavened.'

Luke 13:22 And he was going through cities and villages, teaching, and making progress toward Jerusalem;

Luke 13:23. and a certain one said to him, `Sir, are those saved few?' and he said unto them,

Luke 13:24 `Be striving to go in through the straight gate, because many, I say to you, will seek to go in, and shall not be able;

Luke 13:25 from the time the master of the house may have risen up, and may have shut the door, and ye may begin without to stand, and to knock at the door, saying, Lord, lord, open to us, and he answering shall say to you, I have not known you whence yeare,

Luke 13:26 then ye may begin to say, We did eat before thee, and did drink, and in our broad places thou didst teach;

Luke 13:27 and he shall say, I say to you, I have not known you whence ye are; depart from me, all ye workers of the unrighteousness.

Luke 13:28 `There shall be there the weeping and the gnashing of the teeth, when ye may see Abraham, and Isaac, and Jacob, and all the prophets, in the reign of God, and yourselves being cast out without;

Luke 13:29 and they shall come from east and west, and from north and south, and shall recline in the reign of God,

Luke 13:30 and lo, there are last who shall be first, and there are first who shall be last.'

Luke 13:31. On that day there came near certain Pharisees, saying to him, `Go forth, and be going on hence, for Herod doth wish to kill thee;'

Luke 13:32 and he said to them, `Having gone, say to this fox, Lo, I cast forth demons, and perfect cures to-day and to-morrow, and the third [day] I am being perfected;

Luke 13:33 but it behoveth me to-day, and to-morrow, and the [day] following, to go on, because it is not possible for a prophet to perish out of Jerusalem.

Luke 13:34 `Jerusalem, Jerusalem, that is killing the prophets, and stoning those sent unto her, how often did I will to gather together thy children, as a hen her brood under the wings, and ye did not will.

Luke 13:35 `Lo, your house is being left to you desolate, and verily I say to you--ye may not see me, till it may come, when ye may say, Blessed [is] he who is coming in the name of the Lord.'

Luke 14:1. And it came to pass, on his going into the house of a certain one of the chiefs of the Pharisees, on a sabbath, to eat bread, that they were watching him,

Luke 14:2 and lo, there was a certain dropsical man before him;

Luke 14:3 and Jesus answering spake to the lawyers and Pharisees, saying, Ìs it lawful on the sabbath-day to heal?'

Luke 14:4 and they were silent, and having taken hold of [him], he healed him, and let [him] go;

Luke 14:5 and answering them he said, Òf which of you shall an ass or ox fall into a pit, and he will not immediately draw it up on the sabbath-day?'

Luke 14:6 and they were not able to answer him again unto these things.

Luke 14:7. And he spake a simile unto those called, marking how they were choosing out the first couches, saying unto them,

Luke 14:8 `When thou mayest be called by any one to marriage-feasts, thou mayest not recline on the first couch, lest a more honourable than thou may have been called by him,

Luke 14:9 and he who did call thee and him having come shall say to thee, Give to this one place, and then thou mayest begin with shame to occupy the last place.

Luke 14:10 `But, when thou mayest be called, having gone on, recline in the last place, that when he who called thee may come, he may say to thee, Friend, come up higher; then thou shalt have glory before those reclining with thee;

Luke 14:11 because every one who is exalting himself shall be humbled, and he who is humbling himself shall be exalted.'

Luke 14:12 And he said also to him who did call him, `When thou mayest make a dinner or a supper, be not calling thy friends, nor thy brethren, nor thy kindred, nor rich neighbours, lest they may also call thee again, and a recompense may come to thee;

Luke 14:13 but when thou mayest make a feast, be calling poor, maimed, lame, blind,

Luke 14:14 and happy thou shalt be, because they have not to recompense thee, for it shall be recompensed to thee in the rising again of the righteous.'

Luke 14:15. And one of those reclining with him, having heard these things, said to him, `Happy [is] he who shall eat bread in the reign of God;'

Luke 14:16 and he said to him, À certain man made a great supper, and called many,

Luke 14:17 and he sent his servant at the hour of the supper to say to those having been called, Be coming, because now are all things ready.

Luke 14:18 Ànd they began with one consent all to excuse themselves: The first said to him, A field I bought, and I have need to go forth and see it; I beg of thee, have me excused.

Luke 14:19 Ànd another said, Five yoke of oxen I bought, and I go on to prove them; I beg of thee, have me excused:

Luke 14:20 and another said, A wife I married, and because of this I am not able to come.

Luke 14:21 Ànd that servant having come, told to his lord these things, then the master of the house, having been angry, said to his servant, Go forth quickly to the broad places and lanes of the city, and the poor, and maimed, and lame, and blind, bring in hither.

Luke 14:22 Ànd the servant said, Sir, it hath been done as thou didst command, and still there is room.

Luke 14:23 Ànd the lord said unto the servant, Go forth to the ways and hedges, and constrain to come in, that my house may be filled;

Luke 14:24 for I say to you, that none of those men who have been called shall taste of my supper.'

Luke 14:25. And there were going on with him great multitudes, and having turned, he said unto them,

Luke 14:26 Ìf any one doth come unto me, and doth not hate his own father, and mother, and wife, and children, and brothers, and sisters, and yet even his own life, he is not able to be my disciple;

Luke 14:27 and whoever doth not bear his cross, and come after me, is not able to be my disciple.

Luke 14:28 `For who of you, willing to build a tower, doth not first, having sat down, count the expence, whether he have the things for completing?

Luke 14:29 lest that he having laid a foundation, and not being able to finish, all who are beholding may begin to mock him,

Luke 14:30 saying--This man began to build, and was not able to finish.

Luke 14:31 Òr what king going on to engage with another king in war, doth not, having sat down, first consult if he be able with ten thousand to meet him who with twenty thousand is coming against him?

Luke 14:32 and if not so--he being yet a long way off--having sent an embassy, he doth ask the things for peace.

Luke 14:33 `So, then, every one of you who doth not take leave of all that he himself hath, is not able to be my disciple.

Luke 14:34 `The salt [is] good, but if the salt doth become tasteless, with what shall it be seasoned?

Luke 14:35 neither for land nor for manure is it fit--they cast it without. He who is having ears to hear--let him hear.'

Luke 15:1. And all the tax-gatherers and the sinners were coming nigh to him, to hear him,

Luke 15:2 and the Pharisees and the scribes were murmuring, saying--This one doth receive sinners, and doth eat with them.'

Luke 15:3 And he spake unto them this simile, saying,

Luke 15:4 `What man of you having a hundred sheep, and having lost one out of them, doth not leave behind the ninety-nine in the wilderness, and go on after the lost one, till he may find it?

Luke 15:5 and having found, he doth lay [it] on his shoulders rejoicing,

Luke 15:6 and having come to the house, he doth call together the friends and the neighbours, saying to them, Rejoice with me, because I found my sheep--the lost one.

Luke 15:7 Ì say to you, that so joy shall be in the heaven over one sinner reforming, rather than over ninety-nine righteous men, who have no need of reformation.

Luke 15:8 Òr what woman having ten drachms, if she may lose one drachm, doth not light a lamp, and sweep the house, and seek carefully till that she may find?

Luke 15:9 and having found, she doth call together the female friends and the neighbours, saying, Rejoice with me, for I found the drachm that I lost.

Luke 15:10 `So I say to you, joy doth come before the messengers of God over one sinner reforming.'

Luke 15:11. And he said, À certain man had two sons,

Luke 15:12 and the younger of them said to the father, Father, give me the portion of the substance falling to [me], and he divided to them the living.

Luke 15:13 Ànd not many days after, having gathered all together, the younger son went abroad to a far country, and there he scattered his substance, living riotously;

Luke 15:14 and he having spent all, there came a mighty famine on that country, and himself began to be in want;

Luke 15:15 and having gone on, he joined himself to one of the citizens of that country, and he sent him to the fields to feed swine,

Luke 15:16 and he was desirous to fill his belly from the husks that the swine were eating, and no one was giving to him.

Luke 15:17 Ànd having come to himself, he said, How many hirelings of my father have a superabundance of bread, and I here with hunger am perishing!

Luke 15:18 having risen, I will go on unto my father, and will say to him, Father, I did sin--to the heaven, and before thee,

Luke 15:19 and no more am I worthy to be called thy son; make me as one of thy hirelings.

Luke 15:20 Ànd having risen, he went unto his own father, and he being yet far distant, his father saw him, and was moved with compassion, and having ran he fell upon his neck and kissed him;

Luke 15:21 and the son said to him, Father, I did sin--to the heaven, and before thee, and no more am I worthy to be called thy son.

Luke 15:22 Ànd the father said unto his servants, Bring forth the first robe, and clothe him, and give a ring for his hand, and sandals for the feet;

Luke 15:23 and having brought the fatted calf, kill [it], and having eaten, we may be merry,

Luke 15:24 because this my son was dead, and did live again, and he was lost, and was found; and they began to be merry.

Luke 15:25 Ànd his elder son was in a field, and as, coming, he drew nigh to the house, he heard music and dancing,

Luke 15:26 and having called near one of the young men, he was inquiring what these things might be,

Luke 15:27 and he said to him--Thy brother is arrived, and thy father did kill the fatted calf, because in health he did receive him back.

Luke 15:28 And he was angry, and would not go in, therefore his father, having come forth, was entreating him;

Luke 15:29 and he answering said to the father, Lo, so many years I do serve thee, and never thy command did I transgress, and to me thou didst never give a kid, that with my friends I might make merry;

Luke 15:30 but when thy son--this one who did devour thy living with harlots--came, thou didst kill to him the fatted calf.

Luke 15:31 And he said to him, Child, thou art always with me, and all my things are thine;

Luke 15:32 but to be merry, and to be glad, it was needful, because this thy brother was dead, and did live again, he was lost, and was found.'

Luke 16:1. And he said also unto his disciples, A certain man was rich, who had a steward, and he was accused to him as scattering his goods;

Luke 16:2 and having called him, he said to him, What [is] this I hear about thee? render the account of thy stewardship, for thou mayest not any longer be steward.

Luke 16:3 And the steward said in himself, What shall I do, because my lord doth take away the stewardship from me? to dig I am not able, to beg I am ashamed: --

Luke 16:4 I have known what I shall do, that, when I may be removed from the stewardship, they may receive me to their houses.

Luke 16:5 And having called near each one of his lord's debtors, he said to the first, How much dost thou owe to my lord?

Luke 16:6 and he said, A hundred baths of oil; and he said to him, Take thy bill, and having sat down write fifty.

Luke 16:7 Afterward to another he said, And thou, how much dost thou owe? and he said, A hundred cors of wheat; and he saith to him, Take thy bill, and write eighty.

Luke 16:8 And the lord commended the unrighteous steward that he did prudently, because the sons of this age are more prudent than the sons of the light, in respect to their generation.

Luke 16:9 and I say to you, Make to yourselves friends out of the mammon of unrighteousness, that when ye may fail, they may receive you to the age-during tabernacles.

Luke 16:10 `He who is faithful in the least, [is] also faithful in much; and he who in the least [is] unrighteous, is also unrighteous in much;

Luke 16:11 if, then, in the unrighteous mammon ye became not faithful--the true who will entrust to you?

Luke 16:12 and if in the other's ye became not faithful--your own, who shall give to you?

Luke 16:13 `No domestic is able to serve two lords, for either the one he will hate, and the other he will love; or one he will hold to, and of the other he will be heedless; ye are not able to serve God and mammon.'

Luke 16:14 And also the Pharisees, being lovers of money, were hearing all these things, and were deriding him,

Luke 16:15 and he said to them, `Ye are those declaring yourselves righteous before men, but God doth know your hearts; because that which among men is high, [is] abomination before God;

Luke 16:16 the law and the prophets [are] till John; since then the reign of God is proclaimed good news, and every one doth press into it;

Luke 16:17 and it is easier to the heaven and the earth to pass away, than of the law one tittle to fall.

Luke 16:18 Èvery one who is sending away his wife, and marrying another, doth commit adultery; and every one who is marrying her sent away from a husband doth commit adultery.

Luke 16:19. Ànd--a certain man was rich, and was clothed in purple and fine linen, making merry sumptuously every day,

Luke 16:20 and there was a certain poor man, by name Lazarus, who was laid at his porch, full of sores,

Luke 16:21 and desiring to be filled from the crumbs that are falling from the table of the rich man; yea, also the dogs, coming, were licking his sores.

Luke 16:22 Ànd it came to pass, that the poor man died, and that he was carried away by the messengers to the bosom of Abraham--and the rich man also died, and was buried;

Luke 16:23 and in the hades having lifted up his eyes, being in torments, he doth see Abraham afar off, and Lazarus in his bosom,

Luke 16:24 and having cried, he said, Father Abraham, deal kindly with me, and send Lazarus, that he may dip the tip of his finger in water, and may cool my tongue, because I am distressed in this flame.

Luke 16:25 Ànd Abraham said, Child, remember that thou did receive--thou--thy good things in thy life, and Lazarus in like manner the evil things, and now he is comforted, and thou art distressed;

Luke 16:26 and besides all these things, between us and you a great chasm is fixed, so that they who are willing to go over from hence unto you are not able, nor do they from thence to us pass through.

Luke 16:27 Ànd he said, I pray thee, then, father, that thou mayest send him to the house of my father,

Luke 16:28 for I have five brothers, so that he may thoroughly testify to them, that they also may not come to this place of torment.

Luke 16:29 Àbraham saith to him, They have Moses and the prophets, let them hear them;

Luke 16:30 and he said, No, father Abraham, but if any one from the dead may go unto them, they will reform.

Luke 16:31 And he said to him, If Moses and the prophets they do not hear, neither if one may rise out of the dead will they be persuaded.'

Luke 17:1. And he said unto the disciples, Ìt is impossible for the stumbling blocks not to come, but woe [to him] through whom they come;

Luke 17:2 it is more profitable to him if a weighty millstone is put round about his neck, and he hath been cast into the sea, than that he may cause one of these little ones to stumble.

Luke 17:3 `Take heed to yourselves, and, if thy brother may sin in regard to thee, rebuke him, and if he may reform, forgive him,

Luke 17:4 and if seven times in the day he may sin against thee, and seven times in the day may turn back to thee, saying, I reform; thou shalt forgive him.'

Luke 17:5 And the apostles said to the Lord, Àdd to us faith;'

Luke 17:6 and the Lord said, Ìf ye had faith as a grain of mustard, ye would have said to this sycamine, Be uprooted, and be planted in the sea, and it would have obeyed you.

Luke 17:7 `But, who is he of you-- having a servant ploughing or feeding--who, to him having come in out of the field, will say, Having come near, recline at meat?

Luke 17:8 but will not [rather] say to him, Prepare what I may sup, and having girded thyself about, minister to me, till I eat and drink, and after these things thou shalt eat and drink?

Luke 17:9 Hath he favour to that servant because he did the things directed? I think not.

Luke 17:10 `So also ye, when ye may have done all the things directed you, say--We are unprofitable servants, because that which we owed to do--we have done.'

Luke 17:11. And it came to pass, in his going on to Jerusalem, that he passed through the midst of Samaria and Galilee,

Luke 17:12 and he entering into a certain village, there met him ten leprous men, who stood afar off,

Luke 17:13 and they lifted up the voice, saying, `Jesus, master, deal kindly with us;'

Luke 17:14 and having seen [them], he said to them, `Having gone on, shew yourselves to the priests;' and it came to pass, in their going, they were cleansed,

Luke 17:15 and one of them having seen that he was healed did turn back, with a loud voice glorifying God,

Luke 17:16 and he fell upon [his] face at his feet, giving thanks to him, and he was a Samaritan.

Luke 17:17 And Jesus answering said, `Were not the ten cleansed, and the nine--where?

Luke 17:18 There were not found who did turn back to give glory to God, except this alien;'

Luke 17:19 and he said to him, `Having risen, be going on, thy faith hath saved thee.'

Luke 17:20. And having been questioned by the Pharisees, when the reign of God doth come, he answered them, and said, `The reign of God doth not come with observation;

Luke 17:21 nor shall they say, Lo, here; or lo, there; for lo, the reign of God is within you.'

Luke 17:22 And he said unto his disciples, `Days will come, when ye shall desire to see one of the days of the Son of Man, and ye shall not behold [it];

Luke 17:23 and they shall say to you, Lo, here; or lo, there; ye may not go away, nor follow;

Luke 17:24 for as the lightning that is lightening out of the one [part] under heaven, to the other part under heaven doth shine, so shall be also the Son of Man in his day;

Luke 17:25 and first it behoveth him to suffer many things, and to be rejected by this generation.

Luke 17:26 Ànd, as it came to pass in the days of Noah, so shall it be also in the days of the Son of Man;

Luke 17:27 they were eating, they were drinking, they were marrying, they were given in marriage, till the day that Noah entered into the ark, and the deluge came, and destroyed all;

Luke 17:28 in like manner also, as it came to pass in the days of Lot; they were eating, they were drinking, they were buying, they were selling, they were planting, they were building;

Luke 17:29 and on the day Lot went forth from Sodom, He rained fire and brimstone from heaven, and destroyed all.

Luke 17:30 Àccording to these things it shall be, in the day the Son of Man is revealed;

Luke 17:31 in that day, he who shall be on the house top, and his vessels in the house, let him not come down to take them away; and he in the field, in like manner, let him not turn backward;

Luke 17:32 remember the wife of Lot.

Luke 17:33 Whoever may seek to save his life, shall lose it; and whoever may lose it, shall preserve it.

Luke 17:34 Ì say to you, In that night, there shall be two men on one couch, the one shall be taken, and the other shall be left;

Luke 17:35 two women shall be grinding at the same place together, the one shall be taken, and the other shall be left;

Luke 17:36 two men shall be in the field, the one shall be taken, and the other left.'

Luke 17:37 And they answering say to him, `Where, sir?' and he said to them, `Where the body [is], there will the eagles be gathered together.'

Luke 18:1. And he spake also a simile to them, that it behoveth [us] always to pray, and not to faint,

Luke 18:2 saying, À certain judge was in a certain city--God he is not fearing, and man he is not regarding--

Luke 18:3 and a widow was in that city, and she was coming unto him, saying, Do me justice on my opponent,

Luke 18:4 and he would not for a time, but after these things he said in himself, Even if God I do not fear, and man do not regard,

Luke 18:5 yet because this widow doth give me trouble, I will do her justice, lest, perpetually coming, she may plague me.'

Luke 18:6 And the Lord said, `Hear ye what the unrighteous judge saith:

Luke 18:7 and shall not God execute the justice to His choice ones, who are crying unto Him day and night-- bearing long in regard to them?

Luke 18:8 I say to you, that He will execute the justice to them quickly; but the Son of Man having come, shall he find the faith upon the earth?'

Luke 18:9. And he spake also unto certain who have been trusting in themselves that they were righteous, and have been despising the rest, this simile:

Luke 18:10 `Two men went up to the temple to pray, the one a Pharisee, and the other a tax-gatherer;

Luke 18:11 the Pharisee having stood by himself, thus prayed: God, I thank Thee that I am not as the rest of men, rapacious, unrighteous, adulterers, or even as this tax-gatherer;

Luke 18:12 I fast twice in the week, I give tithes of all things--as many as I possess.

Luke 18:13 Ànd the tax-gatherer, having stood afar off, would not even the eyes lift up to the heaven, but was smiting on his breast, saying, God be propitious to me--the sinner!

Luke 18:14 I say to you, this one went down declared righteous, to his house, rather than that one: for every one who is exalting himself shall be humbled, and he who is humbling himself shall be exalted.'

Luke 18:15. And they were bringing near also the babes, that he may touch them, and the disciples having seen did rebuke them,

Luke 18:16 and Jesus having called them near, said, `Suffer the little children to come unto me, and forbid them not, for of such is the reign of God;

Luke 18:17 verily I say to you, Whoever may not receive the reign of God as a little child, may not enter into it.'

Luke 18:18. And a certain ruler questioned him, saying, `Good teacher, what having done--shall I inherit life age-during?'

Luke 18:19 And Jesus said to him, `Why me dost thou call good? no one [is] good, except One--God;

Luke 18:20 the commands thou hast known: Thou mayest not commit adultery, Thou mayest do no murder, Thou mayest not steal, Thou mayest not bear false witness, Honour thy father and thy mother.'

Luke 18:21 And he said, Àll these I did keep from my youth;'

Luke 18:22 and having heard these things, Jesus said to him, `Yet one thing to thee is lacking; all things--as many as thou hast--sell, and distribute to the poor, and thou shalt have treasure in heaven, and come, be following me;'

Luke 18:23 and he, having heard these things, became very sorrowful, for he was exceeding rich.

Luke 18:24 And Jesus having seen him become very sorrowful, said, `How hardly shall those having riches enter into the reign of God!

Luke 18:25 for it is easier for a camel through the eye of a needle to enter, than for a rich man into the reign of God to enter.'

Luke 18:26 And those who heard, said, Ànd who is able to be saved?'

Luke 18:27 and he said, `The things impossible with men are possible with God.'

Luke 18:28 And Peter said, `Lo, we left all, and did follow thee;'

Luke 18:29 and he said to them, `Verily I say to you, that there is not one who left house, or parents, or brothers, or wife, or children, for the sake of the reign of God,

Luke 18:30 who may not receive back manifold more in this time, and in the coming age, life age-during.'

Luke 18:31. And having taken the twelve aside, he said unto them, `Lo, we go up to Jerusalem, and all things shall be completed--that have been written through the prophets--to the Son of Man,

Luke 18:32 for he shall be delivered up to the nations, and shall be mocked, and insulted, and spit upon,

Luke 18:33 and having scourged they shall put him to death, and on the third day he shall rise again.'

Luke 18:34 And they none of these things understood, and this saying was hid from them, and they were not knowing the things said.

Luke 18:35. And it came to pass, in his coming nigh to Jericho, a certain blind man was sitting beside the way begging,

Luke 18:36 and having heard a multitude going by, he was inquiring what this may be,

Luke 18:37 and they brought him word that Jesus the Nazarene doth pass by,

Luke 18:38 and he cried out, saying, `Jesus, Son of David, deal kindly with me;'

Luke 18:39 and those going before were rebuking him, that he might be silent, but he was much more crying out, `Son of David, deal kindly with me.'

Luke 18:40 And Jesus having stood, commanded him to be brought unto him, and he having come nigh, he questioned him,

Luke 18:41 saying, `What wilt thou I shall do to thee?' and he said, `Sir, that I may receive sight.'

Luke 18:42 And Jesus said to him, `Receive thy sight; thy faith hath saved thee;'

Luke 18:43 and presently he did receive sight, and was following him, glorifying God; and all the people, having seen, did give praise to God.

Luke 19:1. And having entered, he was passing through Jericho,

Luke 19:2 and lo, a man, by name called Zaccheus, and he was a chief tax-gatherer, and he was rich,

Luke 19:3 and he was seeking to see Jesus, who he is, and was not able for the multitude, because in stature he was small,

Luke 19:4 and having run forward before, he went up on a sycamore, that he may see him, because through that [way] he was about to pass by.

Luke 19:5 And as Jesus came up to the place, having looked up, he saw him, and said unto him, `Zaccheus, having hastened, come down, for to-day in thy house it behoveth me to remain;'

Luke 19:6 and he having hastened did come down, and did receive him rejoicing;

Luke 19:7 and having seen [it], they were all murmuring, saying--`With a sinful man he went in to lodge!'

Luke 19:8 And Zaccheus having stood, said unto the Lord, `Lo, the half of my goods, sir, I give to the poor, and if of any one anything I did take by false accusation, I give back fourfold.'

Luke 19:9 And Jesus said unto him--`To-day salvation did come to this house, inasmuch as he also is a son of Abraham;

Luke 19:10 for the Son of Man came to seek and to save the lost.'

Luke 19:11. And while they are hearing these things, having added he spake a simile, because of his be-ing nigh to Jerusalem, and of their thinking that the reign of God is about presently to be made manifest.

Luke 19:12 He said therefore, À certain man of birth went on to a far country, to take to himself a kingdom, and to return,

Luke 19:13 and having called ten servants of his own, he gave to them ten pounds, and said unto them, Do business--till I come;

Luke 19:14 and his citizens were hating him, and did send an embassy after him, saying, We do not wish this one to reign over us.

Luke 19:15 Ànd it came to pass, on his coming back, having taken the kingdom, that he commanded these servants to be called to him, to whom he gave the money, that he might know what any one had done in business.

Luke 19:16 Ànd the first came near, saying, Sir, thy pound did gain ten pounds;

Luke 19:17 and he said to him, Well done, good servant, because in a very little thou didst become faithful, be having authority over ten cities.

Luke 19:18 Ànd the second came, saying, Sir, thy pound made five pounds;

Luke 19:19 and he said also to this one, And thou, become thou over five cities.

Luke 19:20 And another came, saying, Sir, lo, thy pound, that I had lying away in a napkin;

Luke 19:21 for I was afraid of thee, because thou art an austere man; thou takest up what thou didst not lay down, and reapest what thou didst not sow.

Luke 19:22 And he saith to him, Out of thy mouth I will judge thee, evil servant: thou knewest that I am an austere man, taking up what I did not lay down, and reaping what I did not sow!

Luke 19:23 and wherefore didst thou not give my money to the bank, and I, having come, with interest might have received it?

Luke 19:24 And to those standing by he said, Take from him the pound, and give to him having the ten pounds--

Luke 19:25 (and they said to him, Sir, he hath ten pounds) --

Luke 19:26 for I say to you, that to every one having shall be given, and from him not having, also what he hath shall be taken from him,

Luke 19:27 but those my enemies, who did not wish me to reign over them, bring hither and slay before me.'

Luke 19:28. And having said these things, he went on before, going up to Jerusalem.

Luke 19:29 And it came to pass, as he came nigh to Bethphage and Bethany, unto the mount called of the Olives, he sent two of his disciples,

Luke 19:30 having said, Go away to the village over-against, in which, entering into, ye shall find a colt bound, on which no one of men did ever sit, having loosed it, bring [it];

Luke 19:31 and if any one doth question you, Wherefore do ye loose [it]? thus ye shall say to him--The Lord hath need of it.'

Luke 19:32 And those sent, having gone away, found according as he said to them,

Luke 19:33 and while they are loosing the colt, its owners said unto them, `Why loose ye the colt?'

Luke 19:34 and they said, `The Lord hath need of it;'

Luke 19:35 and they brought it unto Jesus, and having cast their garments upon the colt, they did set Jesus upon it.

Luke 19:36 And as he is going, they were spreading their garments in the way,

Luke 19:37 and as he is coming nigh now, at the descent of the mount of the Olives, the whole multitude of the disciples began rejoicing to praise God with a great voice for all the mighty works they had seen,

Luke 19:38 saying, `blessed [is] he who is coming, a king in the name of the Lord; peace in heaven, and glory in the highest.'

Luke 19:39 And certain of the Pharisees from the multitude said unto him, `Teacher, rebuke thy disciples;'

Luke 19:40 and he answering said to them, Ì say to you, that, if these shall be silent, the stones will cry out!'

Luke 19:41. And when he came nigh, having seen the city, he wept over it,

Luke 19:42 saying--Ìf thou didst know, even thou, at least in this thy day, the things for thy peace; but now they were hid from thine eyes.

Luke 19:43 `Because days shall come upon thee, and thine enemies shall cast around thee a rampart, and compass thee round, and press thee on every side,

Luke 19:44 and lay thee low, and thy children within thee, and they shall not leave in thee a stone upon a stone, because thou didst not know the time of thy inspection.'

Luke 19:45 And having entered into the temple, he began to cast forth those selling in it, and those buying,

Luke 19:46 saying to them, Ìt hath been written, My house is a house of prayer--but ye made it a den of robbers.'

Luke 19:47 And he was teaching daily in the temple, but the chief priests and the scribes were seeking to destroy him--also the chiefs of the people--

Luke 19:48 and they were not finding what they shall do, for all the people were hanging on him, hearing him.

Luke 20:1. And it came to pass, on one of those days, as he is teaching the people in the temple, and proclaiming good news, the chief priests and the scribes, with the elders, came upon [him],

Luke 20:2 and spake unto him, saying, `Tell us by what authority thou dost these things? or who is he that gave to thee this authority?'

Luke 20:3 And he answering said unto them, Ì will question you--I also--one thing, and tell me:

Luke 20:4 the baptism of John, from heaven was it, or from men?'

Luke 20:5 And they reasoned with themselves, saying--Ìf we may say, From heaven, he will say, Wherefore, then, did ye not believe him?

Luke 20:6 and if we may say, From men, all the people will stone us, for they are having been persuaded John to be a prophet.'

Luke 20:7 And they answered, that they knew not whence [it was],

Luke 20:8 and Jesus said to them, `Neither do I say to you by what authority I do these things.'

Luke 20:9. And he began to speak unto the people this simile: À certain man planted a vineyard, and gave it out to husbandmen, and went abroad for a long time,

Luke 20:10 and at the season he sent unto the husbandmen a servant, that from the fruit of the vineyard they may give to him, but the husbandmen having beat him, did send [him] away empty.

Luke 20:11 Ànd he added to send another servant, and they that one also having beaten and dishonoured, did send away empty;

Luke 20:12 and he added to send a third, and this one also, having wounded, they did cast out.

Luke 20:13 Ànd the owner of the vineyard said, What shall I do? I will send my son--the beloved, perhaps having seen this one, they will do reverence;

Luke 20:14 and having seen him, the husbandmen reasoned among themselves, saying, This is the heir; come, we may kill him, that the inheritance may become ours;

Luke 20:15 and having cast him outside of the vineyard, they killed [him]; what, then, shall the owner of the vineyard do to them?

Luke 20:16 He will come, and destroy these husbandmen, and will give the vineyard to others.' And having heard, they said, `Let it not be!'

Luke 20:17 and he, having looked upon them, said, `What, then, is this that hath been written: A stone that the builders rejected--this became head of a corner?

Luke 20:18 every one who hath fallen on that stone shall be broken, and on whom it may fall, it will crush him to pieces.'

Luke 20:19 And the chief priests and the scribes sought to lay hands on him in that hour, and they feared the people, for they knew that against them he spake this simile.

Luke 20:20. And, having watched [him], they sent forth liers in wait, feigning themselves to be righteous, that they might take hold of his word, to deliver him up to the rule and to the authority of the governor,

Luke 20:21 and they questioned him, saying, `Teacher, we have known that thou dost say and teach rightly, and dost not accept a person, but in truth the way of God dost teach;

Luke 20:22 Is it lawful to us to give tribute to Caesar or not?'

Luke 20:23 And he, having perceived their craftiness, said unto them, `Why me do ye tempt?

Luke 20:24 shew me a denary; of whom hath it an image and superscription?' and they answering said, Òf Caesar:'

Luke 20:25 and he said to them, `Give back, therefore, the things of Caesar to Caesar, and the things of God to God;'

Luke 20:26 and they were not able to take hold on his saying before the people, and having wondered at his answer, they were silent.

Luke 20:27. And certain of the Sadducees, who are denying that there is a rising again, having come near, questioned him,

Luke 20:28 saying, `Teacher, Moses wrote to us, If any one's brother may die, having a wife, and he may die childless--that his brother may take the wife, and may raise up seed to his brother.

Luke 20:29 `There were, then, seven brothers, and the first having taken a wife, died childless,

Luke 20:30 and the second took the wife, and he died childless,

Luke 20:31 and the third took her, and in like manner also the seven-- they left not children, and they died;

Luke 20:32 and last of all died also the woman:

Luke 20:33 in the rising again, then, of which of them doth she become wife? --for the seven had her as wife.'

Luke 20:34 And Jesus answering said to them, `The sons of this age do marry and are given in marriage,

Luke 20:35 but those accounted worthy to obtain that age, and the rising again that is out of the dead, neither marry, nor are they given in marriage;

Luke 20:36 for neither are they able to die any more--for they are like messengers--and they are sons of God, being sons of the rising again.

Luke 20:37 Ànd that the dead are raised, even Moses shewed at the Bush, since he doth call the Lord, the God of Abraham, and the God of Isaac, and the God of Jacob;

Luke 20:38 and He is not a God of dead men, but of living, for all live to Him.'

Luke 20:39. And certain of the scribes answering said, `Teacher, thou didst say well;'

Luke 20:40 and no more durst they question him anything.

Luke 20:41 And he said unto them, `How do they say the Christ to be son of David,

Luke 20:42 and David himself saith in the Book of Psalms, The Lord said to my lord, Sit thou on my right hand,

Luke 20:43 till I shall make thine enemies thy footstool;

Luke 20:44 David, then, doth call him lord, and how is he his son?'

Luke 20:45 And, all the people hearing, he said to his disciples,

Luke 20:46 `Take heed of the scribes, who are wishing to walk in long robes, and are loving salutations in the markets, and first seats in the synagogues, and first couches in the suppers,

Luke 20:47 who devour the houses of the widows, and for a pretence make long prayers, these shall receive more abundant judgment.'

Luke 21:1. And having looked up, he saw those who did cast their gifts to the treasury--rich men,

Luke 21:2 and he saw also a certain poor widow casting there two mites,

Luke 21:3 and he said, `Truly I say to you, that this poor widow did cast in more than all;

Luke 21:4 for all these out of their superabundance did cast into the gifts to God, but this one out of her want, all the living that she had, did cast in.'

Luke 21:5. And certain saying about the temple, that with goodly stones

and devoted things it hath been adorned, he said,

Luke 21:6 `These things that ye behold--days will come, in which there shall not be left a stone upon a stone, that shall not be thrown down.'

Luke 21:7 And they questioned him, saying, `Teacher, when, then, shall these things be? and what [is] the sign when these things may be about to happen?'

Luke 21:8 And he said, `See--ye may not be led astray, for many shall come in my name, saying--I am [he], and the time hath come nigh; go not on then after them;

Luke 21:9 and when ye may hear of wars and uprisings, be not terrified, for it behoveth these things to happen first, but the end [is] not immediately.'

Luke 21:10 Then said he to them, `Nation shall rise against nation, and kingdom against kingdom,

Luke 21:11 great shakings also in every place, and famines, and pestilences, there shall be; fearful things also, and great signs from heaven there shall be;

Luke 21:12 and before all these, they shall lay on you their hands, and persecute, delivering up to synagogues and prisons, being brought before kings and governors for my name's sake;

Luke 21:13 and it shall become to you for a testimony.

Luke 21:14 `Settle, then, to your hearts, not to meditate beforehand to reply,

Luke 21:15 for I will give to you a mouth and wisdom that all your opposers shall not be able to refute or resist.

Luke 21:16 Ànd ye shall be delivered up also by parents, and brothers, and kindred, and friends, and they shall put of you to death;

Luke 21:17 and ye shall be hated by all because of my name--

Luke 21:18 and a hair out of your head shall not perish;

Luke 21:19 in your patience possess ye your souls.

Luke 21:20. Ànd when ye may see Jerusalem surrounded by encampments, then know that come nigh did her desolation;

Luke 21:21 then those in Judea, let them flee to the mountains; and those in her midst, let them depart out; and those in the countries, let them not come in to her;

Luke 21:22 because these are days of vengeance, to fulfil all things that have been written.

Luke 21:23 Ànd woe to those with child, and to those giving suck, in those days; for there shall be great distress on the land, and wrath on this people;

Luke 21:24 and they shall fall by the mouth of the sword, and shall be led captive to all the nations, and Jerusalem shall be trodden down by nations, till the times of nations be fulfilled.

Luke 21:25 Ànd there shall be signs in sun, and moon, and stars, and on the land [is] distress of nations with perplexity, sea and billow roaring;

Luke 21:26 men fainting at heart from fear, and expectation of the things coming on the world, for the powers of the heavens shall be shaken.

Luke 21:27 Ànd then they shall see the Son of Man, coming in a cloud, with power and much glory;

Luke 21:28 and these things beginning to happen bend yourselves back, and lift up your heads, because your redemption doth draw nigh.'

Luke 21:29. And he spake a simile to them: `See the fig-tree, and all the trees,

Luke 21:30 when they may now cast forth, having seen, of yourselves ye know that now is the summer nigh;

Luke 21:31 so also ye, when ye may see these things happening, ye know that near is the reign of God;

Luke 21:32 verily I say to you--This generation may not pass away till all may have come to pass;

Luke 21:33 the heaven and the earth shall pass away, but my words may not pass away.

Luke 21:34 Ànd take heed to yourselves, lest your hearts may be weighed down with surfeiting, and drunkenness, and anxieties of life, and suddenly that day may come on you,

Luke 21:35 for as a snare it shall come on all those dwelling on the face of all the land,

Luke 21:36 watch ye, then, in every season, praying that ye may be accounted worthy to escape all these things that are about to come to pass, and to stand before the Son of Man.'

Luke 21:37 And he was during the days in the temple teaching, and during the nights, going forth, he was lodging at the mount called of Olives;

Luke 21:38 and all the people were coming early unto him in the temple to hear him.

Luke 22:1. And the feast of the unleavened food was coming nigh, that is called Passover,

Luke 22:2 and the chief priests and the scribes were seeking how they may take him up, for they were afraid of the people.

Luke 22:3 And the Adversary entered into Judas, who is surnamed Iscariot, being of the number of the twelve,

Luke 22:4 and he, having gone away, spake with the chief priests and the magistrates, how he might deliver him up to them,

Luke 22:5 and they rejoiced, and covenanted to give him money,

Luke 22:6 and he agreed, and was seeking a favourable season to deliver him up to them without tumult.

Luke 22:7. And the day of the unleavened food came, in which it was behoving the passover to be sacrificed,

Luke 22:8 and he sent Peter and John, saying, `Having gone on, prepare to us the passover, that we may eat;'

Luke 22:9 and they said to him, `Where wilt thou that we might prepare?'

Luke 22:10 And he said to them, `Lo, in your entering into the city, there shall meet you a man, bearing a pitcher of water, follow him to the house where he doth go in,

Luke 22:11 and ye shall say to the master of the house, The Teacher saith to thee, Where is the guest-chamber where the passover with my disciples I may eat?

Luke 22:12 and he shall show you a large upper room furnished, there make ready;'

Luke 22:13 and they, having gone away, found as he hath said to them, and they made ready the passover.

Luke 22:14 And when the hour come, he reclined (at meat), and the twelve apostles with him,

Luke 22:15 and he said unto them, `With desire I did desire to eat this passover with you before my suffering,

Luke 22:16 for I say to you, that no more may I eat of it till it may be fulfilled in the reign of God.'

Luke 22:17 And having taken a cup, having given thanks, he said, `Take this and divide to yourselves,

Luke 22:18 for I say to you that I may not drink of the produce of the vine till the reign of God may come.'

Luke 22:19 And having taken bread, having given thanks, he brake and gave to them, saying, `This is my body, that for you is being given, this do ye--to remembrance of me.'

Luke 22:20 In like manner, also, the cup after the supping, saying, `This cup [is] the new covenant in my blood, that for you is being poured forth.

Luke 22:21. `But, lo, the hand of him delivering me up [is] with me on the table,

Luke 22:22 and indeed the Son of Man doth go according to what hath been determined; but woe to that man through whom he is being delivered up.'

Luke 22:23 And they began to reason among themselves, who then of them it may be, who is about to do this thing.

Luke 22:24 And there happened also a strife among them--who of them is accounted to be greater.

Luke 22:25 And he said to them, `The kings of the nations do exercise lordship over them, and those exercising authority upon them are called benefactors;

Luke 22:26 but ye [are] not so, but he who is greater among you--let him be as the younger; and he who is leading, as he who is ministering;

Luke 22:27 for who is greater? he who is reclining (at meat), or he who is ministering? is it not he who is reclining (at meat)? and I--I am in your midst as he who is ministering.

Luke 22:28 And ye--ye are those who have remained with me in my temptations,

Luke 22:29 and I appoint to you, as my Father did appoint to me, a kingdom,

Luke 22:30 that ye may eat and may drink at my table, in my kingdom, and may sit on thrones, judging the twelve tribes of Israel.'

Luke 22:31 And the Lord said, `Simon, Simon, lo, the Adversary did ask you for himself to sift as the wheat,

Luke 22:32 and I besought for thee, that thy faith may not fail; and thou, when thou didst turn, strengthen thy brethren.'

Luke 22:33 And he said to him, `Sir, with thee I am ready both to prison and to death to go;'

Luke 22:34 and he said, Ì say to thee, Peter, a cock shall not crow to-day, before thrice thou mayest disown knowing me.'

Luke 22:35 And he said to them, `When I sent you without bag, and scrip, and sandals, did ye lack anything?' and they said, `Nothing.'

Luke 22:36 Then said he to them, `But, now, he who is having a bag, let him take [it] up, and in like manner also a scrip; and he who is not having, let him sell his garment, and buy a sword,

Luke 22:37 for I say to you, that yet this that hath been written it behoveth to be fulfilled in me: And with lawless ones he was reckoned, for also the things concerning me have an end.'

Luke 22:38 And they said, `Sir, lo, here [are] two swords;' and he said to them, Ìt is sufficient.'

Luke 22:39. And having gone forth, he went on, according to custom, to the mount of the Olives, and his disciples also followed him,

Luke 22:40 and having come to the place, he said to them, `Pray ye not to enter into temptation.'

Luke 22:41 And he was withdrawn from them, as it were a stone's cast, and having fallen on the knees he was praying,

Luke 22:42 saying, `Father, if Thou be counselling to make this cup pass from me--;but, not my will, but Thine be done.' --

Luke 22:43 And there appeared to him a messenger from heaven strengthening him;

Luke 22:44 and having been in agony, he was more earnestly praying, and his sweat became, as it were, great drops of blood falling upon the ground.

Luke 22:45 And having risen up from the prayer, having come unto the disciples, he found them sleeping from the sorrow,

Luke 22:46 and he said to them, `Why do ye sleep? having risen, pray that ye may not enter into temptation.'

Luke 22:47. And while he is speaking, lo, a multitude, and he who is called Judas, one of the twelve, was coming before them, and he came nigh to Jesus to kiss him,

Luke 22:48 and Jesus said to him, `Judas, with a kiss the Son of Man dost thou deliver up?'

Luke 22:49 And those about him, having seen what was about to be, said to him, `Sir, shall we smite with a sword?'

Luke 22:50 And a certain one of them smote the servant of the chief priest, and took off his right ear,

Luke 22:51 and Jesus answering said, `Suffer ye thus far,' and having touched his ear, he healed him.

Luke 22:52 And Jesus said to those having come upon him--chief priests, and magistrates of the temple, and elders--Às upon a robber have ye come forth, with swords and sticks?

Luke 22:53 while daily I was with you in the temple, ye did stretch forth no hands against me; but this is your hour and the power of the darkness.'

Luke 22:54. And having taken him, they led and brought him to the house of the chief priest. And Peter was following afar off,

Luke 22:55 and they having kindled a fire in the midst of the court, and having sat down together, Peter was sitting in the midst of them,

Luke 22:56 and a certain maid having seen him sitting at the light, and having earnestly looked at him, she said, Ànd this one was with him!'

Luke 22:57 and he disowned him, saying, `Woman, I have not known him.'

Luke 22:58 And after a little, another having seen him, said, Ànd thou art of them!' and Peter said, `Man, I am not.'

Luke 22:59 And one hour, as it were, having intervened, a certain other was confidently affirming, saying, Òf a truth this one also was with him, for he is also a Galilean;'

Luke 22:60 and Peter said, `Man, I have not known what thou sayest;' and presently, while he is speaking, a cock crew.

Luke 22:61 And the Lord having turned did look on Peter, and Peter remembered the word of the Lord, how he said to him--`Before a cock shall crow, thou mayest disown me thrice;'

Luke 22:62 and Peter having gone without, wept bitterly.

Luke 22:63. And the men who were holding Jesus were mocking him, beating [him];

Luke 22:64 and having blindfolded him, they were striking him on the face, and were questioning him, saying, `Prophesy who he is who smote thee?'

Luke 22:65 and many other things, speaking evilly, they spake in regard to him.

Luke 22:66 And when it became day there was gathered together the eldership of the people, chief priests also, and scribes, and they led him up to their own sanhedrim,

Luke 22:67 saying, Ìf thou be the Christ, tell us.' And he said to them, Ìf I may tell you, ye will not believe;

Luke 22:68 and if I also question [you], ye will not answer me or send me away;

Luke 22:69 henceforth, there shall be the Son of Man sitting on the right hand of the power of God.'

Luke 22:70 And they all said, `Thou, then, art the Son of God?' and he said unto them, `Ye say [it], because I am;'

Luke 22:71 and they said, `What need yet have we of testimony? for we ourselves did hear [it] from his mouth.'

Luke 23:1. And having risen, the whole multitude of them did lead him to Pilate,

Luke 23:2 and began to accuse him, saying, `This one we found perverting the nation, and forbidding to give tribute to Caesar, saying himself to be Christ a king.'

Luke 23:3 And Pilate questioned him, saying, `Thou art the king of the Jews?' and he answering him, said, `Thou dost say [it].'

Luke 23:4 And Pilate said unto the chief priests, and the multitude, Ì find no fault in this man;'

Luke 23:5 and they were the more urgent, saying--`He doth stir up the people, teaching throughout the whole of Judea--having begun from Galilee--unto this place.'

Luke 23:6 And Pilate having heard of Galilee, questioned if the man is a Galilean,

Luke 23:7 and having known that he is from the jurisdiction of Herod, he sent him back unto Herod, he being also in Jerusalem in those days.

Luke 23:8 And Herod having seen Jesus did rejoice exceedingly, for he was wishing for a long [time] to see him, because of hearing many things about him, and he was hoping some sign to see done by him,

Luke 23:9 and was questioning him in many words, and he answered him nothing.

Luke 23:10 And the chief priests and the scribes stood vehemently accusing him,

Luke 23:11 and Herod with his soldiers having set him at nought, and having mocked, having put around him gorgeous apparel, did send him back to Pilate,

Luke 23:12 and both Pilate and Herod became friends on that day with one another, for they were before at enmity between themselves.

Luke 23:13. And Pilate having called together the chief priests, and the rulers, and the people,

Luke 23:14 said unto them, `Ye brought to me this man as perverting the people, and lo, I before you having examined, found in this man no fault in those things ye bring forward against him;

Luke 23:15 no, nor yet Herod, for I sent you back unto him, and lo, nothing worthy of death is having been done by him;

Luke 23:16 having chastised, therefore, I will release him,'

Luke 23:17 for it was necessary for him to release to them one at every feast,

Luke 23:18 and they cried out--the whole multitude--saying, Àway with this one, and release to us Barabbas,'

Luke 23:19 who had been, because of a certain sedition made in the city, and murder, cast into prison.

Luke 23:20 Pilate again then--wishing to release Jesus--called to them,

Luke 23:21 but they were calling out, saying, `Crucify, crucify him.'

Luke 23:22 And he a third time said unto them, `Why, what evil did he? no cause of death did I find in him; having chastised him, then, I will release [him].'

Luke 23:23 And they were pressing with loud voices asking him to be crucified, and their voices, and those of the chief priests, were prevailing,

Luke 23:24 and Pilate gave judgment for their request being done,

Luke 23:25 and he released him who because of sedition and murder hath been cast into the prison, whom they were asking, and Jesus he gave up to their will.

Luke 23:26. And as they led him away, having taken hold on Simon, a certain Cyrenian, coming from the field, they put on him the cross, to bear [it] behind Jesus.

Luke 23:27 And there was following him a great multitude of the people, and of women, who also were beating themselves and lamenting him,

Luke 23:28 and Jesus having turned unto them, said, `Daughters of Jerusalem, weep not for me, but for yourselves weep ye, and for your children;

Luke 23:29 for, lo, days do come, in which they shall say, Happy the barren, and wombs that did not bare, and paps that did not give suck;

Luke 23:30 then they shall begin to say to the mountains, Fall on us, and to the hills, Cover us; --

Luke 23:31 for, if in the green tree they do these things--in the dry what may happen?'

Luke 23:32. And there were also others--two evil-doers--with him, to be put to death;

Luke 23:33 and when they came to the place that is called Skull, there they crucified him and the evil-doers, one on the right hand and one on the left.

Luke 23:34 And Jesus said, `Father, forgive them, for they have not known what they do;' and parting his garments they cast a lot.

Luke 23:35 And the people were standing, looking on, and the rulers also were sneering with them, saying, Òthers he saved, let him save himself, if this be the Christ, the choice one of God.'

Luke 23:36 And mocking him also were the soldiers, coming near and offering vinegar to him,

Luke 23:37 and saying, Ìf thou be the king of the Jews, save thyself.'

Luke 23:38 And there was also a superscription written over him, in letters of Greek, and Roman, and Hebrew, `This is the King of the Jews.'

Luke 23:39 And one of the evil-doers who were hanged, was speaking evil of him, saying, Ìf thou be the Christ, save thyself and us.'

Luke 23:40 And the other answering, was rebuking him, saying, `Dost thou not even fear God, that thou art in the same judgment?

Luke 23:41 and we indeed righteously, for things worthy of what we did we receive back, but this one did nothing out of place;'

Luke 23:42 and he said to Jesus, `Remember me, lord, when thou mayest come in thy reign;'

Luke 23:43 and Jesus said to him, `Verily I say to thee, To-day with me thou shalt be in the paradise.'

Luke 23:44. And it was, as it were, the sixth hour, and darkness came over all the land till the ninth hour,

Luke 23:45 and the sun was darkened, and the vail of the sanctuary was rent in the midst,

Luke 23:46 and having cried with a loud voice, Jesus said, `Father, to Thy hands I commit my spirit;' and these things having said, he breathed forth the spirit.

Luke 23:47 And the centurion having seen what was done, did glorify God, saying, `Really this man was righteous;'

Luke 23:48 and all the multitudes who were come together to this sight, beholding the things that came to pass, smiting their breasts did turn back;

Luke 23:49 and all his acquaintances stood afar off, and women who did follow him from Galilee, beholding these things.

Luke 23:50. And lo, a man, by name Joseph, being a counsellor, a man good and righteous,

Luke 23:51 --he was not consenting to their counsel and deed--from Arimathea, a city of the Jews, who also himself was expecting the reign of God,

Luke 23:52 he, having gone near to Pilate, asked the body of Jesus,

Luke 23:53 and having taken it down, he wrapped it in fine linen, and placed it in a tomb hewn out, where no one was yet laid.

Luke 23:54 And the day was a preparation, and sabbath was approaching,

Luke 23:55 and the women also who have come with him out of Galilee having followed after, beheld the tomb, and how his body was placed,

Luke 23:56 and having turned back, they made ready spices and ointments, and on the sabbath, indeed, they rested, according to the command.

Luke 24:1. And on the first of the sabbaths, at early dawn, they came to the tomb, bearing the spices they made ready, and certain [others] with them,

Luke 24:2 and they found the stone having been rolled away from the tomb,

Luke 24:3 and having gone in, they found not the body of the Lord Jesus.

Luke 24:4 And it came to pass, while they are perplexed about this, that lo, two men stood by them in glittering apparel,

Luke 24:5 and on their having become afraid, and having inclined the face to the earth, they said to them, `Why do ye seek the living with the dead?

Luke 24:6 he is not here, but was raised; remember how he spake to you, being yet in Galilee,

Luke 24:7 saying--It behoveth the Son of Man to be delivered up to the hands of sinful men, and to be crucified, and the third day to rise again.'

Luke 24:8 And they remembered his sayings,

Luke 24:9 and having turned back from the tomb told all these things to the eleven, and to all the rest.

Luke 24:10 And it was the Magdalene Mary, and Joanna, and Mary of James, and the other women with them, who told unto the apostles these things,

Luke 24:11 and their sayings appeared before them as idle talk, and they were not believing them.

Luke 24:12 And Peter having risen, did run to the tomb, and having stooped down he seeth the linen clothes lying alone, and he went away to his own home, wondering at that which was come to pass.

Luke 24:13. And, lo, two of them were going on during that day to a village, distant sixty furlongs from Jerusalem, the name of which [is] Emmaus,

Luke 24:14 and they were conversing with one another about all these things that have happened.

Luke 24:15 And it came to pass in their conversing and reasoning together, that Jesus himself, having come nigh, was going on with them,

Luke 24:16 and their eyes were holden so as not to know him,

Luke 24:17 and he said unto them, `What [are] these words that ye exchange with one another, walking, and ye are sad?'

Luke 24:18 And the one, whose name was Cleopas, answering, said unto him, Àrt thou alone such a stranger in Jerusalem, that thou hast not known the things that came to pass in it in these days?'

Luke 24:19 And he said to them, `What things?' And they said to him, `The things about Jesus of Nazareth, who became a man--a prophet--powerful in deed and word, before God and all the people,

Luke 24:20 how also the chief priests and our rulers did deliver him up to a judgment of death, and crucified him;

Luke 24:21 and we were hoping that he it is who is about to redeem Israel, and also with all these things, this third day is passing to-day, since these things happened.

Luke 24:22 Ànd certain women of ours also astonished us, coming early to the tomb,

Luke 24:23 and not having found his body, they came, saying also to have seen an apparition of messengers, who say he is alive,

Luke 24:24 and certain of those with us went away unto the tomb, and found as even the women said, and him they saw not.'

Luke 24:25 And he said unto them, Ò inconsiderate and slow in heart, to believe on all that the prophets spake!

Luke 24:26 Was it not behoving the Christ these things to suffer, and to enter into his glory?'

Luke 24:27 and having begun from Moses, and from all the prophets, he was expounding to them in all the Writings the things about himself.

Luke 24:28 And they came nigh to the village whither they were going, and he made an appearance of going on further,

Luke 24:29 and they constrained him, saying, `Remain with us, for it is toward evening,' and the day did decline, and he went in to remain with them.

Luke 24:30 And it came to pass, in his reclining (at meat) with them, having taken the bread, he blessed, and having broken, he was giving to them,

Luke 24:31 and their eyes were opened, and they recognized him, and he became unseen by them.

Luke 24:32 And they said one to another, `Was not our heart burning within us, as he was speaking to us in the way, and as he was opening up to us the Writings?'

Luke 24:33 And they, having risen up the same hour, turned back to Jerusalem, and found gathered together the eleven, and those with them,

Luke 24:34 saying--`The Lord was raised indeed, and was seen by Simon;'

Luke 24:35 and they were telling the things in the way, and how he was made known to them in the breaking of the bread,

Luke 24:36. and as they are speaking these things, Jesus himself stood in the midst of them, and saith to them, `Peace--to you;'

Luke 24:37 and being amazed, and becoming affrighted, they were thinking themselves to see a spirit.

Luke 24:38 And he said to them, `Why are ye troubled? and wherefore do reasonings come up in your hearts?

Luke 24:39 see my hands and my feet, that I am he; handle me and see, because a spirit hath not flesh and bones, as ye see me having.'

Luke 24:40 And having said this, he shewed to them the hands and the feet,

Luke 24:41 and while they are not believing from the joy, and wondering, he said to them, `Have ye anything here to eat?'

Luke 24:42 and they gave to him part of a broiled fish, and of an honeycomb,

Luke 24:43 and having taken, he did eat before them,

Luke 24:44 and he said to them, `These [are] the words that I spake unto you, being yet with you, that it behoveth to be fulfilled all the things that are written in the Law of Moses, and the Prophets, and the Psalms, about me.'

Luke 24:45 Then opened he up their understanding to understand the Writings,

Luke 24:46 and he said to them-- `Thus it hath been written, and thus it was behoving the Christ to suffer, and to rise out of the dead the third day,

Luke 24:47 and reformation and remission of sins to be proclaimed in his name to all the nations, beginning from Jerusalem:

Luke 24:48 and ye--ye are witnesses of these things.

Luke 24:49 Ànd, lo, I do send the
promise of my Father upon you, but
ye--abide ye in the city of Jerusalem
till ye be clothed with power from
on high.'

Luke 24:50. And he led them forth
without--unto Bethany, and having
lifted up his hands he did bless
them,

Luke 24:51 and it came to pass, in
his blessing them, he was parted
from them, and was borne up to the
heaven;

Luke 24:52 and they, having bowed
before him, did turn back to Jerusalem with great joy,

Luke 24:53 and were continually in
the temple, praising and blessing
God. Amen.

John

John 1:1. In the beginning was the Word, and the Word was with God, and the Word was God;

John 1:2 this one was in the beginning with God;

John 1:3 all things through him did happen, and without him happened not even one thing that hath happened.

John 1:4 In him was life, and the life was the light of men,

John 1:5. and the light in the darkness did shine, and the darkness did not perceive it.

John 1:6 There came a man--having been sent from God--whose name [is] John,

John 1:7 this one came for testimony, that he might testify about the Light, that all might believe through him;

John 1:8 that one was not the Light, but--that he might testify about the Light.

John 1:9 He was the true Light, which doth enlighten every man, coming to the world;

John 1:10 in the world he was, and the world through him was made, and the world did not know him:

John 1:11 to his own things he came, and his own people did not receive him;

John 1:12 but as many as did receive him to them he gave authority to become sons of God--to those believing in his name,

John 1:13 who--not of blood nor of a will of flesh, nor of a will of man but--of God were begotten.

John 1:14 And the Word became flesh, and did tabernacle among us, and we beheld his glory, glory as of an only begotten of a father, full of grace and truth.

John 1:15. John doth testify concerning him, and hath cried, saying, `This was he of whom I said, He who after me is coming, hath come before me, for he was before me;'

John 1:16 and out of his fulness did we all receive, and grace over-against grace;

John 1:17 for the law through Moses was given, the grace and the truth through Jesus Christ did come;

John 1:18 God no one hath ever seen; the only begotten Son, who is on the bosom of the Father--he did declare.

John 1:19. And this is the testimony of John, when the Jews sent out of

Jerusalem priests and Levites, that they might question him, `Who art thou?'

John 1:20 and he confessed and did not deny, and confessed--`I am not the Christ.'

John 1:21 And they questioned him, `What then? Elijah art thou?' and he saith, `I am not.' --`The prophet art thou?' and he answered, `No.'

John 1:22 They said then to him, `Who art thou, that we may give an answer to those sending us? what dost thou say concerning thyself?'

John 1:23 He said, `I [am] a voice of one crying in the wilderness: Make straight the way of the Lord, as said Isaiah the prophet.'

John 1:24 And those sent were of the Pharisees,

John 1:25 and they questioned him and said to him, `Why, then, dost thou baptize, if thou art not the Christ, nor Elijah, nor the prophet?'

John 1:26 John answered them, saying, `I baptize with water, but in midst of you he hath stood whom ye have not known, this one it is who is coming after me, who hath been before me,

John 1:27 of whom I am not worthy that I may loose the cord of his sandal.'

John 1:28 These things came to pass in Bethabara, beyond the Jordan, where John was baptizing,

John 1:29. on the morrow John seeth Jesus coming unto him, and saith, `Lo, the Lamb of God, who is taking away the sin of the world;

John 1:30 this is he concerning whom I said, After me doth come a man, who hath come before me, because he was before me:

John 1:31 and I knew him not, but, that he might be manifested to Israel, because of this I came with the water baptizing.

John 1:32 And John testified, saying--`I have seen the Spirit coming down, as a dove, out of heaven, and it remained on him;

John 1:33 and I did not know him, but he who sent me to baptize with water, He said to me, On whomsoever thou mayest see the Spirit coming down, and remaining on him, this is he who is baptizing with the Holy Spirit;

John 1:34 and I have seen, and have testified, that this is the Son of God.'

John 1:35 On the morrow, again, John was standing, and two of his disciples,

John 1:36 and having looked on Jesus walking, he saith, `Lo, the Lamb of God;'

John 1:37. and the two disciples heard him speaking, and they followed Jesus.

John 1:38 And Jesus having turned, and having beheld them following, saith to them, `What seek ye?' and they said to them, `Rabbi, (which is, being interpreted, Teacher,) where remainest thou?'

John 1:39 He saith to them, `Come and see;' they came, and saw where he doth remain, and with him they remained that day and the hour was about the tenth.

John 1:40 Andrew, the brother of Simon Peter, was one of the two who heard from John, and followed him;

John 1:41 this one doth first find his own brother Simon, and saith to him, `We have found the Messiah,' (which is, being interpreted, The Anointed,)

John 1:42 and he brought him unto Jesus: and having looked upon him, Jesus saith, `Thou art Simon, the son of Jonas, thou shalt be called Cephas,' (which is interpreted, A rock.)

John 1:43. On the morrow, he willed to go forth to Galilee, and he findeth Philip, and saith to him, `Be following me.'

John 1:44 And Philip was from Bethsaida, of the city of Andrew and Peter;

John 1:45 Philip findeth Nathanael, and saith to him, `Him of whom Moses wrote in the Law, and the prophets, we have found, Jesus the son of Joseph, who [is] from Nazareth;'

John 1:46 and Nathanael said to him, `Out of Nazareth is any good thing able to be?' Philip said to him, `Come and see.'

John 1:47 Jesus saw Nathanael coming unto him, and he saith concerning him, `Lo, truly an Israelite, in whom guile is not;'

John 1:48 Nathanael saith to him, `Whence me dost thou know?' Jesus answered and said to him, `Before Philip's calling thee--thou being under the fig-tree--I saw thee.'

John 1:49 Nathanael answered and saith to him, `Rabbi, thou art the Son of God, thou art the king of Israel.'

John 1:50 Jesus answered and said to him, `Because I said to thee, I saw thee under the fig-tree, thou dost believe; greater things than these thou shalt see;'

John 1:51 and he saith to him, `Verily, verily, I say to you, henceforth ye shall see the heaven opened, and the messengers of God going up and coming down upon the Son of Man.'

John 2:1. And the third day a marriage happened in Cana of Galilee, and the mother of Jesus was there,

John 2:2 and also Jesus was called, and his disciples, to the marriage;

John 2:3 and wine having failed, the mother of Jesus saith unto him, `Wine they have not;'

John 2:4 Jesus saith to her, `What-- to me and to thee, woman? not yet is mine hour come.'

John 2:5 His mother saith to the ministrants, `Whatever he may say to you--do.'

John 2:6 And there were there six water-jugs of stone, placed according to the purifying of the Jews, holding each two or three measures.

John 2:7 Jesus saith to them, `Fill the water-jugs with water;' and they filled them--unto the brim;

John 2:8 and he saith to them, `Draw out, now, and bear to the director of the apartment;' and they bare.

John 2:9 And as the director of the apartment tasted the water become wine, and knew not whence it is, (but the ministrants knew, who have drawn the water,) the director of the feast doth call the bridegroom,

John 2:10 and saith to him, Èvery man, at first, the good wine doth set forth; and when they may have drunk freely, then the inferior; thou didst keep the good wine till now.'

John 2:11 This beginning of the signs did Jesus in Cana of Galilee, and manifested his glory, and his disciples believed in him;

John 2:12. after this he went down to Capernaum, he, and his mother, and his brethren, and his disciples; and there they remained not many days.

John 2:13 And the passover of the Jews was nigh, and Jesus went up to Jerusalem,

John 2:14 and he found in the temple those selling oxen, and sheep, and doves, and the money-changers sitting,

John 2:15 and having made a whip of small cords, he put all forth out of the temple, also the sheep, and the oxen; and of the money-changers he poured out the coins, and the tables he overthrew,

John 2:16 and to those selling the doves he said, `Take these things hence; make not the house of my Father a house of merchandise.'

John 2:17 And his disciples remembered that it is written, `The zeal of Thy house did eat me up;'

John 2:18 the Jews then answered and said to him, `What sign dost thou shew to us--that thou dost these things?'

John 2:19 Jesus answered and said to them, `Destroy this sanctuary, and in three days I will raise it up.'

John 2:20 The Jews, therefore, said, `Forty and six years was this sanctuary building, and wilt thou in three days raise it up?'

John 2:21 but he spake concerning the sanctuary of his body;

John 2:22 when, then, he was raised out of the dead, his disciples remembered that he said this to them, and they believed the Writing, and the word that Jesus said.

John 2:23. And as he was in Jerusalem, in the passover, in the feast, many believed in his name, beholding his signs that he was doing;

John 2:24 and Jesus himself was not trusting himself to them, because of his knowing all [men],

John 2:25 and because he had no need that any should testify concerning man, for he himself was knowing what was in man.

John 3:1. And there was a man of the Pharisees, Nicodemus his name, a ruler of the Jews,

John 3:2 this one came unto him by night, and said to him, `Rabbi, we have known that from God thou hast come--a teacher, for no one these signs is able to do that thou dost, if God may not be with him.'

John 3:3 Jesus answered and said to him, `Verily, verily, I say to thee, If any one may not be born from above, he is not able to see the reign of God;'

John 3:4 Nicodemus saith unto him, `How is a man able to be born, being old? is he able into the womb of his mother a second time to enter, and to be born?'

John 3:5 Jesus answered, `Verily, verily, I say to thee, If any one may not be born of water, and the Spirit, he is not able to enter into the reign of God;

John 3:6 that which hath been born of the flesh is flesh, and that which hath been born of the Spirit is spirit.

John 3:7 `Thou mayest not wonder that I said to thee, It behoveth you to be born from above;

John 3:8 the Spirit where he willeth doth blow, and his voice thou dost hear, but thou hast not known whence he cometh, and whither he goeth; thus is every one who hath been born of the Spirit.'

John 3:9 Nicodemus answered and said to him, `How are these things able to happen?'

John 3:10 Jesus answered and said to him, `Thou art the teacher of Israel--and these things thou dost not know!

John 3:11 `Verily, verily, I say to thee--What we have known we speak, and what we have seen we testify, and our testimony ye do not receive;

John 3:12 if the earthly things I said to you, and ye do not believe, how, if

I shall say to you the heavenly things, will ye believe?

John 3:13 and no one hath gone up to the heaven, except he who out of the heaven came down--the Son of Man who is in the heaven.

John 3:14 Ànd as Moses did lift up the serpent in the wilderness, so it behoveth the Son of Man to be lifted up,

John 3:15 that every one who is believing in him may not perish, but may have life age-during,

John 3:16 for God did so love the world, that His Son--the only begotten--He gave, that every one who is believing in him may not perish, but may have life age-during.

John 3:17 For God did not send His Son to the world that he may judge the world, but that the world may be saved through him;

John 3:18 he who is believing in him is not judged, but he who is not believing hath been judged already, because he hath not believed in the name of the only begotten Son of God.

John 3:19 Ànd this is the judgment, that the light hath come to the world, and men did love the darkness rather than the light, for their works were evil;

John 3:20 for every one who is doing wicked things hateth the light, and doth not come unto the light, that his works may not be detected;

John 3:21 but he who is doing the truth doth come to the light, that his works may be manifested, that in God they are having been wrought.'

John 3:22. After these things came Jesus and his disciples to the land of Judea, and there he did tarry with them, and was baptizing;

John 3:23 and John was also baptizing in Aenon, nigh to Salem, because there were many waters there, and they were coming and were being baptized--

John 3:24 for John was not yet cast into the prison--

John 3:25 there arose then a question from the disciples of John with [some] Jews about purifying,

John 3:26 and they came unto John, and said to him, `Rabbi, he who was with thee beyond the Jordan, to whom thou didst testify, lo, this one is baptizing, and all are coming unto him.'

John 3:27 John answered and said, À man is not able to receive anything, if it may not have been given him from the heaven;

John 3:28 ye yourselves do testify to me that I said, I am not the Christ, but, that I am having been sent before him;

John 3:29 he who is having the bride is bridegroom, and the friend of the bridegroom, who is standing and hearing him, with joy doth rejoice because of the voice of the bridegroom; this, then, my joy hath been fulfilled.

John 3:30 `Him it behoveth to increase, and me to become less;

John 3:31 he who from above is coming is above all; he who is from the earth, from the earth he is, and from the earth he speaketh; he who from the heaven is coming is above all.

John 3:32 Ànd what he hath seen and heard this he doth testify, and his testimony none receiveth;

John 3:33 he who is receiving his testimony did seal that God is true;

John 3:34 for he whom God sent, the sayings of God he speaketh; for not by measure doth God give the Spirit;

John 3:35 the Father doth love the Son, and all things hath given into his hand;

John 3:36 he who is believing in the Son, hath life age-during; and he who is not believing the Son, shall not see life, but the wrath of God doth remain upon him.'

John 4:1. When therefore the Lord knew that the Pharisees heard that Jesus more disciples doth make and baptize than John,

John 4:2 (though indeed Jesus himself was not baptizing, but his disciples,)

John 4:3 he left Judea and went away again to Galilee,

John 4:4. and it was behoving him to go through Samaria.

John 4:5 He cometh, therefore, to a city of Samaria, called Sychar, near to the place that Jacob gave to Joseph his son;

John 4:6 and there was there a well of Jacob. Jesus therefore having been weary from the journeying, was sitting thus on the well; it was as it were the sixth hour;

John 4:7 there cometh a woman out of Samaria to draw water. Jesus saith to her, `Give me to drink;'

John 4:8 for his disciples were gone away to the city, that they may buy victuals;

John 4:9 the Samaritan woman therefore saith to him, `How dost thou, being a Jew, ask drink from me, being a Samaritan woman?' for Jews have no dealing with Samaritans.

John 4:10 Jesus answered and said to her, Ìf thou hadst known the gift of God, and who it is who is saying to thee, Give me to drink, thou wouldest have asked him, and he would have given thee living water.'

John 4:11 The woman saith to him, `Sir, thou hast not even a vessel to draw with, and the well is deep; whence, then, hast thou the living water?

John 4:12 Art thou greater than our father Jacob, who did give us the well, and himself out of it did drink, and his sons, and his cattle?'

John 4:13 Jesus answered and said to her, `Every one who is drinking of this water shall thirst again;

John 4:14 but whoever may drink of the water that I will give him, may not thirst--to the age; and the water that I will give him shall become in him a well of water, springing up to life age-during.'

John 4:15 The woman saith unto him, `Sir, give me this water, that I may not thirst, nor come hither to draw.'

John 4:16 Jesus saith to her, `Go, call thy husband, and come hither;'

John 4:17 the woman answered and said, `I have not a husband.' Jesus saith to her, `Well didst thou say--A husband I have not;

John 4:18 for five husbands thou hast had, and, now, he whom thou hast is not thy husband; this hast thou said truly.'

John 4:19 The woman saith to him, `Sir, I perceive that thou art a prophet;

John 4:20 our fathers in this mountain did worship, and ye--ye say that in Jerusalem is the place where it behoveth to worship.'

John 4:21 Jesus saith to her, `Woman, believe me, that there doth come an hour, when neither in this mountain, nor in Jerusalem, shall ye worship the Father;

John 4:22 ye worship what ye have not known; we worship what we have known, because the salvation is of the Jews;

John 4:23 but, there cometh an hour, and it now is, when the true worshippers will worship the Father in spirit and truth, for the Father also doth seek such to worship him;

John 4:24 God [is] a Spirit, and those worshipping Him, in spirit and truth it doth behove to worship.'

John 4:25 The woman saith to him, `I have known that Messiah doth come, who is called Christ, when that one may come, he will tell us all things;'

John 4:26 Jesus saith to her, `I am [he], who am speaking to thee.'

John 4:27. And upon this came his disciples, and were wondering that with a woman he was speaking, no one, however, said, `What seekest thou?' or `Why speakest thou with her?'

John 4:28 The woman then left her water-jug, and went away to the city, and saith to the men,

John 4:29 `Come, see a man, who told me all things--as many as I did; is this the Christ?'

John 4:30 They went forth therefore out of the city, and were coming unto him.

John 4:31 And in the meanwhile his disciples were asking him, saying, `Rabbi, eat;'

John 4:32 and he said to them, `I have food to eat that ye have not known.'

John 4:33 The disciples then said one to another, `Did any one bring him anything to eat?'

John 4:34 Jesus saith to them, `My food is, that I may do the will of Him who sent me, and may finish His work;

John 4:35 do not say that it is yet four months, and the harvest cometh; lo, I say to you, Lift up your eyes, and see the fields, that they are white unto harvest already.

John 4:36 And he who is reaping doth receive a reward, and doth gather fruit to life age-during, that both he who is sowing and he who is reaping may rejoice together;

John 4:37 for in this the saying is the true one, that one is the sower and another the reaper.

John 4:38 I sent you to reap that on which ye have not laboured; others laboured, and ye into their labour have entered.

John 4:39 And from that city many believed in him, of the Samaritans, because of the word of the woman testifying, --`He told me all things--as many as I did.'

John 4:40 When, then, the Samaritans came unto him, they were asking him to remain with them, and he remained there two days;

John 4:41 and many more did believe because of his word,

John 4:42 and said to the woman--`No more because of thy speaking do we believe; for we ourselves have heard and known that this is truly the Saviour of the world--the Christ.'

John 4:43. And after the two days he went forth thence, and went away to Galilee,

John 4:44 for Jesus himself testified that a prophet in his own country shall not have honour;

John 4:45 when then, he came to Galilee, the Galileans received him, having seen all things that he did in Jerusalem in the feast--for they also went to the feast.

John 4:46 Jesus came, therefore, again to Cana of Galilee, where he made the water wine, and there was a certain courtier, whose son was ailing in Capernaum,

John 4:47 he, having heard that Jesus is come out of Judea to Galilee, went away unto him, and was asking him that he may come down and may heal his son, for he was about to die.

John 4:48 Jesus then said unto him, `If signs and wonders ye may not see, ye will not believe.'

John 4:49 The courtier saith unto him, `Sir, come down before my child die;'

John 4:50 Jesus saith to him, `Be going on; thy son doth live.' And the man believed the word that Jesus said to him, and was going on,

John 4:51 and he now going down, his servants met him, and told, saying--`Thy child doth live;'

John 4:52 he inquired then of them the hour in which he became better, and they said to him--`Yesterday at the seventh hour the fever left him;'

John 4:53 then the father knew that [it was] in that hour in which Jesus said to him--`Thy son doth live,' and he himself believed, and his whole house;

John 4:54 this again a second sign did Jesus, having come out of Judea to Galilee.

John 5:1. After these things there was a feast of the Jews, and Jesus went up to Jerusalem,

John 5:2 and there is in Jerusalem by the sheep -[gate] a pool that is called in Hebrew Bethesda, having five porches,

John 5:3 in these were lying a great multitude of the ailing, blind, lame, withered, waiting for the moving of the water,

John 5:4 for a messenger at a set time was going down in the pool, and was troubling the water, the first then having gone in after the troubling of the water, became whole of whatever sickness he was held.

John 5:5 and there was a certain man there being in ailment thirty and eight years,

John 5:6 him Jesus having seen lying, and having known that he is already a long time, he saith to him, `Dost thou wish to become whole?'

John 5:7 The ailing man answered him, `Sir, I have no man, that, when the water may be troubled, he may put me into the pool, and while I am coming, another doth go down before me.'

John 5:8 Jesus saith to him, `Rise, take up thy couch, and be walking;'

John 5:9 and immediately the man became whole, and he took up his couch, and was walking, and it was a sabbath on that day,

John 5:10 the Jews then said to him that hath been healed, `It is a sabbath; it is not lawful to thee to take up the couch.'

John 5:11 He answered them, `He who made me whole--that one said to me, Take up thy couch, and be walking;'

John 5:12 they questioned him, then, `Who is the man who is saying to thee, Take up thy couch and be walking?'

John 5:13 But he that was healed had not known who he is, for Jesus did move away, a multitude being in the place.

John 5:14 After these things, Jesus findeth him in the temple, and said to him, `Lo, thou hast become whole; sin no more, lest something worse may happen to thee.'

John 5:15 The man went away, and told the Jews that it is Jesus who made him whole,

John 5:16 and because of this were the Jews persecuting Jesus, and seeking to kill him, because these things he was doing on a sabbath.

John 5:17. And Jesus answered them, `My Father till now doth work, and I work;'

John 5:18 because of this, then, were the Jews seeking the more to kill him, because not only was he breaking the sabbath, but he also called God his own Father, making himself equal to God.

John 5:19 Jesus therefore responded and said to them, `Verily, verily, I say to you, The Son is not able to do anything of himself, if he may not see the Father doing anything; for whatever things He may do, these also the Son in like manner doth;

John 5:20 for the Father doth love the Son, and doth shew to him all things that He himself doth; and greater works than these He will shew him, that ye may wonder.

John 5:21 `For, as the Father doth raise the dead, and doth make alive, so also the Son doth make alive whom he willeth;

John 5:22 for neither doth the Father judge any one, but all the judgment He hath given to the Son,

John 5:23 that all may honour the Son according as they honour the Father; he who is not honouring the Son, doth not honour the Father who sent him.

John 5:24 `Verily, verily, I say to you--He who is hearing my word, and is believing Him who sent me, hath life age-during, and to judgment he doth not come, but hath passed out of the death to the life.

John 5:25 `Verily, verily, I say to you--There cometh an hour, and it now is, when the dead shall hear the voice of the Son of God, and those having heard shall live;

John 5:26 for, as the Father hath life in himself, so He gave also to the Son to have life in himself,

John 5:27 and authority He gave him also to do judgment, because he is Son of Man.

John 5:28 `Wonder not at this, because there doth come an hour in which all those in the tombs shall hear his voice,

John 5:29 and they shall come forth; those who did the good things to a rising again of life, and those who practised the evil things to a rising again of judgment.

John 5:30 Ì am not able of myself to do anything; according as I hear I judge, and my judgment is righteous, because I seek not my own will, but the will of the Father who sent me.

John 5:31. Ìf I testify concerning myself, my testimony is not true;

John 5:32 another there is who is testifying concerning me, and I have known that the testimony that he doth testify concerning me is true;

John 5:33 ye have sent unto John, and he hath testified to the truth.

John 5:34 `But I do not receive testimony from man, but these things I say that ye may be saved;

John 5:35 he was the burning and shining lamp, and ye did will to be glad, for an hour, in his light.

John 5:36 `But I have the testimony greater than John's, for the works that the Father gave me, that I might finish them, the works themselves that I do, they testify concerning me, that the Father hath sent me.

John 5:37 Ànd the Father who sent me Himself hath testified concerning me; ye have neither heard His voice at any time, nor His appearance have ye seen;

John 5:38 and His word ye have not remaining in you, because whom He sent, him ye do not believe.

John 5:39 `Ye search the Writings, because ye think in them to have life age-during, and these are they that are testifying concerning me;

John 5:40 and ye do not will to come unto me, that ye may have life;

John 5:41 glory from man I do not receive,

John 5:42 but I have known you, that the love of God ye have not in yourselves.

John 5:43 Ì have come in the name of my Father, and ye do not receive me; if another may come in his own name, him ye will receive;

John 5:44 how are ye able--ye--to believe, glory from one another receiving, and the glory that [is] from God alone ye seek not?

John 5:45 `Do not think that I will accuse you unto the Father; there is who is accusing you, Moses--in whom ye have hoped;

John 5:46 for if ye were believing Moses, ye would have been believing me, for he wrote concerning me;

John 5:47 but if his writings ye believe not, how shall ye believe my sayings?'

John 6:1. After these things Jesus went away beyond the sea of Galilee (of Tiberias),

John 6:2 and there was following him a great multitude, because they were seeing his signs that he was doing on the ailing;

John 6:3 and Jesus went up to the mount, and he was there sitting with his disciples,

John 6:4 and the passover was nigh, the feast of the Jews.

John 6:5 Jesus then having lifted up [his] eyes and having seen that a great multitude doth come to him, saith unto Philip, `Whence shall we buy loaves, that these may eat?' --

John 6:6 and this he said, trying him, for he himself had known what he was about to do.

John 6:7 Philip answered him, `Two hundred denaries' worth of loaves are not sufficient to them, that each of them may receive some little;'

John 6:8 one of his disciples--Andrew, the brother of Simon Peter--saith to him,

John 6:9 `There is one little lad here who hath five barley loaves, and two fishes, but these--what are they to so many?'

John 6:10 And Jesus said, `Make the men to sit down;' and there was much grass in the place, the men then sat down, in number, as it were, five thousand,

John 6:11 and Jesus took the loaves, and having given thanks he distributed to the disciples, and the disciples to those reclining, in like manner, also of the little fishes as much as they wished.

John 6:12 And when they were filled, he saith to his disciples, `Gather together the broken pieces that are over, that nothing may be lost;'

John 6:13 they gathered together, therefore, and filled twelve hand-baskets with broken pieces, from the five barley loaves that were over to those having eaten.

John 6:14 The men, then, having seen the sign that Jesus did, said--`This is truly the Prophet, who is coming to the world;'

John 6:15. Jesus, therefore, having known that they are about to come, and to take him by force that they may make him king, retired again to the mountain himself alone.

John 6:16 And when evening came, his disciples went down to the sea,

John 6:17 and having entered into the boat, they were going over the sea to Capernaum, and darkness had already come, and Jesus had not come unto them,

John 6:18 the sea also--a great wind blowing--was being raised,

John 6:19 having pushed onwards, therefore, about twenty-five or thirty furlongs, they behold Jesus walking on the sea, and coming nigh to the boat, and they were afraid;

John 6:20 and he saith to them, I am [he], be not afraid;'

John 6:21 they were willing then to receive him into the boat, and immediately the boat came unto the land to which they were going.

John 6:22. On the morrow, the multitude that was standing on the other side of the sea, having seen that there was no other little boat there except one--that into which his disciples entered--and that Jesus went not in with his disciples into the littleboat, but his disciples went away alone,

John 6:23 (and other little boats came from Tiberias, nigh the place where they did eat the bread, the Lord having given thanks),

John 6:24 when therefore the multitude saw that Jesus is not there, nor his disciples, they also themselves did enter into the boats, and came to Capernaum seeking Jesus;

John 6:25 and having found him on the other side of the sea, they said to him, 'Rabbi, when hast thou come hither?'

John 6:26 Jesus answered them and said, 'Verily, verily, I say to you, Ye seek me, not because ye saw signs, but because ye did eat of the loaves, and were satisfied;

John 6:27 work not for the food that is perishing, but for the food that is remaining to life age-during, which the Son of Man will give to you, for him did the Father seal--[even] God.'

John 6:28. They said therefore unto him, 'What may we do that we may work the works of God?'

John 6:29 Jesus answered and said to them, 'This is the work of God, that ye may believe in him whom He did send.'

John 6:30 They said therefore to him, 'What sign, then, dost thou, that we may see and may believe thee? what dost thou work?

John 6:31 our fathers the manna did eat in the wilderness, according as it is having been written, Bread out of the heaven He gave them to eat.'

John 6:32 Jesus, therefore, said to them, 'Verily, verily, I say to you, Moses did not give you the bread out of the heaven; but my Father doth give you the true bread out of the heaven;

John 6:33 for the bread of God is that which is coming down out of the heaven, and giving life to the world.'

John 6:34 They said, therefore, unto him, `Sir, always give us this bread.'

John 6:35 And Jesus said to them, Ì am the bread of the life; he who is coming unto me may not hunger, and he who is believing in me may not thirst--at any time;

John 6:36 but I said to you, that ye also have seen me, and ye believe not;

John 6:37 all that the Father doth give to me will come unto me; and him who is coming unto me, I may in no wise cast without,

John 6:38 because I have come down out of the heaven, not that I may do my will, but the will of Him who sent me.

John 6:39 Ànd this is the will of the Father who sent me, that all that He hath given to me I may not lose of it, but may raise it up in the last day;

John 6:40 and this is the will of Him who sent me, that every one who is beholding the Son, and is believing in him, may have life age-during, and I will raise him up in the last day.'

John 6:41 The Jews, therefore, were murmuring at him, because he said, Ì

am the bread that came down out of the heaven;'

John 6:42 and they said, Ìs not this Jesus, the son of Joseph, whose father and mother we have known? how then saith this one--Out of the heaven I have come down?'

John 6:43 Jesus answered, therefore, and said to them, `Murmur not one with another;

John 6:44 no one is able to come unto me, if the Father who sent me may not draw him, and I will raise him up in the last day;

John 6:45 it is having been written in the prophets, And they shall be all taught of God; every one therefore who heard from the Father, and learned, cometh to me;

John 6:46 not that any one hath seen the Father, except he who is from God, he hath seen the Father.

John 6:47 `Verily, verily, I say to you, He who is believing in me, hath life age-during;

John 6:48 I am the bread of the life;

John 6:49 your fathers did eat the manna in the wilderness, and they died;

John 6:50 this is the bread that out of the heaven is coming down, that any one may eat of it, and not die.

John 6:51 Ì am the living bread that came down out of the heaven; if any one may eat of this bread he shall live--to the age; and the bread also that I will give is my flesh, that I will give for the life of the world.'

John 6:52 The Jews, therefore, were striving with one another, saying, `How is this one able to give us [his] flesh to eat?'

John 6:53 Jesus, therefore, said to them, `Verily, verily, I say to you, If ye may not eat the flesh of the Son of Man, and may not drink his blood, ye have no life in yourselves;

John 6:54 he who is eating my flesh, and is drinking my blood, hath life age-during, and I will raise him up in the last day;

John 6:55 for my flesh truly is food, and my blood truly is drink;

John 6:56 he who is eating my flesh, and is drinking my blood, doth remain in me, and I in him.

John 6:57 Àccording as the living Father sent me, and I live because of the Father, he also who is eating me, even that one shall live because of me;

John 6:58 this is the bread that came down out of the heaven; not as your fathers did eat the manna, and died; he who is eating this bread shall live--to the age.'

John 6:59 These things he said in a synagogue, teaching in Capernaum;

John 6:60. many, therefore, of his disciples having heard, said, `This word is hard; who is able to hear it?'

John 6:61 And Jesus having known in himself that his disciples are murmuring about this, said to them, `Doth this stumble you?

John 6:62 if then ye may behold the Son of Man going up where he was before?

John 6:63 the spirit it is that is giving life; the flesh doth not profit anything; the sayings that I speak to you are spirit, and they are life;

John 6:64 but there are certain of you who do not believe;' for Jesus had known from the beginning who they are who are not believing, and who is he who will deliver him up,

John 6:65 and he said, `Because of this I have said to you--No one is able to come unto me, if it may not have been given him from my Father.'

John 6:66 From this [time] many of his disciples went away backward, and were no more walking with him,

John 6:67 Jesus, therefore, said to the twelve, `Do ye also wish to go away?'

John 6:68 Simon Peter, therefore, answered him, `Sir, unto whom shall we go? thou hast sayings of life age-during;

John 6:69 and we have believed, and we have known, that thou art the Christ, the Son of the living God.'

John 6:70 Jesus answered them, `Did not I choose you--the twelve? and of you--one is a devil.

John 6:71 And he spake of Judas, Simon's [son], Iscariot, for he was about to deliver him up, being one of the twelve.

John 7:1. And Jesus was walking after these things in Galilee, for he did not wish to walk in Judea, because the Jews were seeking to kill him,

John 7:2 and the feast of the Jews was nigh--that of tabernacles--

John 7:3 his brethren, therefore, said unto him, `Remove hence, and go away to Judea, that thy disciples also may behold thy works that thou dost;

John 7:4 for no one in secret doth anything, and himself seeketh to be in public; if thou dost these things--manifest thyself to the world;'

John 7:5 for not even were his brethren believing in him.

John 7:6 Jesus, therefore, saith to them, `My time is not yet present, but your time is always ready;

John 7:7 the world is not able to hate you, but me it doth hate, because I testify concerning it that its works are evil.

John 7:8 Ye--go ye up to this feast; I do not yet go up to this feast, because my time hath not yet been fulfilled;'

John 7:9 and saying these things to them, he remained in Galilee.

John 7:10 And when his brethren went up, then also he himself went up to the feast, not manifestly, but as in secret;

John 7:11 the Jews, therefore, were seeking him, in the feast, and said, `Where is that one?'

John 7:12 and there was much murmuring about him among the multitudes, some indeed said--`He is good;' and others said, `No, but he leadeth astray the multitude;'

John 7:13 no one, however, was speaking freely about him, through fear of the Jews.

John 7:14. And it being now the middle of the feast, Jesus went up to the temple, and he was teaching,

John 7:15 and the Jews were wondering, saying, `How hath this one known letters--not having learned?'

John 7:16 Jesus answered them and said, `My teaching is not mine, but His who sent me;

John 7:17 if any one may will to do His will, he shall know concerning the teaching, whether it is of God, or--I do speak from myself.

John 7:18 `He who is speaking from himself his own glory doth seek, but he who is seeking the glory of him who sent him, this one is true, and unrighteousness is not in him;

John 7:19 hath not Moses given you the law? and none of you doth the law; why me do ye seek to kill?'

John 7:20 The multitude answered and said, `Thou hast a demon, who doth seek to kill thee?'

John 7:21 Jesus answered and said to them, Òne work I did, and ye all wonder,

John 7:22 because of this, Moses hath given you the circumcision--not that it is of Moses, but of the fathers--and on a sabbath ye circumcise a man;

John 7:23 if a man doth receive circumcision on a sabbath that the law of Moses may not be broken, are ye wroth with me that I made a man all whole on a sabbath?

John 7:24 judge not according to appearance, but the righteous judgment judge.'

John 7:25 Certain, therefore, of the Jerusalemites said, Ìs not this he whom they are seeking to kill?

John 7:26 and, lo, he doth speak freely, and they say nothing to him; did the rulers at all know truly that this is truly the Christ?

John 7:27 but this one--we have known whence he is; and the Christ, when he doth come, no one doth know whence he is.'

John 7:28 Jesus cried, therefore, in the temple, teaching and saying, `Ye have both known me, and ye have known whence I am; and I have not come of myself, but He who sent me is true, whom ye have not known;

John 7:29 and I have known Him, because I am from Him, and He did send me.'

John 7:30 They were seeking, therefore, to seize him, and no one laid the hand on him, because his hour had not yet come,

John 7:31 and many out of the multitude did believe in him, and said--`The Christ--when he may come--will he do more signs than these that this one did?'

John 7:32 The Pharisees heard the multitude murmuring these things concerning him, and the Pharisees and the chief priests sent officers that they may take him;

John 7:33 Jesus, therefore, said to them, `Yet a little time I am with you, and I go away unto Him who sent me;

John 7:34 ye will seek me, and ye shall not find; and where I am, ye are not able to come.'

John 7:35 The Jews, therefore, said among themselves, `Whither is this one about to go that we shall not find him? --to the dispersion of the Greeks is he about to go? and to teach the Greeks;

John 7:36 what is this word that he said, Ye will seek me, and ye shall not find? and, Where I am, ye are not able to come?'

John 7:37. And in the last, the great day of the feast, Jesus stood and cried, saying, Ìf any one doth thirst, let him come unto me and drink;

John 7:38 he who is believing in me, according as the Writing said, Rivers out of his belly shall flow of living water;'

John 7:39 and this he said of the Spirit, which those believing in him were about to receive; for not yet was the Holy Spirit, because Jesus was not yet glorified.

John 7:40 Many, therefore out of the multitude, having heard the word, said, `This is truly the Prophet;'

John 7:41 others said, `This is the Christ;' and others said, `Why, out of Galilee doth the Christ come?

John 7:42 Did not the Writing say, that out of the seed of David, and from Bethlehem--the village where David was--the Christ doth come?'

John 7:43 A division, therefore, arose among the multitude because of him.

John 7:44 And certain of them were willing to seize him, but no one laid hands on him;

John 7:45. the officers came, therefore, unto the chief priests and Pharisees, and they said to them, `Wherefore did ye not bring him?'

John 7:46 The officers answered, `Never so spake man--as this man.'

John 7:47 The Pharisees, therefore, answered them, `Have ye also been led astray?

John 7:48 did any one out of the rulers believe in him? or out of the Pharisees?

John 7:49 but this multitude, that is not knowing the law, is accursed.'

John 7:50 Nicodemus saith unto them--he who came by night unto him--being one of them,

John 7:51 `Doth our law judge the man, if it may not hear from him first, and know what he doth?'

John 7:52 They answered and said to him, Àrt thou also out of Galilee? search and see, that a prophet out of Galilee hath not risen;'

John 7:53 and each one went on to his house, but Jesus went on to the mount of the Olives.

John 8:1. And at dawn he came again to the temple,

John 8:2 and all the people were coming unto him, and having sat down, he was teaching them;

John 8:3 and the scribes and the Pharisees bring unto him a woman having been taken in adultery, and having set her in the midst,

John 8:4 they say to him, `Teacher, this woman was taken in the very crime--committing adultery,

John 8:5 and in the law, Moses did command us that such be stoned; thou, therefore, what dost thou say?'

John 8:6 and this they said, trying him, that they might have to accuse him. And Jesus, having stooped down, with the finger he was writing on the ground,

John 8:7 and when they continued asking him, having bent himself back, he said unto them, `The sinless of you--let him first cast the stone at her;'

John 8:8 and again having stooped down, he was writing on the ground,

John 8:9 and they having heard, and by the conscience being convicted, were going forth one by one, having begun from the elders--unto the last; and Jesus was left alone, and the woman standing in the midst.

John 8:10 And Jesus having bent himself back, and having seen no one but the woman, said to her, `Woman, where are those--thine ac-cusers? did no one pass sentence upon thee?'

John 8:11 and she said, `No one, Sir;' and Jesus said to her, `Neither do I pass sentence on thee; be going on, and no more sin.'

John 8:12. Again, therefore, Jesus spake to them, saying, Ì am the light of the world; he who is following me shall not walk in the darkness, but he shall have the light of the life.'

John 8:13 The Pharisees, therefore, said to him, `Thou of thyself dost testify, thy testimony is not true;'

John 8:14 Jesus answered and said to them, Ànd if I testify of myself-- my testimony is true, because I have known whence I came, and whither I go, and ye--ye have not known whence I come, or whither I go.

John 8:15 `Ye according to the flesh do judge; I do not judge any one,

John 8:16 and even if I do judge my judgment is true, because I am not alone, but I and the Father who sent me;

John 8:17 and also in your law it hath been written, that the testimony of two men are true;

John 8:18 I am [one] who is testify-ing of myself, and the Father who sent me doth testify of me.'

John 8:19 They said, therefore, to him, `Where is thy father?' Jesus an-swered, `Ye have neither known me nor my Father: if me ye had known, my Father also ye had known.'

John 8:20 These sayings spake Jesus in the treasury, teaching in the temple, and no one seized him, because his hour had not yet come;

John 8:21. therefore said Jesus again to them, Ì go away, and ye will seek me, and in your sin ye shall die; whither I go away, ye are not able to come.'

John 8:22 The Jews, therefore, said, `Will he kill himself, because he saith, Whither I go away, ye are not able to come?'

John 8:23 and he said to them, `Ye are from beneath, I am from above; ye are of this world, I am not of this world;

John 8:24 I said, therefore, to you, that ye shall die in your sins, for if ye may not believe that I am [he], ye shall die in your sins.'

John 8:25 They said, therefore, to him, `Thou--who art thou?' and Jesus said to them, Èven what I did speak of to you at the beginning;

John 8:26 many things I have to speak concerning you and to judge, but He who sent me is true, and I-- what things I heard from Him--these I say to the world.'

John 8:27 They knew not that of the Father he spake to them;

John 8:28 Jesus, therefore, said to them, `When ye may lift up the Son of Man then ye will know that I am [he]; and of myself I do nothing, but according as my Father did teach me, these things I speak;

John 8:29 and He who sent me is with me; the Father did not leave me alone, because I, the things pleasing to Him, do always.'

John 8:30 As he is speaking these things, many believed in him;

John 8:31. Jesus, therefore, said unto the Jews who believed in him, Ìf ye may remain in my word, truly my disciples ye are, and ye shall know the truth,

John 8:32 and the truth shall make you free.'

John 8:33 They answered him, `Seed of Abraham we are; and to no one have we been servants at any time; how dost thou say--Ye shall become free?'

John 8:34 Jesus answered them, `Verily, verily, I say to you--Every one who is committing sin, is a servant of the sin,

John 8:35 and the servant doth not remain in the house--to the age, the son doth remain--to the age;

John 8:36 if then the son may make you free, in reality ye shall be free.

John 8:37 Ì have known that ye are seed of Abraham, but ye seek to kill me, because my word hath no place in you;

John 8:38. I--that which I have seen with my Father do speak, and ye, therefore, that which ye have seen with your father--ye do.'

John 8:39 They answered and said to him, Òur father is Abraham;' Jesus saith to them, Ìf children of Abraham ye were, the works of Abraham ye were doing;

John 8:40 and now, ye seek to kill me--a man who hath spoken to you the truth I heard from God; this Abraham did not;

John 8:41 ye do the works of your father.' They said, therefore, to him, `We of whoredom have not been born; one Father we have--God;'

John 8:42 Jesus then said to them, Ìf God were your father, ye were loving me, for I came forth from God, and am come; for neither have I come of myself, but He sent me;

John 8:43 wherefore do ye not know my speech? because ye are not able to hear my word.

John 8:44 `Ye are of a father--the devil, and the desires of your father ye will to do; he was a man-slayer from the beginning, and in the truth he hath not stood, because there is no truth in him; when one may speak the falsehood, of his own he speaketh, because he is a liar--also his father.

John 8:45 Ànd because I say the truth, ye do not believe me.

John 8:46. Who of you doth convict me of sin? and if I speak truth, wherefore do ye not believe me?

John 8:47 he who is of God, the sayings of God he doth hear; because of this ye do not hear, because of God ye are not.'

John 8:48 The Jews, therefore, answered and said to him, `Do we not say well, that thou art a Samaritan, and hast a demon?'

John 8:49 Jesus answered, Ì have not a demon, but I honour my Father, and ye dishonour me;

John 8:50 and I do not seek my own glory; there is who is seeking and is judging;

John 8:51. verily, verily, I say to you, If any one may keep my word, death he may not see--to the age.'

John 8:52 The Jews, therefore, said to him, `Now we have known that thou hast a demon; Abraham did die, and the prophets, and thou dost say, If any one may keep my word, he shall not taste of death--to the age!

John 8:53 Art thou greater than our father Abraham, who died? and the prophets died; whom dost thou make thyself?'

John 8:54 Jesus answered, Ìf I glorify myself, my glory is nothing; it is my Father who is glorifying me, of whom ye say that He is your God;

John 8:55 and ye have not known Him, and I have known Him, and if I say that I have not known Him, I shall be like you--speaking falsely; but I have known Him, and His word I keep;

John 8:56 Abraham, your father, was glad that he might see my day; and he saw, and did rejoice.'

John 8:57 The Jews, therefore, said unto him, `Thou art not yet fifty years old, and Abraham hast thou seen?'

John 8:58 Jesus said to them, `Verily, verily, I say to you, Before Abraham's coming--I am;'

John 8:59 they took up, therefore, stones that they may cast at him, but Jesus hid himself, and went forth out of the temple, going through the midst of them, and so passed by.

John 9:1. And passing by, he saw a man blind from birth,

John 9:2 and his disciples asked him, saying, `Rabbi, who did sin, this one or his parents, that he should be born blind?'

John 9:3 Jesus answered, `Neither did this one sin nor his parents, but that the works of God may be manifested in him;

John 9:4 it behoveth me to be working the works of Him who sent me while it is day; night doth come, when no one is able to work: --

John 9:5 when I am in the world, I am a light of the world.'

John 9:6 These things saying, he spat on the ground, and made clay of the spittle, and rubbed the clay on the eyes of the blind man, and said to him,

John 9:7 `Go away, wash at the pool of Siloam,' which is, interpreted, Sent. He went away, therefore, and did wash, and came seeing;

John 9:8. the neighbours, therefore, and those seeing him before, that he was blind, said, `Is not this he who is sitting and begging?'

John 9:9 others said--`This is he;' and others--`He is like to him;' he himself said, --`I am [he].'

John 9:10 They said, therefore, to him, `How were thine eyes opened?'

John 9:11 he answered and said, `A man called Jesus made clay, and rubbed my eyes, and said to me, Go away to the pool of Siloam, and wash; and having gone away and having washed, I received sight;'

John 9:12 they said, therefore, to him, `Where is that one?' he saith, `I have not known.'

John 9:13. They bring him to the Pharisees who once [was] blind,

John 9:14 and it was a sabbath when Jesus made the clay, and opened his eyes.

John 9:15 Again, therefore, the Pharisees also were asking him how he received sight, and he said to them, `Clay he did put upon my eyes, and I did wash--and I see.'

John 9:16 Of the Pharisees, therefore, certain said, `This man is not from God, because the sabbath he doth not keep;' others said, `How is a man--a sinful one--able to do such signs?' and there was a division among them.

John 9:17 They said to the blind man again, `Thou--what dost thou say of him--that he opened thine eyes?'

John 9:18 and he said--`He is a prophet.' The Jews, therefore, did not believe concerning him that he was blind and did receive sight, till that they called the parents of him who received sight,

John 9:19 and they asked them, saying, Ìs your son, of whom ye say that he was born blind? how then now doth he see?'

John 9:20 His parents answered them and said, `We have known that this is our son, and that he was born blind;

John 9:21 and how he now seeth, we have not known; or who opened his eyes, we have not known; him-self is of age, ask him; he himself shall speak concerning himself.'

John 9:22 These things said his parents, because they were afraid of the Jews, for already had the Jews agreed together, that if any one may confess him--Christ, he may be put out of the synagogue;

John 9:23 because of this his parents said--`He is of age, ask him.'

John 9:24 They called, therefore, a second time the man who was blind, and they said to him, `Give glory to God, we have known that this man is a sinner;'

John 9:25 he answered, therefore, and said, Ìf he be a sinner--I have not known, one thing I have known, that, being blind, now I see.'

John 9:26 And they said to him again, `What did he to thee? how did he open thine eyes?'

John 9:27 He answered them, Ì told you already, and ye did not hear; why again do ye wish to hear? do ye also wish to become his disciples?'

John 9:28 They reviled him, therefore, and said, `Thou art his disciple, and we are Moses' disciples;

John 9:29 we have known that God hath spoken to Moses, but this one--we have not known whence he is.'

John 9:30 The man answered and said to them, `Why, in this is a wonderful thing, that ye have not known whence he is, and he opened my eyes!

John 9:31 and we have known that God doth not hear sinners, but, if any one may be a worshipper of God, and may do His will, him He doth hear;

John 9:32 from the age it was not heard, that any one did open eyes of one who hath been born blind;

John 9:33 if this one were not from God, he were not able to do anything.'

John 9:34 They answered and said to him, Ìn sins thou wast born altogether, and thou dost teach us!' and they cast him forth without.

John 9:35. Jesus heard that they cast him forth without, and having found him, he said to him, `Dost thou believe in the Son of God?'

John 9:36 he answered and said, `Who is he, sir, that I may believe in him?'

John 9:37 And Jesus said to him, `Thou hast both seen him, and he who is speaking with thee is he;'

John 9:38 and he said, Ì believe, sir,' and bowed before him.

John 9:39. And Jesus said, `For judgment I to this world did come, that those not seeing may see, and those seeing may become blind.'

John 9:40 And those of the Pharisees who were with him heard these things, and they said to him, Àre we also blind?'

John 9:41 Jesus said to them, Ìf ye were blind, ye were not having had sin, but now ye say--We see, therefore doth your sin remain.

John 10:1. `Verily, verily, I say to you, He who is not entering through the door to the fold of the sheep, but is going up from another side, that one is a thief and a robber;

John 10:2 and he who is entering through the door is shepherd of the sheep;

John 10:3 to this one the doorkeeper doth open, and the sheep hear his voice, and his own sheep he doth call by name, and doth lead them forth;

John 10:4 and when his own sheep he may put forth, before them he goeth on, and the sheep follow him, because they have known his voice;

John 10:5 and a stranger they will not follow, but will flee from him, because they have not known the voice of strangers.'

John 10:6 This similitude spake Jesus to them, and they knew not what the things were that he was speaking to them;

John 10:7 Jesus said therefore again to them, `Verily, verily, I say to you-- I am the door of the sheep;

John 10:8 all, as many as came before me, are thieves and robbers, but the sheep did not hear them;

John 10:9 I am the door, through me if any one may come in, he shall be saved, and he shall come in, and go out, and find pasture.

John 10:10 `The thief doth not come, except that he may steal, and kill, and destroy; I came that they may have life, and may have [it] abundantly.

John 10:11 Ì am the good shepherd; the good shepherd his life layeth down for the sheep;

John 10:12 and the hireling, and not being a shepherd, whose own the sheep are not, doth behold the wolf coming, and doth leave the sheep, and doth flee; and the wolf catcheth them, and scattereth the sheep;

John 10:13 and the hireling doth flee because he is an hireling, and is not caring for the sheep.

John 10:14 Ì am the good shepherd, and I know my [sheep], and am known by mine,

John 10:15 according as the Father doth know me, and I know the Father, and my life I lay down for the sheep,

John 10:16 and other sheep I have that are not of this fold, these also it behoveth me to bring, and my voice they will hear, and there shall become one flock--one shepherd.

John 10:17 `Because of this doth the Father love me, because I lay down my life, that again I may take it;

John 10:18 no one doth take it from me, but I lay it down of myself; authority I have to lay it down, and authority I have again to take it; this command I received from my Father.'

John 10:19. Therefore, again, there came a division among the Jews, because of these words,

John 10:20 and many of them said, `He hath a demon, and is mad, why do ye hear him?'

John 10:21 others said, `These sayings are not those of a demoniac; is a demon able blind men's eyes to open?'

John 10:22. And the dedication in Jerusalem came, and it was winter,

John 10:23 and Jesus was walking in the temple, in the porch of Solomon,

John 10:24 the Jews, therefore, came round about him, and said to him, `Till when our soul dost thou hold in suspense? if thou art the Christ, tell us freely.'

John 10:25 Jesus answered them, Ì told you, and ye do not believe; the works that I do in the name of my Father, these testify concerning me;

John 10:26 but ye do not believe, for ye are not of my sheep,

John 10:27 according as I said to you: My sheep my voice do hear, and I know them, and they follow me,

John 10:28 and life age-during I give to them, and they shall not perish--to the age, and no one shall pluck them out of my hand;

John 10:29 my Father, who hath given to me, is greater than all, and no one is able to pluck out of the hand of my Father;

John 10:30 I and the Father are one.'

John 10:31 Therefore, again, did the Jews take up stones that they may stone him;

John 10:32 Jesus answered them, `Many good works did I shew you from my Father; because of which work of them do ye stone me?'

John 10:33 The Jews answered him, saying, `For a good work we do not stone thee, but for evil speaking, and because thou, being a man, dost make thyself God.'

John 10:34 Jesus answered them, Ìs it not having been written in your law: I said, ye are gods?

John 10:35 if them he did call gods unto whom the word of God came, (and the Writing is not able to be broken,)

John 10:36 of him whom the Father did sanctify, and send to the world,

do ye say--Thou speakest evil, because I said, Son of God I am?

John 10:37 if I do not the works of my Father, do not believe me;

John 10:38 and if I do, even if me ye may not believe, the works believe, that ye may know and may believe that in me [is] the Father, and I in Him.'

John 10:39. Therefore were they seeking again to seize him, and he went forth out of their hand,

John 10:40 and went away again to the other side of the Jordan, to the place where John was at first baptizing, and remained there,

John 10:41 and many came unto him, and said--`John, indeed, did no sign, and all things, as many as John said about this one were true;'

John 10:42 and many did believe in him there.

John 11:1. And there was a certain one ailing, Lazarus, from Bethany, of the village of Mary and Martha her sister--

John 11:2 and it was Mary who did anoint the Lord with ointment, and did wipe his feet with her hair, whose brother Lazarus was ailing--

John 11:3 therefore sent the sisters unto him, saying, `Sir, lo, he whom thou dost love is ailing;'

John 11:4 and Jesus having heard, said, `This ailment is not unto death, but for the glory of God, that the Son of God may be glorified through it.'

John 11:5 And Jesus was loving Martha, and her sister, and Lazarus,

John 11:6 when, therefore, he heard that he is ailing, then indeed he remained in the place in which he was two days,

John 11:7 then after this, he saith to the disciples, `We may go to Judea again;'

John 11:8 the disciples say to him, `Rabbi, now were the Jews seeking to stone thee, and again thou dost go thither!'

John 11:9 Jesus answered, Àre there not twelve hours in the day? if any one may walk in the day, he doth not stumble, because the light of this world he doth see;

John 11:10 and if any one may walk in the night, he stumbleth, because the light is not in him.'

John 11:11 These things he said, and after this he saith to them, `Lazarus our friend hath fallen asleep, but I go on that I may awake him;'

John 11:12 therefore said his disciples, `Sir, if he hath fallen asleep, he will be saved;'

John 11:13 but Jesus had spoken about his death, but they thought that about the repose of sleep he speaketh.

John 11:14 Then, therefore, Jesus said to them freely, `Lazarus hath died;

John 11:15 and I rejoice, for your sake, (that ye may believe,) that I was not there; but we may go to him;'

John 11:16 therefore said Thomas, who is called Didymus, to the fellow-disciples, `We may go--we also, that we may die with him,'

John 11:17. Jesus, therefore, having come, found him having been four days already in the tomb.

John 11:18 And Bethany was nigh to Jerusalem, about fifteen furlongs off,

John 11:19 and many of the Jews had come unto Martha and Mary, that they might comfort them concerning their brother;

John 11:20 Martha, therefore, when she heard that Jesus doth come, met him, and Mary kept sitting in the house.

John 11:21 Martha, therefore, said unto Jesus, `Sir, if thou hadst been here, my brother had not died;

John 11:22 but even now, I have known that whatever thou mayest ask of God, God will give to thee;'

John 11:23 Jesus saith to her, `Thy brother shall rise again.'

John 11:24 Martha saith to him, `I have known that he will rise again, in the rising again in the last day;'

John 11:25 Jesus said to her, `I am the rising again, and the life; he who is believing in me, even if he may die, shall live;

John 11:26 and every one who is living and believing in me shall not die--to the age;

John 11:27 believest thou this?' she saith to him, `Yes, sir, I have believed that thou art the Christ, the Son of God, who is coming to the world.'

John 11:28 And these things having said, she went away, and called Mary her sister privately, saying, `The Teacher is present, and doth call thee;'

John 11:29 she, when she heard, riseth up quickly, and doth come to him;

John 11:30 and Jesus had not yet come to the village, but was in the place where Martha met him;

John 11:31 the Jews, therefore, who were with her in the house, and were comforting her, having seen Mary that she rose up quickly and went forth, followed her, saying-- `She doth go away to the tomb, that she may weep there.'

John 11:32 Mary, therefore, when she came where Jesus was, having seen him, fell at his feet, saying to him, `Sir, if thou hadst been here, my brother had not died;'

John 11:33. Jesus, therefore, when he saw her weeping, and the Jews who came with her weeping, did groan in the spirit, and troubled himself, and he said,

John 11:34 `Where have ye laid him?' they say to him, `Sir, come and see;'

John 11:35 Jesus wept.

John 11:36 The Jews, therefore, said, `Lo, how he was loving him!'

John 11:37 and certain of them said, `Was not this one, who did open the eyes of the blind man, able to cause that also this one might not have died?'

John 11:38 Jesus, therefore, again groaning in himself, cometh to the tomb, and it was a cave, and a stone was lying upon it,

John 11:39 Jesus saith, `Take ye away the stone;' the sister of him who hath died--Martha--saith to him, `Sir, already he stinketh, for he is four days dead;'

John 11:40 Jesus saith to her, `Said I not to thee, that if thou mayest believe, thou shalt see the glory of God?'

John 11:41 They took away, therefore, the stone where the dead was laid, and Jesus lifted his eyes upwards, and said, `Father, I thank Thee, that Thou didst hear me;

John 11:42 and I knew that Thou always dost hear me, but, because of the multitude that is standing by, I said [it], that they may believe that Thou didst send me.'

John 11:43 And these things saying, with a loud voice he cried out, `Lazarus, come forth;'

John 11:44 and he who died came forth, being bound feet and hands with grave-clothes, and his visage with a napkin was bound about; Jesus saith to them, `Loose him, and suffer to go.'

John 11:45. Many, therefore, of the Jews who came unto Mary, and beheld what Jesus did, believed in him;

John 11:46 but certain of them went away unto the Pharisees, and told them what Jesus did;

John 11:47 the chief priests, therefore, and the Pharisees, gathered together a sanhedrim, and said, `What may we do? because this man doth many signs?

John 11:48 if we may let him alone thus, all will believe in him; and the Romans will come, and will take away both our place and nation.'

John 11:49 and a certain one of them, Caiaphas, being chief priest of that year, said to them, `Ye have not known anything,

John 11:50 nor reason that it is good for us that one man may die for the people, and not the whole nation perish.'

John 11:51 And this he said not of himself, but being chief priest of that year, he did prophesy that Jesus was about to die for the nation,

John 11:52 and not for the nation only, but that also the children of God, who have been scattered abroad, he may gather together into one.

John 11:53 From that day, therefore, they took counsel together that they may kill him;

John 11:54 Jesus, therefore, was no more freely walking among the Jews, but went away thence to the region nigh the wilderness, to a city called Ephraim, and there he tarried with his disciples.

John 11:55 And the passover of the Jews was nigh, and many went up to Jerusalem out of the country before the passover, that they might purify themselves;

John 11:56 they were seeking, therefore, Jesus, and said one with another, standing in the temple, `What doth appear to you--that he may not come to the feast?'

John 11:57 and both the chief priests and the Pharisees had given a command, that if any one may know where he is, he may shew [it], so that they may seize him.

John 12:1. Jesus, therefore, six days before the passover, came to Bethany, where was Lazarus, who had died, whom he raised out of the dead;

John 12:2 they made, therefore, to him a supper there, and Martha was ministering, and Lazarus was one of those reclining together (at meat) with him;

John 12:3 Mary, therefore, having taken a pound of ointment of spikenard, of great price, anointed the feet of Jesus and did wipe with her hair his feet, and the house was filled from the fragrance of the ointment.

John 12:4 Therefore saith one of his disciples--Judas Iscariot, of Simon, who is about to deliver him up--

John 12:5 `Wherefore was not this ointment sold for three hundred denaries, and given to the poor?'

John 12:6 and he said this, not because he was caring for the poor, but because he was a thief, and had the bag, and what things were put in he was carrying.

John 12:7 Jesus, therefore, said, `Suffer her; for the day of my embalming she hath kept it,

John 12:8 for the poor ye have always with yourselves, and me ye have not always.'

John 12:9 A great multitude, therefore, of the Jews knew that he is there, and they came, not because of Jesus only, but that Lazarus also they may see, whom he raised out of the dead;

John 12:10 and the chief priests took counsel, that also Lazarus they may kill,

John 12:11 because on account of him many of the Jews were going away, and were believing in Jesus.

John 12:12. On the morrow, a great multitude that came to the feast, having heard that Jesus doth come to Jerusalem,

John 12:13 took the branches of the palms, and went forth to meet him, and were crying, `Hosanna, blessed [is] he who is coming in the name of the Lord--the king of Israel;'

John 12:14 and Jesus having found a young ass did sit upon it, according as it is written,

John 12:15 `Fear not, daughter of Sion, lo, thy king doth come, sitting on an ass' colt.'

John 12:16 And these things his disciples did not know at the first, but when Jesus was glorified, then they remembered that these things were having been written about him, and these things they did to him.

John 12:17 The multitude, therefore, who are with him, were testifying that he called Lazarus out of the tomb, and did raise him out of the dead;

John 12:18 because of this also did the multitude meet him, because they heard of his having done this sign,

John 12:19 the Pharisees, therefore, said among themselves, `Ye see that ye do not gain anything, lo, the world did go after him.'

John 12:20. And there were certain Greeks out of those coming up that they may worship in the feast,

John 12:21 these then came near to Philip, who [is] from Bethsaida of Galilee, and were asking him, saying, `Sir, we wish to see Jesus;'

John 12:22 Philip cometh and telleth Andrew, and again Andrew and Philip tell Jesus.

John 12:23 And Jesus responded to them, saying, `The hour hath come that the Son of Man may be glorified;

John 12:24 verily, verily, I say to you, if the grain of the wheat, having fallen to the earth, may not die, itself remaineth alone; and if it may die, it doth bear much fruit;

John 12:25 he who is loving his life shall lose it, and he who is hating his

life in this world--to life age-during shall keep it;

John 12:26 if any one may minister to me, let him follow me, and where I am, there also my ministrant shall be; and if any one may minister to me--honour him will the Father.

John 12:27. `Now hath my soul been troubled, and what? shall I say-- Father, save me from this hour? -- but because of this I came to this hour;

John 12:28 Father, glorify Thy name.' There came, therefore, a voice out of the heaven, Ì both glorified, and again I will glorify [it];'

John 12:29 the multitude, therefore, having stood and heard, were saying that there hath been thunder; others said, À messenger hath spoken to him.'

John 12:30 Jesus answered and said, `Not because of me hath this voice come, but because of you;

John 12:31 now is a judgment of this world, now shall the ruler of this world be cast forth;

John 12:32 and I, if I may be lifted up from the earth, will draw all men unto myself.'

John 12:33 And this he said signifying by what death he was about to die;

John 12:34 the multitude answered him, `We heard out of the law that the Christ doth remain--to the age; and how dost thou say, That it behoveth the Son of Man to be lifted up? who is this--the Son of Man?'

John 12:35 Jesus, therefore, said to them, `Yet a little time is the light with you; walk while ye have the light, that darkness may not overtake you; and he who is walking in the darkness hath not known where he goeth;

John 12:36 while ye have the light, believe in the light, that sons of light ye may become.' These things spake Jesus, and having gone away, he was hid from them,

John 12:37. yet he having done so many signs before them, they were not believing in him,

John 12:38 that the word of Isaiah the prophet might be fulfilled, which he said, `Lord, who gave credence to our report? and the arm of the Lord--to whom was it revealed?'

John 12:39 Because of this they were not able to believe, that again Isaiah said,

John 12:40 `He hath blinded their eyes, and hardened their heart, that they might not see with the eyes, and understand with the heart, and turn back, and I might heal them;'

John 12:41 these things said Isaiah, when he saw his glory, and spake of him.

John 12:42. Still, however, also out of the rulers did many believe in him, but because of the Pharisees they were not confessing, that they might not be put out of the synagogue,

John 12:43 for they loved the glory of men more than the glory of God.

John 12:44. And Jesus cried and said, `He who is believing in me, doth not believe in me, but in Him who sent me;

John 12:45 and he who is beholding me, doth behold Him who sent me;

John 12:46 I a light to the world have come, that every one who is believing in me--in the darkness may not remain;

John 12:47 and if any one may hear my sayings, and not believe, I--I do not judge him, for I came not that I might judge the world, but that I might save the world.

John 12:48 `He who is rejecting me, and not receiving my sayings, hath one who is judging him, the word that I spake, that will judge him in the last day,

John 12:49 because I spake not from myself, but the Father who sent me, He did give me a command, what I may say, and what I may speak,

John 12:50 and I have known that His command is life age-during; what, therefore, I speak, according as the Father hath said to me, so I speak.'

John 13:1. And before the feast of the passover, Jesus knowing that his hour hath come, that he may remove out of this world unto the Father, having loved his own who [are] in the world--to the end he loved them.

John 13:2 And supper being come, the devil already having put [it] into the heart of Judas of Simon, Iscariot, that he may deliver him up,

John 13:3 Jesus knowing that all things the Father hath given to him--into [his] hands, and that from God he came forth, and unto God he goeth,

John 13:4 doth rise from the supper, and doth lay down his garments, and having taken a towel, he girded himself;

John 13:5 afterward he putteth water into the basin, and began to wash the feet of his disciples, and to wipe with the towel with which he was being girded.

John 13:6 He cometh, therefore, unto Simon Peter, and that one saith to him, `Sir, thou--dost thou wash my feet?'

John 13:7 Jesus answered and said to him, `That which I do thou hast not known now, but thou shalt know after these things;'

John 13:8 Peter saith to him, `Thou mayest not wash my feet--to the

age.' Jesus answered him, Ìf I may not wash thee, thou hast no part with me;'

John 13:9 Simon Peter saith to him, `Sir, not my feet only, but also the hands and the head.'

John 13:10 Jesus saith to him, `He who hath been bathed hath no need save to wash his feet, but he is clean altogether; and ye are clean, but not all;'

John 13:11 for he knew him who is delivering him up; because of this he said, `Ye are not all clean.'

John 13:12 When, therefore, he washed their feet, and took his garments, having reclined (at meat) again, he said to them, `Do ye know what I have done to you?

John 13:13 ye call me, The Teacher and The Lord, and ye say well, for I am;

John 13:14 if then I did wash your feet--the Lord and the Teacher--ye also ought to wash one another's feet.

John 13:15 `For an example I gave to you, that, according as I did to you, ye also may do;

John 13:16 verily, verily, I say to you, a servant is not greater than his lord, nor an apostle greater than he who sent him;

John 13:17 if these things ye have known, happy are ye, if ye may do them;

John 13:18. not concerning you all do I speak; I have known whom I chose for myself; but that the Writing may be fulfilled: He who is eating the bread with me, did lift up against me his heel.

John 13:19 `From this time I tell you, before its coming to pass, that, when it may come to pass, ye may believe that I am [he];

John 13:20 verily, verily, I say to you, he who is receiving whomsoever I may send, doth receive me; and he who is receiving me, doth receive Him who sent me.'

John 13:21 These things having said, Jesus was troubled in the spirit, and did testify, and said, `Verily, verily, I say to you, that one of you will deliver me up;'

John 13:22 the disciples were looking, therefore, one at another, doubting concerning whom he speaketh.

John 13:23 And there was one of his disciples reclining (at meat) in the bosom of Jesus, whom Jesus was loving;

John 13:24 Simon Peter, then, doth beckon to this one, to inquire who he may be concerning whom he speaketh,

John 13:25 and that one having leant back on the breast of Jesus, respondeth to him, `Sir, who is it?'

John 13:26 Jesus answereth, `That one it is to whom I, having dipped the morsel, shall give it;' and having dipped the morsel, he giveth [it] to Judas of Simon, Iscariot.

John 13:27 And after the morsel, then the Adversary entered into that one, Jesus, therefore, saith to him, `What thou dost--do quickly;'

John 13:28 and none of those reclining at meat knew for what intent he said this to him,

John 13:29 for certain were thinking, since Judas had the bag, that Jesus saith to him, `Buy what we have need of for the feast;' or that he may give something to the poor;

John 13:30 having received, therefore, the morsel, that one immediately went forth, and it was night.

John 13:31. When, therefore, he went forth, Jesus saith, `Now was the Son of Man glorified, and God was glorified in him;

John 13:32 if God was glorified in him, God also will glorify him in Himself; yea, immediately He will glorify him.

John 13:33 `Little children, yet a little am I with you; ye will seek me, and, according as I said to the Jews-- Whither I go away, ye are not able to come, to you also I do say [it] now.

John 13:34 À new commandment I give to you, that ye love one another; according as I did love you, that ye also love one another;

John 13:35 in this shall all know that ye are my disciples, if ye may have love one to another.'

John 13:36. Simon Peter saith to him, `Sir, whither dost thou go away?' Jesus answered him, `Whither I go away, thou art not able now to follow me, but afterward thou shalt follow me.'

John 13:37 Peter saith to him, `Sir, wherefore am I not able to follow thee now? my life for thee I will lay down;'

John 13:38 Jesus answered him, `Thy life for me thou wilt lay down! verily, verily, I say to thee, a cock will not crow till thou mayest deny me thrice.'

John 14:1. `Let not your heart be troubled, believe in God, also in me believe;

John 14:2 in the house of my Father are many mansions; and if not, I would have told you; I go on to prepare a place for you;

John 14:3 and if I go on and prepare for you a place, again do I come, and will receive you unto myself, that where I am ye also may be;

John 14:4. and whither I go away ye have known, and the way ye have known.'

John 14:5 Thomas saith to him, `Sir, we have not known whither thou goest away, and how are we able to know the way?'

John 14:6 Jesus saith to him, Ì am the way, and the truth, and the life, no one doth come unto the Father, if not through me;

John 14:7 if ye had known me, my Father also ye would have known, and from this time ye have known Him, and have seen Him.'

John 14:8 Philip saith to him, `Sir, shew to us the Father, and it is enough for us;'

John 14:9 Jesus saith to him, `So long time am I with you, and thou hast not known me, Philip? he who hath seen me hath seen the Father; and how dost thou say, Shew to us the Father?

John 14:10 Believest thou not that I [am] in the Father, and the Father is in me? the sayings that I speak to you, from myself I speak not, and the Father who is abiding in me, Himself doth the works;

John 14:11 believe me, that I [am] in the Father, and the Father in me; and if not, because of the works themselves, believe me.

John 14:12. `Verily, verily, I say to you, he who is believing in me, the works that I do--that one also shall do, and greater than these he shall do, because I go on to my Father;

John 14:13 and whatever ye may ask in my name, I will do, that the Father may be glorified in the Son;

John 14:14 if ye ask anything in my name I will do [it].

John 14:15. Ìf ye love me, my commands keep,

John 14:16 and I will ask the Father, and another Comforter He will give to you, that he may remain with you--to the age;

John 14:17 the Spirit of truth, whom the world is not able to receive, because it doth not behold him, nor know him, and ye know him, because he doth remain with you, and shall be in you.

John 14:18. Ì will not leave you bereaved, I come unto you;

John 14:19 yet a little, and the world doth no more behold me, and ye behold me, because I live, and ye shall live;

John 14:20 in that day ye shall know that I [am] in my Father, and ye in me, and I in you;

John 14:21 he who is having my commands, and is keeping them, that one it is who is loving me, and he who is loving me shall be loved by my Father, and I will love him, and will manifest myself to him.'

John 14:22 Judas saith to him, (not the Iscariot), `Sir, what hath come to pass, that to us thou are about to manifest thyself, and not to the world?'

John 14:23 Jesus answered and said to him, Ìf any one may love me, my word he will keep, and my Father will love him, and unto him we will come, and abode with him we will make;

John 14:24 he who is not loving me, my words doth not keep; and the word that ye hear is not mine, but the Father's who sent me.

John 14:25. `These things I have spoken to you, remaining with you,

John 14:26 and the Comforter, the Holy Spirit, whom the Father will send in my name, he will teach you all things, and remind you of all things that I said to you.

John 14:27 `Peace I leave to you; my peace I give to you, not according as the world doth give do I give to you; let not your heart be troubled, nor let it be afraid;

John 14:28. ye heard that I said to you--I go away, and I come unto you; if ye did love me, ye would have rejoiced that I said--I go on to the Father, because my Father is greater than I.

John 14:29 Ànd now I have said [it] to you before it come to pass, that when it may come to pass, ye may believe;

John 14:30 I will no more talk much with you, for the ruler of this world doth come, and in me he hath nothing;

John 14:31 but that the world may know that I love the Father, and according as the Father gave me command so I do; arise, we may go hence.

John 15:1. Ì am the true vine, and my Father is the husbandman;

John 15:2 every branch in me not bearing fruit, He doth take it away, and every one bearing fruit, He doth cleanse by pruning it, that it may bear more fruit;

John 15:3 already ye are clean, because of the word that I have spoken to you;

John 15:4 remain in me, and I in you, as the branch is not able to bear fruit of itself, if it may not remain in the vine, so neither ye, if ye may not remain in me.

John 15:5 Ì am the vine, ye the branches; he who is remaining in me, and I in him, this one doth bear much fruit, because apart from me ye are not able to do anything;

John 15:6 if any one may not remain in me, he was cast forth without as the branch, and was withered, and they gather them, and cast to fire, and they are burned;

John 15:7 if ye may remain in me, and my sayings in you may remain, whatever ye may wish ye shall ask, and it shall be done to you.

John 15:8 Ìn this was my Father glorified, that ye may bear much fruit, and ye shall become my disciples.

John 15:9. According as the Father did love me, I also loved you, remain in my love;

John 15:10 if my commandments ye may keep, ye shall remain in my love, according as I the commands of my Father have kept, and do remain in His love;

John 15:11 these things I have spoken to you, that my joy in you may remain, and your joy may be full.

John 15:12 `This is my command, that ye love one another, according as I did love you;

John 15:13 greater love than this hath no one, that any one his life may lay down for his friends;

John 15:14 ye are my friends, if ye may do whatever I command you;

John 15:15 no more do I call you servants, because the servant hath not known what his lord doth, and you I have called friends, because all things that I heard from my Father, I did make known to you.

John 15:16 `Ye did not choose out me, but I chose out you, and did appoint you, that ye might go away, and might bear fruit, and your fruit might remain, that whatever ye may ask of the Father in my name, He may give you.

John 15:17 `These things I command you, that ye love one another;

John 15:18. if the world doth hate you, ye know that it hath hated me before you;

John 15:19 if of the world ye were, the world its own would have been loving, and because of the world ye are not--but I chose out of the world--because of this the world hateth you.

John 15:20 `Remember the word that I said to you, A servant is not greater than his lord; if me they did persecute, you also they will persecute; if my word they did keep, yours also they will keep;

John 15:21 but all these things will they do to you, because of my name, because they have not known Him who sent me;

John 15:22 if I had not come and spoken to them, they were not having sin; but now pretext they have not for their sin.

John 15:23 `He who is hating me, doth hate also my Father;

John 15:24 if I did not do among them the works that no other hath done, they were not having sin, and now they have both seen and hated both me and my Father;

John 15:25 but--that the word may be fulfilled that was written in their law--They hated me without a cause.

John 15:26. Ànd when the Comforter may come, whom I will send to you from the Father--the Spirit of truth, who from the Father doth come forth, he will testify of me;

John 15:27 and ye also do testify, because from the beginning ye are with me.

John 16:1. `These things I have spoken to you, that ye may not be stumbled,

John 16:2 out of the synagogues they will put you; but an hour doth come, that every one who hath killed you, may think to offer service unto God;

John 16:3 and these things they will do to you, because they did not know the Father, nor me.

John 16:4 `But these things I have spoken to you, that when the hour may come, ye may remember them, that I said [them] to you, and these things to you from the beginning I did not say, because I was with you;

John 16:5 and now I go away to Him who sent me, and none of you doth ask me, Whither dost thou go?

John 16:6 but because these things I have said to you, the sorrow hath filled your heart.

John 16:7. `But I tell you the truth; it is better for you that I go away, for if I may not go away, the Comforter will not come unto you, and if I go on, I will send Him unto you;

John 16:8 and having come, He will convict the world concerning sin, and concerning righteousness, and concerning judgment;

John 16:9 concerning sin indeed, because they do not believe in me;

John 16:10 and concerning righteousness, because unto my Father I go away, and no more do ye behold me;

John 16:11 and concerning judgment, because the ruler of this world hath been judged.

John 16:12 Ì have yet many things to say to you, but ye are not able to bear [them] now;

John 16:13 and when He may come--the Spirit of truth--He will guide you to all the truth, for He will not speak from Himself, but as many things as He will hear He will speak, and the coming things He will tell you;

John 16:14 He will glorify me, because of mine He will take, and will tell to you.

John 16:15 Àll things, as many as the Father hath, are mine; because of this I said, That of mine He will take, and will tell to you;

John 16:16. a little while, and ye do not behold me, and again a little while, and ye shall see me, because I go away unto the Father.'

John 16:17 Therefore said [some] of his disciples one to another, `What is this that he saith to us, A little while, and ye do not behold me, and again a little while, and ye shall see me, and, Because I go away unto the Father?'

John 16:18 they said then, `What is this he saith--the little while? we have not known what he saith.'

John 16:19 Jesus, therefore, knew that they were wishing to ask him, and he said to them, `Concerning this do ye seek one with another, because I said, A little while, and you do not behold me, and again a little while, and ye shall see me?

John 16:20 verily, verily, I say to you, that ye shall weep and lament, and the world will rejoice; and ye shall be sorrowful, but your sorrow joy will become.

John 16:21 `The woman, when she may bear, hath sorrow, because her hour did come, and when she may bear the child, no more doth she remember the anguish, because of the joy that a man was born to the world.

John 16:22 Ànd ye, therefore, now, indeed, have sorrow; and again I will see you, and your heart shall rejoice, and your joy no one doth take from you,

John 16:23. and in that day ye will question me nothing; verily, verily, I say to you, as many things as ye may ask of the Father in my name, He will give you;

John 16:24 till now ye did ask nothing in my name; ask, and ye shall receive, that your joy may be full.

John 16:25 `These things in similitudes I have spoken to you, but there cometh an hour when no more in similitudes will I speak to you, but freely of the Father, will tell you.

John 16:26 İn that day, in my name ye will make request, and I do not say to you that I will ask the Father for you,

John 16:27 for the Father himself doth love you, because me ye have loved, and ye have believed that I from God came forth;

John 16:28 . I came forth from the Father, and have come to the world; again I leave the world, and go on unto the Father.'

John 16:29 His disciples say to him, `Lo, now freely thou dost speak, and no similitude speakest thou;

John 16:30 now we have known that thou hast known all things, and hast no need that any one do question thee; in this we believe that from God thou didst come forth.'

John 16:31 Jesus answered them, `Now do ye believe? lo, there doth come an hour,

John 16:32 and now it hath come, that ye may be scattered, each to his own things, and me ye may leave alone, and I am not alone, because the Father is with me;

John 16:33 these things I have spoken to you, that in me ye may have peace, in the world ye shall have tribulation, but take courage--I have overcome the world.'

John 17:1. These things spake Jesus, and lifted up his eyes to the heaven, and said--`Father, the hour hath come, glorify Thy Son, that Thy Son also may glorify Thee,

John 17:2 according as Thou didst give to him authority over all flesh, that--all that Thou hast given to him--he may give to them life age-during;

John 17:3 and this is the life age-during, that they may know Thee, the only true God, and him whom Thou didst send--Jesus Christ;

John 17:4 I did glorify Thee on the earth, the work I did finish that Thou hast given me, that I may do [it].

John 17:5 Ànd now, glorify me, Thou Father, with Thyself, with the glory that I had before the world was, with Thee;

John 17:6. I did manifest Thy name to the men whom Thou hast given to me out of the world; Thine they were, and to me Thou hast given them, and Thy word they have kept;

John 17:7 now they have known that all things, as many as Thou hast given to me, are from Thee,

John 17:8 because the sayings that Thou hast given to me, I have given to them, and they themselves received, and have known truly, that from Thee I came forth, and they did believe that Thou didst send me.

John 17:9 Ì ask in regard to them; not in regard to the world do I ask, but in regard to those whom Thou hast given to me, because Thine they are,

John 17:10 and all mine are Thine, and Thine [are] mine, and I have been glorified in them;

John 17:11. and no more am I in the world, and these are in the world, and I come unto Thee. Holy Father, keep them in Thy name, whom Thou hast given to me, that they may be one as we;

John 17:12 when I was with them in the world, I was keeping them in Thy name; those whom Thou hast given to me I did guard, and none of them was destroyed, except the son of the destruction, that the Writing may be fulfilled.

John 17:13 Ànd now unto Thee I come, and these things I speak in the world, that they may have my joy fulfilled in themselves;

John 17:14 I have given to them Thy word, and the world did hate them, because they are not of the world, as I am not of the world;

John 17:15 I do not ask that Thou mayest take them out of the world, but that Thou mayest keep them out of the evil.

John 17:16 Òf the world they are not, as I of the world am not;

John 17:17. sanctify them in Thy truth, Thy word is truth;

John 17:18 as Thou didst send me to the world, I also did send them to the world;

John 17:19 and for them do I sanctify myself, that they also themselves may be sanctified in truth.

John 17:20. Ànd not in regard to these alone do I ask, but also in regard to those who shall be believing, through their word, in me;

John 17:21 that they all may be one, as Thou Father [art] in me, and I in Thee; that they also in us may be one, that the world may believe that Thou didst send me.

John 17:22 Ànd I, the glory that thou hast given to me, have given to them, that they may be one as we are one;

John 17:23 I in them, and Thou in me, that they may be perfected into one, and that the world may know that Thou didst send me, and didst love them as Thou didst love me.

John 17:24. `Father, those whom Thou hast given to me, I will that where I am they also may be with me, that they may behold my glory that Thou didst give to me, because Thou didst love me before the foundation of the world.

John 17:25 `Righteous Father, also the world did not know Thee, and I knew Thee, and these have known that Thou didst send me,

John 17:26 and I made known to them Thy name, and will make known, that the love with which Thou lovedst me in them may be, and I in them.'

John 18:1. These things having said, Jesus went forth with his disciples beyond the brook of Kedron, where was a garden, into which he entered, himself and his disciples,

John 18:2 and Judas also, who delivered him up, had known the place, because many times did Jesus assemble there with his disciples.

John 18:3 Judas, therefore, having taken the band and officers out of the chief priests and Pharisees, doth come thither with torches and lamps, and weapons;

John 18:4 Jesus, therefore, knowing all things that are coming upon him, having gone forth, said to them, `Whom do ye seek?'

John 18:5 they answered him, `Jesus the Nazarene;' Jesus saith to them, Ì am [he];' --and Judas who delivered him up was standing with them; --

John 18:6 when, therefore, he said to them--Ì am [he],' they went away backward, and fell to the ground.

John 18:7 Again, therefore, he questioned them, `Whom do ye seek?' and they said, `Jesus the Nazarene;'

John 18:8 Jesus answered, Ì said to you that I am [he]; if, then, me ye seek, suffer these to go away;'

John 18:9 that the word might be fulfilled that he said--`Those whom Thou hast given to me, I did not lose of them even one.'

John 18:10 Simon Peter, therefore, having a sword, drew it, and struck the chief priest's servant, and cut off his right ear--and the name of the servant was Malchus--

John 18:11 Jesus, therefore, said to Peter, `Put the sword into the sheath; the cup that the Father hath given to me, may I not drink it?'

John 18:12 The band, therefore, and the captain, and the officers of the Jews, took hold on Jesus, and bound him,

John 18:13. and they led him away to Annas first, for he was father-in-law of Caiaphas, who was chief priest of that year,

John 18:14 and Caiaphas was he who gave counsel to the Jews, that it is good for one man to perish for the people.

John 18:15 And following Jesus was Simon Peter, and the other disciple, and that disciple was known to the chief priest, and he entered with Jesus to the hall of the chief priest,

John 18:16 and Peter was standing at the door without, therefore went forth the other disciple who was known to the chief priest, and he spake to the female keeping the door, and he brought in Peter.

John 18:17 Then said the maid keeping the door to Peter, Àrt thou also of the disciples of this man?' he saith, Ì am not;'

John 18:18 and the servants and the officers were standing, having made a fire of coals, because it was cold, and they were warming themselves, and Peter was standing with them, and warming himself.

John 18:19 The chief priests, therefore, questioned Jesus concerning his disciples, and concerning his teaching;

John 18:20 Jesus answered him, Ì spake freely to the world, I did always teach in a synagogue, and in the temple, where the Jews do always come together; and in secret I spake nothing;

John 18:21 why me dost thou question? question those having heard what I spake to them; lo, these have known what I said.'

John 18:22 And he having said these things, one of the officers standing by did give Jesus a slap, saying, `Thus dost thou answer the chief priest?'

John 18:23 Jesus answered him, Ìf I spake ill, testify concerning the ill; and if well, why me dost thou smite?'

John 18:24 Annas then sent him bound to Caiaphas the chief priest.

John 18:25 And Simon Peter was standing and warming himself, they said then to him, Àrt thou also of his disciples?' he denied, and said, Ì am not.'

John 18:26 One of the servants of the chief priest, being kinsman of him whose ear Peter cut off, saith, `Did not I see thee in the garden with him?'

John 18:27 again, therefore, Peter denied, and immediately a cock crew.

John 18:28. They led, therefore, Jesus from Caiaphas to the praetorium, and it was early, and they themselves did not enter into the praetorium, that they might not be defiled, but that they might eat the passover;

John 18:29 Pilate, therefore, went forth unto them, and said, `What accusation do ye bring against this man?'

John 18:30 they answered and said to him, `If he were not an evil doer, we had not delivered him to thee.'

John 18:31 Pilate, therefore, said to them, `Take ye him--ye--and according to your law judge him;' the Jews, therefore, said to him, `It is not lawful to us to put any one to death;'

John 18:32 that the word of Jesus might be fulfilled which he said, signifying by what death he was about to die.

John 18:33 Pilate, therefore, entered into the praetorium again, and called Jesus, and said to him, `Thou art the King of the Jews?'

John 18:34 Jesus answered him, `From thyself dost thou say this? or did others say it to thee about me?'

John 18:35 Pilate answered, `Am I a Jew? thy nation, and the chief priests did deliver thee up to me; what didst thou?'

John 18:36 Jesus answered, `My kingdom is not of this world; if my kingdom were of this world, my officers had struggled that I might not be delivered up to Jews; but now my kingdom is not from hence.'

John 18:37 Pilate, therefore, said to him, `Art thou then a king?' Jesus answered, `Thou dost say [it]; because a king I am, I for this have been born, and for this I have come to the world, that I may testify to the truth;

every one who is of the truth, doth hear my voice.'

John 18:38 Pilate saith to him, `What is truth?' and this having said, again he went forth unto the Jews, and saith to them, `I do find no fault in him;

John 18:39 and ye have a custom that I shall release to you one in the passover; will ye, therefore, [that] I shall release to you the king of the Jews?'

John 18:40 therefore they all cried out again, saying, `Not this one--but Barabbas;' and Barabbas was a robber.

John 19:1. Then, therefore, did Pilate take Jesus and scourge [him],

John 19:2 and the soldiers having plaited a crown of thorns, did place [it] on his head, and a purple garment they put around him,

John 19:3 and said, `Hail! the king of the Jews;' and they were giving him slaps.

John 19:4 Pilate, therefore, again went forth without, and saith to them, `Lo, I do bring him to you without, that ye may know that in him I find no fault;'

John 19:5 Jesus, therefore, came forth without, bearing the thorny crown and the purple garment; and he saith to them, `Lo, the man!'

John 19:6 When, therefore, the chief priests and the officers did see him, they cried out, saying, `Crucify, crucify;' Pilate saith to them, `Take ye him--ye, and crucify; for I find no fault in him;'

John 19:7 the Jews answered him, `We have a law, and according to our law he ought to die, for he made himself Son of God.'

John 19:8 When, therefore, Pilate heard this word, he was the more afraid,

John 19:9 and entered again to the praetorium, and saith to Jesus, `Whence art thou?' and Jesus gave him no answer.

John 19:10 Pilate, therefore, saith to him, `To me dost thou not speak? hast thou not known that I have authority to crucify thee, and I have authority to release thee?'

John 19:11 Jesus answered, `Thou wouldest have no authority against me, if it were not having been given thee from above; because of this, he who is delivering me up to thee hath greater sin.'

John 19:12 From this [time] was Pilate seeking to release him, and the Jews were crying out, saying, Ìf this one thou mayest release, thou art not a friend of Caesar; every one making himself a king, doth speak against Caesar.'

John 19:13 Pilate, therefore, having heard this word, brought Jesus without--and he sat down upon the tribunal--to a place called, `Pavement,' and in Hebrew, Gabbatha;

John 19:14 and it was the preparation of the passover, and as it were the sixth hour, and he saith to the Jews, `Lo, your king!'

John 19:15 and they cried out, `Take away, take away, crucify him;' Pilate saith to them, `Your king shall I crucify?' the chief priests answered, `We have no king except Caesar.'

John 19:16. Then, therefore, he delivered him up to them, that he may be crucified, and they took Jesus and led [him] away,

John 19:17 and bearing his cross, he went forth to the place called [Place] of a Skull, which is called in Hebrew Golgotha;

John 19:18 where they crucified him, and with him two others, on this side, and on that side, and Jesus in the midst.

John 19:19. And Pilate also wrote a title, and put [it] on the cross, and it was written, `Jesus the Nazarene, the king of the Jews;'

John 19:20 this title, therefore, read many of the Jews, because the place was nigh to the city where Jesus was crucified, and it was having been written in Hebrew, in Greek, in Roman.

John 19:21 The chief priests of the Jews said, therefore, to Pilate, `Write not--The king of the Jews, but that one said, I am king of the Jews;'

John 19:22 Pilate answered, `What I have written, I have written.'

John 19:23 The soldiers, therefore, when they did crucify Jesus, took his garments, and made four parts, to each soldier a part, also the coat, and the coat was seamless, from the top woven throughout,

John 19:24 they said, therefore, to one another, `We may not rend it, but cast a lot for it, whose it shall be;' that the Writing might be fulfilled, that is saying, `They divided my garments to themselves, and upon my raiment they did cast a lot;' the soldiers, therefore, indeed, did these things.

John 19:25 And there stood by the cross of Jesus his mother, and his mother's sister, Mary of Cleopas, and Mary the Magdalene;

John 19:26 Jesus, therefore, having seen [his] mother, and the disciple standing by, whom he was loving, he saith to his mother, `Woman, lo, thy son;'

John 19:27 afterward he saith to the disciple, `Lo, thy mother;' and from that hour the disciple took her to his own [home].

John 19:28 After this, Jesus knowing that all things now have been finished, that the Writing may be fulfilled, saith, Ì thirst;'

John 19:29 a vessel, therefore, was placed full of vinegar, and they having filled a sponge with vinegar, and having put [it] around a hyssop stalk, did put [it] to his mouth;

John 19:30 when, therefore, Jesus received the vinegar, he said, Ìt hath been finished;' and having bowed the head, gave up the spirit.

John 19:31. The Jews, therefore, that the bodies might not remain on the cross on the sabbath, since it was the preparation, (for that sabbath day was a great one,) asked of Pilate that their legs may be broken, and they taken away.

John 19:32 The soldiers, therefore, came, and of the first indeed they did break the legs, and of the other who was crucified with him,

John 19:33 and having come to Jesus, when they saw him already having been dead, they did not break his legs;

John 19:34 but one of the soldiers with a spear did pierce his side, and immediately there came forth blood and water;

John 19:35 and he who hath seen hath testified, and his testimony is true, and that one hath known that true things he speaketh, that ye also may believe.

John 19:36 For these things came to pass, that the Writing may be fulfilled, À bone of him shall not be broken;'

John 19:37 and again another Writing saith, `They shall look to him whom they did pierce.'

John 19:38. And after these things did Joseph of Arimathea--being a disciple of Jesus, but concealed, through the fear of the Jews--ask of Pilate, that he may take away the body of Jesus, and Pilate gave leave; he came, therefore, and took away the body of Jesus,

John 19:39 and Nicodemus also came--who came unto Jesus by night at the first--bearing a mixture of myrrh and aloes, as it were, a hundred pounds.

John 19:40 They took, therefore, the body of Jesus, and bound it with linen clothes with the spices, according as it was the custom of the Jews to prepare for burial;

John 19:41 and there was in the place where he was crucified a garden, and in the garden a new tomb, in which no one was yet laid;

John 19:42 there, therefore, because of the preparation of the Jews, because the tomb was nigh, they laid Jesus.

John 20:1. And on the first of the sabbaths, Mary the Magdalene doth come early (there being yet darkness) to the tomb, and she seeth the stone having been taken away out of the tomb,

John 20:2 she runneth, therefore, and cometh unto Simon Peter, and unto the other disciple whom Jesus was loving, and saith to them, `They took away the Lord out of the tomb, and we have not known where they laid him.'

John 20:3 Peter, therefore, went forth, and the other disciple, and they were coming to the tomb,

John 20:4 and the two were running together, and the other disciple did run forward more quickly than Peter, and came first to the tomb,

John 20:5 and having stooped down, seeth the linen clothes lying, yet, indeed, he entered not.

John 20:6 Simon Peter, therefore, cometh, following him, and he entered into the tomb, and beholdeth the linen clothes lying,

John 20:7 and the napkin that was upon his head, not lying with the linen clothes, but apart, having been folded up, in one place;

John 20:8 then, therefore, entered also the other disciple who came first unto the tomb, and he saw, and did believe;

John 20:9 for not yet did they know the Writing, that it behoveth him out of the dead to rise again.

John 20:10 The disciples therefore went away again unto their own friends,

John 20:11. and Mary was standing near the tomb, weeping without; as she was weeping, then, she stooped down to the tomb, and beholdeth two messengers in white, sitting,

John 20:12 one at the head, and one at the feet, where the body of Jesus had been laid.

John 20:13 And they say to her, `Woman, why dost thou weep?' she saith to them, `Because they took away my Lord, and I have not known where they laid him;'

John 20:14 and these things having said, she turned backward, and seeth Jesus standing, and she had not known that it is Jesus.

John 20:15 Jesus saith to her, `Woman, why dost thou weep? whom dost thou seek;' she, supposing that he is the gardener, saith to him, `Sir, if thou didst carry him away, tell me where thou didst lay him, and I will take him away;'

John 20:16 Jesus saith to her, `Mary!' having turned, she saith to him, `Rabbouni;' that is to say, `Teacher.'

John 20:17 Jesus saith to her, `Be not touching me, for I have not yet ascended unto my Father; and be going on to my brethren, and say to them, I ascend unto my Father, and your Father, and to my God, and to your God.'

John 20:18 Mary the Magdalene cometh, telling to the disciples that she hath seen the Lord, and [that] these things he said to her.

John 20:19. It being, therefore, evening, on that day, the first of the sabbaths, and the doors having been shut where the disciples were assembled, through fear of the Jews, Jesus came and stood in the midst, and saith to them, `Peace to you;'

John 20:20 and this having said, he shewed them his hands and side; the disciples, therefore, rejoiced, having seen the Lord.

John 20:21 Jesus, therefore, said to them again, `Peace to you; according as the Father hath sent me, I also send you;'

John 20:22 and this having said, he breathed on [them], and saith to them, `Receive the Holy Spirit;

John 20:23 if of any ye may loose the sins, they are loosed to them; if of any ye may retain, they have been retained.'

John 20:24 And Thomas, one of the twelve, who is called Didymus, was not with them when Jesus came;

John 20:25 the other disciples, therefore, said to him, `We have seen the Lord;' and he said to them, `If I may not see in his hands the mark of the nails, and may put my finger to the mark of the nails, and may put my hand to his side, I will not believe.'

John 20:26. And after eight days, again were his disciples within, and Thomas with them; Jesus cometh, the doors having been shut, and he stood in the midst, and said, `Peace to you!'

John 20:27 then he saith to Thomas, `Bring thy finger hither, and see my hands, and bring thy hand, and put [it] to my side, and become not unbelieving, but believing.'

John 20:28 And Thomas answered and said to him, `My Lord and my God;'

John 20:29 Jesus saith to him, `Because thou hast seen me, Thomas, thou hast believed; happy those not having seen, and having believed.'

John 20:30 Many indeed, therefore, other signs also did Jesus before his disciples, that are not written in this book;

John 20:31 and these have been written that ye may believe that Jesus is the Christ, the Son of God, and that believing ye may have life in his name.'

John 21:1. After these things did Jesus manifest himself again to the disciples on the sea of Tiberias, and he did manifest himself thus:

John 21:2 There were together Simon Peter, and Thomas who is called Didymus, and Nathanael from Cana of Galilee, and the [sons] of Zebedee, and two others of his disciples.

John 21:3 Simon Peter saith to them, `I go away to fish;' they say to him, `We go--we also--with thee;' they went forth and entered into the boat immediately, and on that night they caught nothing.

John 21:4 And morning being now come, Jesus stood at the shore, yet indeed the disciples did not know that it is Jesus;

John 21:5 Jesus, therefore, saith to them, `Lads, have ye any meat?'

John 21:6 they answered him, `No;' and he said to them, `Cast the net at the right side of the boat, and ye shall find;' they cast, therefore, and no longer were they able to draw it, from the multitude of the fishes.

John 21:7 That disciple, therefore, whom Jesus was loving saith to Peter, `The Lord it is!' Simon Peter, therefore, having heard that it is the Lord, did gird on the outer coat, (for he was naked,) and did cast himself into the sea;

John 21:8 and the other disciples came by the little boat, for they were not far from the land, but as it were about two hundred cubits off, dragging the net of the fishes;

John 21:9 when, therefore, they came to the land, they behold a fire of coals lying, and a fish lying on it, and bread.

John 21:10 Jesus saith to them, `Bring ye from the fishes that ye caught now;'

John 21:11 Simon Peter went up, and drew the net up on the land, full of great fishes, an hundred fifty and three, and though they were so many, the net was not rent.

John 21:12 Jesus saith to them, `Come ye, dine;' and none of the disciples was venturing to inquire of him, `Who art thou?' knowing that it is the Lord;

John 21:13 Jesus, therefore, doth come and take the bread and give to them, and the fish in like manner;

John 21:14 this [is] now a third time Jesus was manifested to his disciples, having been raised from the dead.

John 21:15. When, therefore, they dined, Jesus saith to Simon Peter, `Simon, [son] of Jonas, dost thou love me more than these?' he saith to him, `Yes, Lord; thou hast known that I dearly love thee;' he saith to him, `Feed my lambs.'

John 21:16 He saith to him again, a second time, `Simon, [son] of Jonas, dost thou love me?' he saith to him,

`Yes, Lord; thou hast known that I dearly love thee;' he saith to him, `Tend my sheep.'

John 21:17 He saith to him the third time, `Simon, [son] of Jonas, dost thou dearly love me?' Peter was grieved that he said to him the third time, `Dost thou dearly love me?' and he said to him, `Lord, thou hast known all things; thou dost know that I dearly love thee.' Jesus saith to him, `Feed my sheep;

John 21:18 verily, verily, I say to thee, When thou wast younger, thou wast girding thyself and wast walking whither thou didst will, but when thou mayest be old, thou shalt stretch forth thy hands, and another will gird thee, and shall carry [thee] whither thou dost not will;'

John 21:19 and this he said, signifying by what death he shall glorify God; and having said this, he saith to him, `Be following me.'

John 21:20. And Peter having turned about doth see the disciple whom Jesus was loving following, (who also reclined in the supper on his breast, and said, `Sir, who is he who is delivering thee up?')

John 21:21 Peter having seen this one, saith to Jesus, `Lord, and what of this one?'

John 21:22 Jesus saith to him, Ìf him I will to remain till I come, what--to thee? be thou following me.' This word, therefore, went forth to the brethren that that disciple doth not die,

John 21:23 yet Jesus did not say to him, that he doth not die, but, Ìf him I will to remain till I come, what--to thee?'

John 21:24 this is the disciple who is testifying concerning these things, and he wrote these things, and we have known that his testimony is true.

John 21:25 And there are also many other things--as many as Jesus did--which, if they may be written one by one, not even the world itself I think to have place for the books written. Amen.

Ingram Content Group UK Ltd.
Milton Keynes UK
UKHW020956130623
423332UK00005B/83